Your College Experience

Brief Twelfth Edition

John N. Gardner
President, John N. Gardner Institute for Excellence in Undergraduate Education
Brevard, North Carolina
Distinguished Professor Emeritus, Library and Information Science
Senior Fellow, National Resource Center for
The First-Year Experience and Students in Transition
University of South Carolina, Columbia

Betsy O. Barefoot
Vice President and Senior Scholar
John N. Gardner Institute for Excellence in Undergraduate Education
Brevard, North Carolina

Bedford/St. Martin's
Boston ■ New York

For Bedford/St. Martin's

Vice President, Editorial, Macmillan Higher Education Humanities: Edwin Hill
Publisher for College Success: Erika Gutierrez
Senior Executive Editor for College Success: Simon Glick
Developmental Editor: Jennifer Jacobson of Ohlinger Publishing Services
Production Editor: Kerri A. Cardone
Senior Production Supervisor: Dennis J. Conroy
Senior Marketing Manager: Christina Shea
Associate Editor: Bethany Gordon
Copy Editor: Janet Renard
Indexer: Steve Csipke
Photo Researcher: Sue McDermott Barlow
Senior Art Director: Anna Palchik
Text Design: Jerilyn Bockorick, Cenveo Publisher Services
Composition: Cenveo Publisher Services
Printing and Binding: RR Donnelley and Sons

Manufactured in the United States of America.

For information, write: Bedford/St. Martin's, 75 Arlington Street, Boston, MA 02116 (617-399-4000)

Acknowledgments
Acknowledgments and copyrights appear at their source throughout the text, which constitutes an extension of the copyright page. It is a violation if the law to reproduce these selections by any means whatsoever without written permission of the copyright holder.

At the time of publication all Internet URLs published in this text were found to accurately link to their intended Web site. If you do find a broken link, please forward the information to collegesuccess@bedfordstmartins.com so that it can be corrected for the next printing.

CONTENTS

preface

Anyone who teaches beginning college students knows how much they have changed in recent years. Today's students are increasingly job focused, technologically adept, and concerned about the future. More than ever, students worry about how they will pay for college. Recently, popular media sources such as the *Washington Post* have raised questions about whether the benefits of college are worth the cost.[1] While it is tempting to focus on the few individuals who succeed without finishing college, we know that for the overwhelming majority of individuals, a college degree is more essential than ever before.

Today, we see diverse students of all ages and backgrounds enrolling in two- and four-year public and private institutions, bringing with them the hopes and dreams that a college education can help fulfill—as well as expectations that may or may not be realistic. *Your College Experience* is designed specifically to give all students the practical help they need to gain self-knowledge, set goals, succeed, and stay in college so that those hopes and dreams have a better chance of becoming realities.

While maintaining its approach on goal setting, the twelfth edition of this text offers a new emphasis on the ten high-impact practices identified by the American Association of Colleges and Universities, and it now incorporates information on the value of peer leaders in supporting students. *Your College Experience* teaches skills and strategies in areas where students often need the most help and that are critical for success in college and the workplace. These include time management, academic reading, test taking, research, and career preparation. At a time when institutions are increasing class sizes and mainstreaming developmental students, students will need more individual attention and the skills to ask for the help they need. Of course, concerns about student retention remain, as do pressures on college success administrators to do more with less. These realities of college and university life mean that giving students strategies they can use immediately is more important than ever.

To help you meet the challenges of engaging and retaining today's students, we have created a complete package of support materials, including an Instructor's Annotated Edition and an Instructor's Manual. In the Instructor's Annotated Edition, you will find clearly marked retention strategies and activities to help you engage and retain students. These activities, and all of the instructor support materials, are valuable for both new and experienced instructors as they prepare to teach the course.

What has not changed in the forty years since the inception of the first-year seminar is our level of commitment to and deep understanding of our students. Although this edition of *Your College Experience* has been significantly revised, it is still based on our collective knowledge and experience in teaching new students. It is grounded in the growing body of research

[1]www.washingtonpost.com/blogs/she-the-people/wp/2014/08/22/do-the-benefits-of-a-college-education-outweigh-the-cost

on student success and retention and includes valuable contributions from leading experts in the field. Most of all, it is a text born from our devotion to students and to their success. Simply put, we do not like to see students fail. We are confident that if students both read and heed the information herein, they will become engaged in the college experience, learn, and persist to graduation.

We have written this text for students of any age in both residential and commuter institutions. Our writing style is intended to convey respect and admiration for students while recognizing their continued need for challenge and support. We have addressed topics that our experience, our research, and our reviewers tell us are concerns for students at any type of college or university and with any kind of educational background. We have also embedded various reading and writing strategies to support students' efforts to comprehend the material and apply the skills presented in each chapter, and we have included technology tools and tips that can enhance students' studying experience.

Your College Experience uses a simple and logical organization. Part One, Foundations, sets the stage by challenging students to explore their purpose for attending college and by helping them learn how to apply that purpose to both short- and long-term goal setting. Students are armed with solid time-management strategies in Chapter Two, and then they explore the topics of emotional intelligence and learning styles. Part Two, Preparing to Learn, enumerates essential learning skills like critical thinking, reading, note taking, studying, and test taking, and guides students in communicating and finding information. Part Three, Preparing for Life, emphasizes practical and realistic considerations such as relationships, diversity, wellness, and money management. Part Four, Next Steps, features a comprehensive chapter on majors and careers with a wealth of tools and strategies that students can use during their first-year experience and beyond.

Whether you are considering this textbook for use in your first-year seminar or have already made a decision to adopt it, we thank you for your interest, and we trust that you will find it to be a valuable teaching aid. We also hope that this book will guide you and your campus in understanding the broad range of issues that can affect student success.

A Revision Focused on Research-Based Strategies to Help Students Succeed

While retaining many of the hallmark features that characterize the Gardner/Barefoot text, we have added new areas of emphasis grounded in the latest research on student success.

1. **A focus on high-impact practices.** An exciting new aspect of the twelfth edition is the inclusion of strategies for using "high-impact practices"—ten educational activities that have been shown to increase student learning, retention, and engagement throughout the undergraduate years.[2] The first chapter of the book introduces the concept of high-impact practices (HIP) for students, lists and describes

[2]G. D. Kuh, *High-Impact Educational Practices: What They Are, Who Has Access to Them, and Why They Matter* (Washington, DC: Association of American Colleges and Universities, 2008). www.aacu.org/leap/hips

them, and discusses their benefits. New annotations in each chapter of the Instructor's Annotated Edition feature suggestions for utilizing one or more HIPs in the context of chapter content. This new category of instructor's annotations is denoted with the heading "HIGH-IMPACT PRACTICE." Also, a special icon identifies content in the features and narrative of the student edition that relates to HIPs. For instance, readers will see the HIP icon adjacent to the Your Turn: Work Together and Your Turn: Write and Reflect activities, and with content coverage related to writing, collaboration, diversity, global learning, or service learning. Furthermore, icons placed within the table of contents and the list of Your Turn features show you where to find HIP material.

2. **An emphasis on motivation and the importance of the choices students make.** Through the narrative and special features, the new edition helps students see how good choices bring them closer to their goals, guides them in understanding how being resilient involves bouncing back from poor choices and making increasingly smarter ones, and motivates them to make these smarter decisions. Each chapter includes a Your Turn: Stay Motivated feature, a Your Turn: Make Good Choices feature, and an ending exercise that invites students to Reflect on Choices through writing. Collegiate success is often determined by both large and small choices that students make in the first term of college, and we want students to be aware of how their choices can dramatically change the outcomes of their college experience.

3. **Updates across all chapters, with extensive revisions to fundamental coverage in one chapter in each major part.** In Chapter 3, Emotional Intelligence, we present strong links between emotional intelligence concepts and the daily events of college life. In Chapter 5, Thinking in College, students explore what college-level thinking involves. Chapter 13, Wellness, presents the mental, physical, and spiritual aspects of wellness. Chapter 15, Majors and Careers, offers effective guidance on and tools for exploring different careers and industries in today's job market and economy. See more information about changes in each chapter on pages xxiv– xxvi.

4. **Assistance for using peer leaders in college success courses.** As many colleges and universities now recognize the importance of upper-level students as coteachers or peer leaders for the first-year seminar, the Instructor's Annotated Edition now includes special annotations for and about them. Each chapter includes suggestions that peer leaders (or the instructor of record) can use in designing special activities that can be led by peer leaders. The Use Your Resources section includes peer leaders as valuable sources for student support.

5. **An increased focus on four-year higher education.** With the publication of a new edition of *Your College Experience* specifically developed for students attending two-year and community colleges, the twelfth edition now focuses more intentionally on the particular issues of students in baccalaureate colleges and universities. Given that students attending open-enrollment institutions are becoming increasingly broad and diverse, the twelfth edition provides support, information, and guidance appropriate for students at all higher education institutions.

The twelfth edition continues the Gardner and Barefoot tradition of helping students self-assess their strengths, practice goal setting, focus on purpose and motivation, and maintain their engagement in this course. A section on goal setting in Chapter 1 gets students thinking immediately about this important skill. Assess Your Strengths and Set Goals boxes early in each chapter ask students to set goals, and Reflect on Choices and Apply What You Have Learned exercises at the end of each chapter ask students to think back on how the chapter relates to choices they make and to apply what they have learned in the chapter to current and future academic work.

The following features return in the twelfth edition, with many exciting enhancements:

Chapter-opening profiles help students see themselves in the text. Each chapter of the text opens with the story of a recent first-year student who has used the strategies presented in the chapter to succeed in college. The profiled students come from diverse backgrounds and attend diverse colleges and universities around the country.

Thought-provoking photographs and cartoons in every chapter—many of them new to this edition—with carefully written titles and captions reinforce concepts in the narrative and encourage critical thinking. For instance, in the Time Management chapter, a captioned photo of NFL coach Pete Carroll and his players encourages students to "Set Priorities like the Pros." In the communication chapter, a new photo of Ellen DeGeneres hosting the Academy Awards provides a great example of audience interaction, and its caption discusses how the comedy icon used to be scared to speak before an audience. In the careers chapter, a new photo of a career fair for military veterans emphasizes the importance of making professional connections.

***Your Turn* collaborative learning activities foster peer-to-peer communication, collaboration, and critical thinking.** These activities can be used in class, as homework, or as group activities to strengthen the bond between students and their college communities. They are organized into four types based on what students are asked to do or to consider: Work Together, Write and Reflect, Make Good Choices, and Stay Motivated. A complete list of all Your Turn activities, organized by type and with page numbers included to make it easy for instructors to assign them, can be found on p. xviii.

***Is This You?* boxes speak directly to students in circumstances that are commonly found among students taking first-year experience courses.** Look for these special messages to first-generation college students, returning students, veterans, students with children, and student athletes. They also cover common first-year issues that many students encounter, such as being disappointed in a class, weight gain, financial problems, and the clash of new ideas with old beliefs. The feature directs students to specific content within the chapter. Here is a list of these features:

Is This You? I Don't Know What I'm Doing Here (Chapter 1)
Is This You? Time Flies (Chapter 2)
Is This You? Older than Average (Chapter 3)
Is This You? Disappointed in My Classes (Chapter 4)

Is This You? When New Knowledge and Old Beliefs Collide (Chapter 5)
Is This You? The Challenge of Being "First" (Chapter 6)
Is This You? Balancing Sports and Study (Chapter 7)
Is This You? Making *A*'s without Studying (Chapter 8)
Is This You? Bouncing Back from a Bad Grade (Chapter 9)
Is This You? Dreading Writing Assignments (Chapter 10)
Is This You? In a Long-Distance Relationship (Chapter 11)
Is This You? From Another Country (Chapter 12)
Is This You? My Favorite Pants Don't Fit (Chapter 13)
Is This You? Too Much Month, Too Little Money (Chapter 14)
Is This You? No Plan for Life after College (Chapter 15)

Coverage of technology and learning. The link between technology and learning is highlighted in every chapter of the twelfth edition with a Tech Tip feature. These features introduce critical technology skills that span the classroom and real life. All Tech Tip features have been extensively revised for the new edition, with titles such as Get Digitally Organized (Chapter 2); Use Blogs and Twitter (Chapter 3); Correlate Online Learning with Your Learning Style (Chapter 4); Take Better Notes in Better Ways (Chapter 7); Use the Cloud (Chapter 8); Conduct Effective Searches (Chapter 10); Build a Digital Persona (Chapter 11); Go Beyond the Filter (new, Chapter 12); and Join the Professional Community (Chapter 15).
Models (including **digital models**) let students see principles in action. Because many students learn best by example, full-size models—more than in any competing book—show realistic examples of strategies for academic success such as using time-management tools, annotating a textbook, using mind maps, and taking notes in various formats. Digital models are included to reflect the tools today's students use in their everyday lives.

Expanded examples from across the curriculum. The text now includes more concrete scenarios, pages, exercises, and problems from STEM, humanities, and social science courses.

***Use Your Resources* boxes connect students to their campus, faculty, and other students.** To help students take more control of their own success, every chapter includes a quick overview of additional resources for support, including learning-assistance centers, books, Web sites, and fellow students—with a prompt for students to add their own ideas.

Skills-based practice exercises provide hands-on, point-of-use reinforcement of major concepts. Students use these exercises to practice skills that they can then apply to other academic courses. For instance, the Time Management chapter includes a tool for students to conduct a Procrastination Self-Assessment, and the test-taking chapter includes a new Test Anxiety Quiz.

Retention Strategies in every chapter of the Instructor's Annotated Edition offer best practices from John Gardner and Betsy Barefoot to help students persist in the first year. In addition, a 16-page insert at the beginning of the Instructor's Annotated Edition includes chapter-specific exercises and activities designed as retention strategies to support writing, critical thinking, working in groups, planning, reflecting, and taking action.

Key Chapter-by-Chapter Revisions

In addition to new features that appear across all chapters of the book, each chapter also features key new and updated content:

Chapter 1, Welcome to Your College Experience, introduces students to the concepts of purpose and goal setting and explores the value of higher education. New to this reorganized chapter is a summary of high-impact practices that are featured throughout the book, an introduction to the role of peer leaders in the college success course, and new material on academic planning and working with an academic adviser. In addition, the authors introduce students to the concept of resilience, a topic that is addressed throughout the new edition.

Chapter 2, Time Management, addresses the tools today's students use to stay organized. This chapter includes information about the relationship between locus of control and one's ability to manage time. Students are guided in using time-management tools and understanding how to avoid procrastination. The chapter includes a new procrastination self-assessment and a valuable tool for measuring the impact of distractions.

Chapter 3, Emotional Intelligence, has been improved by linking emotional intelligence concepts to the daily events of college life, with additional explanation on the concepts of resilience and making good choices. The chapter also includes self-assessments that help students evaluate and improve their own level of emotional intelligence.

Chapter 4, How You Learn, introduces students to learning styles and learning preferences. The chapter includes the VARK Inventory, which can be used in class. Also, three other learning-styles theories are described in the chapter: David Kolb's Experiential Learning Theory, the Myers-Briggs Type Indicator, and Howard Gardner's Theory of Multiple Intelligences. A brief version of the Multiple Intelligences Inventory is included. The chapter ends with coverage of learning disabilities to help students know how and when to seek help for themselves or other students.

Chapter 5, Thinking in College, has been heavily revised and reorganized to give students a better understanding of what is involved in college-level thinking and practical strategies on how to achieve that high level of thinking. Students are clearly shown how concepts like fast and slow thinking, problem solving, creativity, and collaboration all relate to critical thinking. The chapter includes a critical-thinking assessment that is new to this edition, as well as a new application of Bloom's Taxonomy.

Chapter 6, Reading to Learn, helps students meet the particular challenges of reading college textbooks across the various disciplines. It introduces them to the steps involved in active reading and explains how to use strategies such as outlining and mapping to understand and retain important content for tests and exams. Strategies for reading with concentration, reading improvement, and monitoring are provided. New visuals include a sample organizer, several new photos, and sample textbook pages from an economics and chemistry textbook, which reflect the text's increased attention to the STEM fields.

Chapter 7, Getting the Most from Class, covers topics such as preparing for class, listening, taking notes, and participating. The chapter introduces students to various note-taking methods, particularly the Cornell method. The chapter's Tech Tip presents helpful note-taking apps. Students are encouraged to overcome any reluctance they might have about asking a question in class or participating out loud in a group discussion.

Chapter 8, Studying, includes an essential focus on the basics—how to study and how to remember. Students are warned about the pitfalls of multitasking and the downsides of trying to study in an environment that is full of distractions. The chapter opens with a new assessment that asks students to determine their willingness to make tough choices to improve their study habits and includes a new figure showing a sample mind map.

Chapter 9, Test Taking, helps students learn how to prepare for tests and exams, understand and deal with test anxiety, and appreciate the value of maintaining academic integrity. The chapter covers different types of tests and different test environments, including online testing. A major theme in the chapter is the importance of being resilient—not allowing a poor grade on a test to negatively affect a student's motivation. A new visual showing a sample page from a math textbook reinforces the value of working practice problems as a great way to study for tests.

Chapter 10, Information Literacy and Communication, connects writing and speaking to the important topic of information literacy. The chapter now more clearly walks students through the steps of the writing process. The chapter emphasizes doing good research and getting comfortable using the resources at the campus library. Students are also introduced to ways to evaluate and cite sources and recognize bias.

Chapter 11, Relationships, includes a major focus on the value of students building positive relationships with their instructors. The chapter also addresses the changing nature of interactions with family members, roommate issues, and romantic relationships. The chapter contains a new section on communicating in a digital age, with a new table outlining best practices for online communication. The chapter's Tech Tip has been reoriented around building a digital persona in an attempt to educate students about being responsible with their online presence, especially as it relates to employment. This chapter also covers the value of involvement in campus life.

Chapter 12, Diversity, takes a broad view of diversity and considers the many advantages of a diverse campus environment that includes differences in gender, race, ethnic group, sexuality, age, economic status, religion, and learning and physical abilities. The chapter advises students to refrain from stereotyping and instead get to know others as individuals before drawing conclusions about an entire group.

Chapter 13, Wellness, takes a new, holistic view of wellness, including mental, physical, and spiritual health. A major focus of this chapter is stress and how to prevent and manage it through proper nutrition, sleep, and exercise. The chapter includes a stress self-assessment exercise and a Tech Tip that introduces students to ways that technology can help monitor health. This chapter includes new coverage of cyberbullying and the latest information about the federal government's actions against sexual assault, including strategies that students can use to protect themselves and others from becoming victims.

Chapter 14, Money, emphasizes the importance of budgeting and gives students a template for designing their own budget. The chapter also explores responsible use of credit and debit cards, and ways for students to obtain and maintain financial aid.

Chapter 15, Majors and Careers, helps students understand how to consider different majors and to make a decision that sets them up for success and fulfillment. The chapter also provides a wealth of guidance on and tools for exploring different careers and industries. This chapter offers a cutting-edge evaluation of the new economy and guidance in developing the right mind-set for creating a strong future, before moving on to discuss clear strategies for career planning, enhancing marketability, conducting industry and company research, gaining experience while in college, and searching for jobs.

Extensive Resources for Instructors

- **LaunchPad for *Your College Experience,* Twelfth Edition.** LaunchPad combines an interactive e-book with high-quality multimedia content and ready-made assessment options, including LearningCurve adaptive quizzing. Prebuilt units are easy to assign or adapt to your material, such as readings, videos, quizzes, discussion groups, and more. LaunchPad also provides access to a grade book that provides a clear window on performance for your whole class, for individual students, and for individual assignments. The result is superior, book-specific content in a breakthrough user interface in which power and simplicity go hand in hand. To package LaunchPad for *Your College Experience* with the text, use ISBN 978-1-319-03845-8. To order LaunchPad standalone, use ISBN 978-1-319-01263-2.
- ***LearningCurve for College Success 2.0.*** *LearningCurve for College Success 2.0* is an online, adaptive, self-quizzing program that quickly learns what students already know and helps them practice what they don't yet understand. LearningCurve motivates students to engage with key concepts before they come to class so that they are ready to participate; it also offers reporting tools to help you discern your students' needs. This updated version of LearningCurve features a larger question pool with new multiple-choice questions. To package *LearningCurve for College Success 2.0* for **free** with the text, use ISBN 978-1-319-03846-5. To order LearningCurve standalone, use ISBN 978-1-4576-7999-5.
- **The Academic and Career Excellence System (ACES).** This instrument measures student strengths in twelve critical areas and prompts students to reflect on their habits, behaviors, attitudes, and skills. Norm-referenced reports indicate whether students are at a high, moderate, or low skill level in particular areas. For more information, go to **macmillanhighered.com/ACES/catalog**.
- **Instructor's Annotated Edition.** A valuable tool for new and experienced instructors alike, the Instructor's Annotated Edition includes the full text of the student edition with abundant marginal annotations, chapter-specific exercises, and helpful suggestions for teaching, fully updated and revised by the authors. In this edition are numerous retention strategies and high-impact practice tips and exercises to help you help your students succeed and stay in school.

- **Instructor's Manual.** The Instructor's Manual includes chapter objectives, teaching suggestions, an introduction to the first-year experience course, a sample lesson plan for each chapter, sample syllabi, final projects for the end of the course, and various case studies that are relevant to the topics covered in the text. The Instructor's Manual is available online.
- **Computerized Test Bank.** The Computerized Test Bank contains more than 800 multiple-choice, true/false, short-answer, and essay questions designed to assess students' understanding of key concepts. This edition features 150 new multiple-choice questions and more challenging scenario-based questions that ask students to apply their understanding to concepts in the text. An answer key is included. A digital text file is also available.
- ***French Fries Are Not Vegetables.*** This comprehensive instructional DVD features multiple resources for class and professional use. Also available online on Video Central: College Success. ISBN 978-0-312-65073-5.
- **Custom Solutions program.** Bedford/St. Martin's Custom Publishing offers the highest-quality books and media, created in consultation with publishing professionals who are committed to the discipline. Make *Your College Experience* more closely fit your course and goals by integrating your own materials, including only the parts of the text you intend to use in your course, or both. Contact your local Bedford/St. Martin's sales representative for more information.
- **CS Select custom database.** The CS Select database allows you to create a textbook for your College Success course that reflects your course objectives and uses just the content you need. Start with one of our core texts, and then rearrange chapters, delete chapters, and add additional content—including your own original content—to create just the book you're looking for. Get started by visiting **macmillanhighered.com/csSelect**.
- **TradeUp.** Bring more value and choice to your students' first-year experience by packaging *Your College Experience*, Twelfth Edition, with one of a thousand titles from Macmillan publishers at a 50 percent discount from the regular price. Contact your local Bedford/St. Martin's sales representative for more information.

Student Resources

- **LaunchPad for *Your College Experience*, Twelfth Edition.** LaunchPad is an online course solution that offers our acclaimed content, including e-books, videos, LearningCurve adaptive quizzes, and more. For more information, see the Extensive Resources for Instructors section. To package LaunchPad for *Your College Experience* with the text, use ISBN 978-1-319-03845-8. To order LaunchPad standalone, use ISBN 978-1-319-01263-2.
- ***LearningCurve for College Success 2.0.*** *LearningCurve for College Success 2.0* is an online, adaptive, self-quizzing program that quickly learns what students already know and helps them practice what they don't yet understand. For more information, see the Extensive Resources for Instructors section. To package *LearningCurve for College Success 2.0* for **free** with the text, use ISBN 978-1-319-03846-5. To order LearningCurve standalone, use ISBN 978-1-4576-7999-5.

- **College Success companion site: macmillanhighered.com/collegesuccess/resources.** The College Success companion site offers a number of tools to use in class, including videos with quizzing, downloadable podcasts, flashcards of key terms, and links to apps that students can use on their phones or computers to reinforce success strategies. From the companion Web site, you can also access instructor materials whenever you need them.
- ***VideoCentral: College Success*** is a premiere collection of videos for the college success classroom. The site features the 30-minute documentary, *French Fries Are Not Vegetables and Other College Lessons: A Documentary of the First Year of College,* which follows five students through the life-changing transition to the first year of college. Learn more at **macmillanhighered.com/videosuccess/catalog**. *VideoCentral* also includes access to sixteen brief Conversation Starters that combine student and instructor interviews on the most important topics taught in first-year seminar courses, and sixteen accompanying video glossary definitions with questions that bring these topics to life.
- **Bedford e-Book to Go for *Your College Experience*, Twelfth Edition**. For roughly half the cost of a print book, **Bedford e-Book to Go** offers an affordable alternative for students. To learn more, visit **macmillanhighered.com/aboutebooks**.
- **Additional e-book formats.** You can also find PDF versions of our books when you shop online at our publishing partners' sites: CourseSmart, Barnes & Noble NookStudy, Kno, CafeScribe, or Chegg.
- ***The Bedford/St. Martin's Planner*** includes everything that students need to plan and use their time effectively, with advice on preparing schedules and to-do lists, along with blank schedules and monthly and weekly calendars for planning. Integrated into the planner are tips and advice on fixing common grammar errors, taking notes, and succeeding on tests; an address book; and an annotated list of useful Web sites. The planner fits easily into a backpack or purse, so students can take it anywhere. To order the planner standalone, use ISBN 978-0-312-57447-5.
- ***Bedford/St. Martin's Insider's Guides.*** These concise and student-friendly booklets on topics that are critical to college success are a perfect complement to your textbook and course. One Insider's Guide can be packaged with *any* Bedford/St. Martin's textbook at no additional cost. Additional Insider's Guides can also be packaged for additional cost. Topics include:
  - New! *Insider's Guide for Adult Learners*
  - New! *Insider's Guide to College Etiquette,* 2e
  - New! *Insider's Guide for Returning Veterans*
  - New! *Insider's Guide to Transferring*
  - *Insider's Guide to Academic Planning*
  - *Insider's Guide to Beating Test Anxiety*
  - *Insider's Guide to Building Confidence*
  - *Insider's Guide to Career Services*
  - *Insider's Guide to College Ethics and Personal Responsibility*
  - *Insider's Guide to Community College*

- *Insider's Guide to Credit Cards,* 2e
- *Insider's Guide to Getting Involved on Campus*
- *Insider's Guide to Global Citizenship*
- *Insider's Guide to Time Management,* 2e

For more information on ordering one of these guides with the text, go to **macmillanhighered.com/collegesuccess**.

- ***Journal Writing: A Beginning.*** Designed to give students an opportunity to use writing as a way to explore their thoughts and feelings, this writing journal includes a generous supply of inspirational quotes placed throughout the pages, tips for journaling, and suggested journal topics. To order the journal standalone, use ISBN 978-0-312-59027-7.

Acknowledgments

Special thanks to the reviewers of this edition, whose wisdom and suggestions guided the creation of the twelfth edition of the text:

Donna Dabney, Norfolk State University
Maria Flynn, West Kentucky Community and Technical College
DeLandra Hunter, Clayton State University
Hector Menchaca, Tarrant County College—Trinity River Campus
Darrah Mugrauer, Delaware Valley College
Amy Nemmetz, University of Wisconsin—Platteville
Heather Ortiz, Ranger College
Jennifer Palcich, University of North Texas
Carolyn Sanders, University of Alabama in Huntsville
Deborah Stephens, East Tennessee State University

We also thank those who reviewed the Instructor's Manual and Test Bank so thoroughly: Margaret Garroway, Howard Community College; Greta Henglein, Martin Methodist College; Patti Richter, Northwestern State University of Louisiana; Mary Kay Skrabalak, University of Alabama; Brenda Tuberville, Rogers State University. We would also like to continue to thank our reviewers from the eleventh, tenth, and ninth editions, as they helped to shape the text you see today.

Eleventh Edition: Erin Barnett, Eastern Kentucky University; Andrea Berta, University of Texas at El Paso; Christie Cruse-Cohen, Rockland Community College; Linda Frank, Harper College; Lauren Kelley, Owens Community College; Mark Lanting, Kankakee Community College; Molly Burke Leon, Indiana University at Bloomington; General McArthur, Moraine Valley Community College; Roarke O'Leary, Long Beach City College; Rachael Orr, University of Missouri; Jennifer Palcich, University of North Texas; Kelda Quintana, Humboldt State University; Carolyn Sanders, University of Alabama in Huntsville; Deb Vetter, Asbury University; Sara Weertz, Angelo State University.

Tenth Edition: Laurie Adamson, Olympic College; Jim Archer, South Plains College; Jennifer L. Guerriero, Valencia Community College; Kevin Johnson, Middle Georgia College; Joseph Kaye, Edison State College; Elizabeth Kennedy, Florida Atlantic University; Kimberly Koledoye, Houston Community College; Joseph Kornoski, Montgomery County Community College; Audra Leverton, Hinds Community College; Rhonda Lee Meadows, West Virginia University; Pamela Moss, Midwestern State University; Marissa Santos, Navarro College; Ysabel M. Sarte, Texas A&M University;

Melanie Steeves, Dean College; Susannah Waldrop, University of South Carolina Upstate; and Shoshana Zeisman, Portland State University.

Ninth Edition: Josie Adamo, Buffalo State College; Leigh A. Adams, Missouri State University—West Plains; Andrés Armijo, University of New Mexico; Camille J. Belolan, Bloomsburg University of Pennsylvania; Richard Conway, Nassau Community College; Matthew Gainous, Ogeechee Technical College; Wendy Grace, Holmes Community College; Janis M. Hausmann, Mount Marty College; Darby Johnsen, Oklahoma City Community College; Tamara Kuzmenkov, Tacoma Community College; Wendy McNeeley, Howard Payne University; Gail Malone Platt, South Plains College; Amy Reese, Baton Rouge Community College; Cristina C. Rodriguez, Los Angeles Pierce College; Rebecca Rogge, Louisiana State University; Janice Waltz, Harrisburg Area Community College; Jodi E. Webb, Bowling Green State University.

As we look to the future, we are excited about the numerous improvements to this text that our creative Bedford/St. Martin's team has made and will continue to make. Special thanks to Edwin Hill, Vice President, Editorial, Macmillan Higher Education Humanities; Simon Glick, Senior Executive Editor for College Success; Jennifer Jacobson, Development Editor of Ohlinger Publishing Services; Bethany Gordon, Associate Editor; Jonathan Douglas, Editorial Assistant; Christina Shea, Senior Marketing Manager; and Greg Erb, Senior Production Editor.

Most of all, we thank you, the users of our book, for you are the true inspirations for our work.

Contributors

Although this text speaks with the voices of its two authors, it represents contributions from many other people. We gratefully acknowledge those contributions and thank these individuals, whose special expertise has made it possible to introduce new students to their college experience through the holistic approach we deeply believe in.

Amber Manning-Ouellette of Southern Illinois University provided guidance on revising the Emotional Intelligence, Thinking in College, and Wellness chapters. Amber is the Director of Enrollment Management for the SIU College of Business, focusing on recruitment and retention strategies for undergraduate students. She holds a B.S. in Psychology and an M.S. in Counselor Education and received her Doctorate in Educational Administration and Higher Education from SIU in May 2015.

Amber enjoys working with first-year students. In her previous position, she coordinated more than one hundred sections of student success courses, designed curricula, implemented faculty training, and assisted in assessment through a University College model. She was also instrumental in the implementation of the First-Year Experience program for incoming SIU students. One of her passions is coordinating a first-year women's leadership course and living learning community to empower her students. Her academic research interests surround first-year student early interventions, at-risk student development programs, sex education, sexual assault, women's leadership, women's cognitive development, and retention initiatives. She is active in the First-Year Experience movement and continues to present and publish her research at national, regional, and institutional conferences.

Given the nature of technology as a moving target, we relied on the work of **Mark Hendrix** of Palm Beach State College to update the Tech Tips for the twelfth edition. Mark heavily revised or rewrote the Tech Tips, providing new themes in several cases, with the goal of providing students with information to increase their productivity when using the apps, software, or hardware described.

Mark has been an educator for over twenty-five years. He taught in adult and community education before earning a master's degree in education from the University of St. Thomas in St. Paul, Minnesota. He has worked as a teacher or program director in a variety of adult and vocational programs and alternative high school programming, in addition to teaching at community colleges and universities in Minnesota, Kansas, and Florida. He has served on numerous boards of community organizations and has helped them creatively and enthusiastically embrace challenges and thrive in a changing environment. Currently, he is an Associate Professor at Palm Beach State College in Palm Beach County, Florida. He has been recognized for his dynamic teaching strategies, use of technology in the classroom, and his ability to work effectively across departments and outside organizations.

Lea Susan Engle rewrote and updated the chapter on information literacy for the previous edition, helping to incorporate the topics of writing and speaking. Lea is a former instructor and first-year experience librarian at Texas A&M University and currently serves as Training Coordinator for the Canvas learning management system at The University of Texas at Austin. Lea earned a B.A. in Women's Studies from the University of Maryland, College Park and holds an M.S. in Information Studies and an M.A. in Women's and Gender Studies from the University of Texas at Austin.

Her professional interests include educational technology, the first-year experience, creative outreach methods, feminist pedagogy, library service to GLBTQ users, formative assessment, taking risks, and fostering cross-campus collaborations. She is a library evangelist, fulfilling her dream of strategically positioning librarians in all areas of academia.

Casey Reid vastly updated the chapter on Time Management to reflect the needs of today's students. Casey graduated in 2002 from Missouri State University with a B.A. in Anthropology and Professional Writing, and in 2004 she received an M.A. in Writing from the same institution. From 2004 through 2011, she worked on the English faculty at Metropolitan Community College (MCC) in Kansas City. From 2011–2014, she was MCC's College Orientation Coordinator, initiating and directing a mandatory first-year seminar class for 6,000–7,000 new students each year. In 2014, she became the Director of Developmental Education Programs at East Central College, where she implements first-year seminars and programs for students in developmental education classes. When she isn't working, she adds balance to her life by running, biking, hiking, reading, spending time with her three rescued dogs, and hanging out with friends and family.

The wealth of resources offered in the Majors and Careers chapter is due in large part to **Heather N. Maietta**. Heather is Associate Vice President of Career and Corporate Engagement at Merrimack College. While at Merrimack, she created Generation Merr1mack, a career and professional development program to support first-generation college students. Generation Merr1mack was a finalist for the 2014 Diversity and Inclusion award from the National Association of Colleges and Employers.

Heather has presented or copresented more than thirty times nationally on topics related to career and professional preparation, and she is a Certified Career Development Facilitator Instructor through the National Career Development Association. Heather has authored articles and research reports in several publications, including About Campus; Career Convergence; and ESource. Heather has also coauthored three textbooks for Kendall/Hunt Publishers. Most recently, she coauthored and edited *The Senior Year: Culminating Experiences and Transitions*, published by The National Resource Center on the First-Year Experience and Students in Transition.

Heather also serves on the Notre Dame Education Center Board of Directors, an organization that provides education and support services for adult learners in the greater Lawrence, Massachusetts, community.

Chris Gurrie is an Assistant Professor and Director of the Speech Communication Program at the University of Tampa. He also teaches first-year experience seminars and advises undergraduate students. He holds a doctorate from Nova Southeastern University, and when he is not teaching he speaks about the concept of immediacy and student-instructor connections. He has published other articles about communication among the Millennial Generation. He contributed the first generation of Tech Tips, which were introduced in the tenth edition, and wrote the *Guide to Teaching with YouTube,* which is available online and as part of the Instructor's Manual.

We would also like to acknowledge and thank the numerous colleagues who have contributed to this book in its previous editions:

Chapters 2, 6, 7, 8, 9: Jeanne L. Higbee, University of Minnesota
Chapter 3: Catherine Andersen, University of Baltimore
Chapters 4, 11: Tom Carskadon, Mississippi State University
Chapter 7: Mary Ellen O'Leary, University of South Carolina
Chapter 10: Charles Curran, Distinguished Professor Emeritus, University of South Carolina at Columbia
Chapter 14: Natala Kleather (Tally) Hart, founding head of the Economic Access Initiative at The Ohio State University; and Kate Trombitas, Director of Development at The Ohio State University College of Nursing
Chapter 15: Philip D. Gardner, Michigan State University

David Shaffer/Getty Images

1 WELCOME TO YOUR COLLEGE EXPERIENCE

YOU WILL EXPLORE

The value of a college education, the college success course, and this textbook

What the college experience is about

The importance of exploring your purpose and setting goals for attending college

The value of academic planning and working with an academic adviser to choose a major and build a program of study

What high-impact practices are and the positive impact they can have on your learning and overall success

John N. Gardner and Betsy O. Barefoot, "Welcome to Your College Experience," from *Your College Experience: Strategies for Success*, Twelfth Edition, pages 3–22. Copyright © 2016 by Bedford/St. Martin's.

Rontavius Jamal Snipes, 23

Biology major
Clayton State University, Georgia

"Working twenty-two hours while taking sixteen credits means that I rarely get enough sleep because I have to stay up late studying. So my biggest goal for now is to find a way to better manage my time."

Setting both long- and short-term goals has always been important to Rontavius Snipes. After high school, when he found himself living in Atlanta and working at a dead-end job, he set his sights on going to college and enrolled at Clayton State University. Now that he's in college, he's majoring in biology with the goal of attending dental school after graduation, and he knows that getting good grades and staying involved on campus will help him achieve that ultimate goal.

Like many students, Rontavius also needs to balance working (he works at a pharmacy 30 miles from campus) with attending and participating in school, so many of his goals have involved small steps. "I am currently the president of the pre-dental student association," he explains. "The group is small, but this semester I plan to attend a leadership seminar to get some extra motivation to be able to lead a successful student organization." He also gets involved on campus in smaller ways by promoting concerts and plays, which helps him stay connected with other students. He acknowledges, however, that working while attending school does have its challenges, which he is still trying to solve. "Working twenty-two hours while taking sixteen credits means that I rarely get enough sleep because I have to stay up late studying. Finding a social life away from my roommates and my girlfriend can be difficult too, so my biggest goal for now is to find a way to better manage my time." Still, Rontavius knows that the hard work will pay off. "Prior to attending college, I never thought about things deeply and took everything at face value. I have greater intuition now and definitely feel that the price I pay for education is well worth it," he says.

In the future, Rontavius hopes to travel the world tackling issues such as poverty, cultural barriers, and the economic glass ceiling that many people face, and his favorite class so far, Sociology 1101, plays nicely into those goals. "That class pushes my life message," he says, "that we should try to understand other cultures and not be so close-minded. I have been the subject of negative stereotypes, and I just love how this class shows how these ways of thinking came about."

To access the LearningCurve study tool, video activities, and more, go to LaunchPad for *Your College Experience*. macmillanhighered.com/gardner12e

Rontavius knows how important a college education is to his future economic status, but he also knows that going to college presents him with many learning opportunities that he couldn't access any other way. He has already discovered how important it is to think deeply and has recognized that he has leadership skills. Rontavius is also encountering challenges, primarily in time management. He has to work and also wants a satisfying personal life. Therefore, he wants strategies to help him better manage his limited time and maintain good grades.

This book is designed to help you both overcome the struggles that face you and explore all that college has to offer. As you read this book, you will

assess your strengths

Think about the topic of this chapter. Do you already have a good understanding of the benefits of college? Do you have a clear sense of purpose? What personal and career goals do you want to pursue in college? Describe the experience you have with setting goals and reaching them. If you are not quite ready to answer these questions yet, return to them as you read through this chapter.

set goals

Think about a challenge you have had in the past with understanding what college is all about or setting personal goals. As you read this chapter, set a goal that relates to chapter material, and be prepared to talk with others in your class about why you selected this goal. For example, you might set a goal to understand the research on the value of a college degree and apply it to your own personal goals for your future.

discover your own strengths, learn to be a good thinker, and become skilled at making good choices. You will develop an appreciation of the power you have to direct the aspects of your life, such as managing relationships with your friends, instructors, and family, selecting out-of-class opportunities to pursue, and allocating your time to school, work, and leisure activities. But the most important skill you will need to learn in college is how to keep learning throughout your life. As you're settling into your new college routine, we want to welcome you to the demanding and rewarding world of higher education and equip you with a set of strategies you can use to do your best.

THE VALUE OF A COLLEGE EDUCATION

American society values higher education, which explains why the United States currently has more than 4,400 colleges and universities. College is the primary way that people achieve upward social mobility or the ability to attain a higher standard of living. That might accurately describe your purpose for being in college: to attain a higher standard of living. In earlier centuries, a high standard of living was almost always a function of family background. Either you were born into power and money or you spent your life working for others who had power and money. In most countries today, however, receiving a college degree helps level the playing field for everyone. A college degree can minimize or eliminate the restrictions to achievement that stem from differences in background, race, ethnicity, family income level, national origin, immigration status, family lineage, and personal connections. Simply put, college participation is about ensuring that more people have the opportunity to be evaluated on the basis of merit rather than family status, money, or other forms of privilege. It makes achieving the American dream possible.

In 1900, fewer than 2 percent of Americans of traditional college age attended college. Today, new technologies and the information explosion are changing the workplace so drastically that to support themselves and their families adequately, most people will need some education beyond high school. In spite of the fact that today more than 67 percent of high school graduates (approximately 18 million students) are attending college, we are seeing a wave of questions in the media about whether or not college is really worth it.

Rontavius, the student profiled at the beginning of this chapter, likely would answer that yes, college is really worth it, but what do the data say? A *New York Times* analysis of data from the Economic Institute (**epi.com**) finds that the answer is "yes." Dramatic differences exist between the earning power of students with a high school diploma and those with a four-year college degree. In 2013, four-year college graduates earned about twice as much per hour as high school graduates. While there are concerns about the cost of college today, the cost of not attending college is even more dramatic. David Autor, an economist from the Massachusetts Institute of Technology, reported that not going to college will, over your lifetime, cost you about half a million dollars.[1]

You can also take a look at Figure 1 to see how earning a college degree will improve your earning potential. This figure breaks down unemployment rates and weekly earnings according to education level. The more education you have, the more likely you are to be employed, and the higher your earnings will be.

Beyond the financial benefits that earning a college degree gives to an individual, society benefits as a whole when people earn college degrees. College is an established process designed to further formal education so that students who attend and graduate will be prepared for certain roles in society. Today, for many, those roles are found predominantly in what has become known as the "information economy," which means that most college graduates will earn their living by creating,

[1]David Leonhardt, "Is College Worth It? Clearly, New Data Say," *The New York Times*, May 27, 2014, www.nytimes.com/2014/05/27/upshot/is-college-worth-it-clearly-new-data-say. html?_r=0, accessed August 7, 2014.

FIGURE 1 › Education Pays

Earning a college degree will improve your earning potential. This figure breaks down unemployment rates and weekly earnings according to education level. Use this information as motivation to make the most of college. The more education you have, the more likely you are to be employed, and the higher your earnings will be.

Source: U.S. Department of Labor, Bureau of Labor Statistics, *Current Population Survey*, 2013.

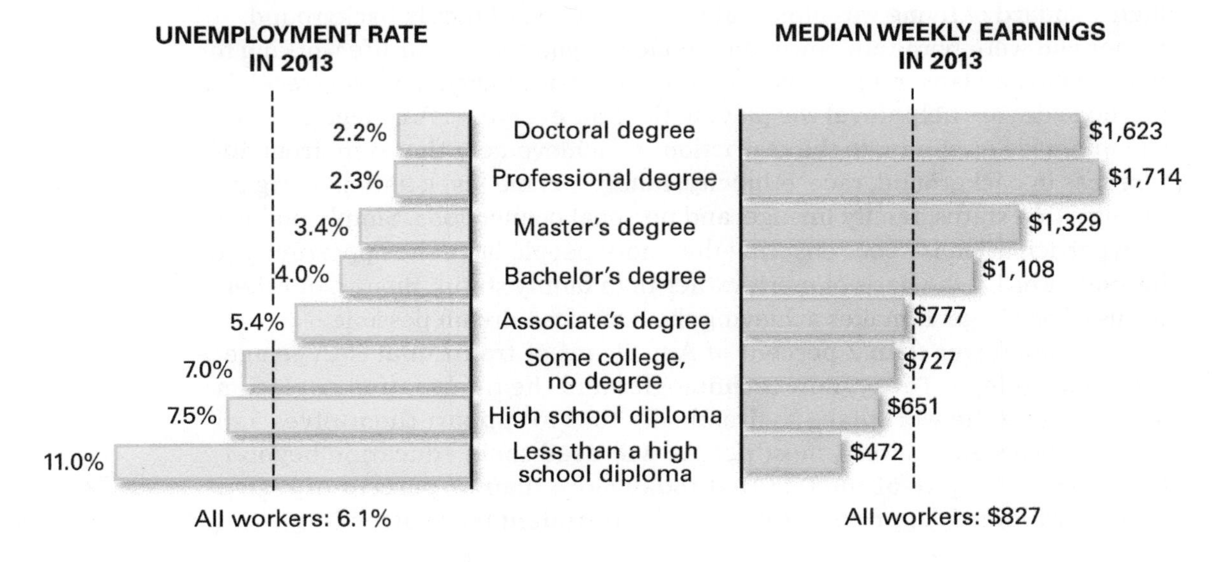

managing, and using information. For others, college is a crucial way for students to prepare for leadership roles in their communities, companies, professions, or military units.

Another reason students get a four-year college degree is to prepare them to continue their education in a graduate or professional school. If you want to become a medical doctor, dentist, lawyer, or college professor, a four-year college degree is just the beginning, but it is a required step on the path to such professions. Let's say you aspire to be a pharmacist and are planning to get a bachelor's degree in chemistry. Your primary purpose for your degree in chemistry is to gain admittance to pharmacy school. Perhaps you have also considered that if your plans should change, having a degree in chemistry will get your foot in the door in several different industries, so another purpose for your degree is having an edge in the job market upon graduation.

The Value of Your College Success Course

Since you are reading this textbook, it is likely that you are enrolled in a first-year seminar, first-year experience, or "college success" course. In this book we use all three names. The course—possibly the most important course you will take—and this textbook—possibly the most important textbook you will read—are all about improving your chances for success in college and beyond. Before you start reading, though, you probably have some questions.

Research conducted by colleges and universities has found that first-year students are far more likely to be successful if they participate in courses and programs designed to teach them how to succeed in college. This course is designed to help you avoid some of the pitfalls—both academic and personal—that trip up many beginning students.

Although your classmates might not say it out loud, many of them share your concerns, doubts, and fears about being in college. This course will provide a supportive environment in which you can share your successes and your frustrations, get to know others who are beginning college, develop lasting relationships with your instructor and some other students, and begin to think about your plans for life after college.

The Value of Your College Success Textbook

As college professors, researchers, and administrators with many years of experience working with first-year students, we're well aware that starting college can be challenging. We also know that if you apply the ideas in this book to your everyday life, you are likely to enjoy your time in college, graduate, and achieve your life goals.

Your instructor may ask you to read every chapter in this book, but even if you're not required to do so, consider this book a resource to answer questions you might have later this year and throughout your college experience. This chapter discusses the value of college, purpose and goal setting, and academic planning; other chapters cover topics such as managing your time, discovering your personal learning style, understanding how your emotions affect your learning and interactions with others, thinking, taking notes, writing and speaking, developing information literacy skills, managing your money, understanding diversity, and maintaining healthy behaviors.

Though some of the textbook's content may seem like common sense, much of it is based on research and the experiences of thousands of college students and educators. And although some topics in this book might have been presented in high school, we find that many college success strategies cannot be properly understood until students are actually in college and have an immediate "need to know."

THE COLLEGE EXPERIENCE

What is the college experience? Depending on who you are, your life circumstances, and why you decided to enroll, college can mean different things. College is often portrayed in books and movies as a place where young people live away from home in ivy-covered residence halls. We frequently see college depicted with a major focus on big-time sports, heavy drinking, and partying. Yes, you'll find some of that at some colleges, but most students today don't move away from home, don't live on campus, and don't see much ivy. College is far more than any single image you might carry around in your head. And college students today come from more walks of life than ever before.

Why College Is Important for You

College is about thinking, and it will help you understand how to become a careful and critical thinker, someone who doesn't believe everything that he or she hears or reads but instead looks for evidence before forming an opinion. Developing solid thinking skills will empower you to make sound decisions throughout your life.

Although college is often thought of as a time when traditional-age students become young adults, we realize that on today's college campuses, many students are already adults. Whatever your age, college can be a time when you take risks, learn new things, and meet new and different people, all in a relatively safe environment. It's OK to experiment in college, within limits, because that's what college is designed for.

College will provide you with numerous opportunities to develop a variety of formal and informal social networks. These networks will help you make friends and develop alliances with faculty members and fellow students who share your interests and goals. Social networking sites such as Facebook and Twitter provide a way to enrich your real-life social networks in college.

College definitely can and should be fun, and we hope it will be for you. You will meet new people, go to athletic events and parties, build camaraderie with new friends, and feel a sense of school spirit. Many college graduates relive memories of college days throughout their lives, fanatically root for their institution's athletic teams, return for homecoming and class reunions, and encourage their own children to attend their alma mater. In fact, you might be a legacy student, someone whose parents or grandparents attended the same institution that you do.

In addition to being fun, college is a lot of work. Being a college student means spending many hours studying each week, staying up late at night, taking high-stakes exams, and possibly working harder than you ever have before. For many students, college becomes much like a job, with defined duties, expectations, and obligations. Most important is that college will be a set of experiences that will help you to further define your goals and achieve your own purpose.

Getting the Most Out of College: High-Impact Practices

Throughout your college experience, you will have the opportunity to participate in activities known as "high-impact practices." High-impact practices are particular activities that research shows have significant positive impact on both your learning and your overall success. One high-impact practice is taking the first-year seminar, which shouldn't surprise you given what you have read in this chapter about the value of this course. Here is a comprehensive list of the ten high-impact practices in which you can participate, listed in the order you are most likely to encounter them. (In this textbook, this icon is used to alert you to these opportunities to enrich your learning.):

1. **first-year seminars** The course in which you find yourself now, designed to prepare you for your college experience.
2. **writing-intensive courses** Courses across the curriculum that engage you in multiple forms of writing for different audiences. This textbook offers various writing activities that make your first-year seminar a writing-intensive course.
3. **collaborative assignments** Learning activities in which you work and solve problems with your classmates in this and other courses.
4. **global learning or diversity experiences** Courses and programs in which you explore cultures, life experiences, and worldviews different from your own.
5. **service-learning** Programs or courses in which you engage in required field-based "experiential learning" and reflection while giving back to your community through service.
6. **learning communities** Programs in which you would take two or more "linked" courses with a group of other students and work closely with one another and with your instructors.
7. **campus-wide common intellectual experiences** Programs in which you would take required "common-core" courses, participate in a required learning community, or engage in other shared experiences such as a "common reading."
8. **undergraduate research** A program that gives you the opportunity to participate in systematic investigation and research working one-to-one with a faculty member.
9. **internships** Direct experience with service-learning or in a work setting often related to your career interests.
10. **capstone courses and projects** Courses or experiences that would require you in the senior year to reflect on what you have learned in all your courses and create a project of some sort that integrates and applies your knowledge.

Does College Seem Like a Strange Land?
Are you a student who has recently come to the United States from another country? Perhaps you have immigrated with family members or on your own. Whatever the situation, learning the unique language, culture, and expectations that exist at a U.S. college can be a challenge. Do instructors' expectations and students' behaviors seem different than what you experienced in your home country? Seek out English as a second language (ESL) courses or programs if you need help you with your English skills. Also, visit the international student counselors to find out how you can continue to increase your understanding of life in the United States, both on and off campus.
Blend Images/Arial Skelley/Getty Images

Some high-impact practices may be activities or courses that are mandatory to fulfill general education or major requirements, but others will be optional. It's a good idea to seek out as many of these practices as you can manage, because doing so will result in heightened learning and greater success for you.

your turn Make Good Choices

The Decision to Become a College Student
Write five reasons that you chose to go to college at this time in your life. Share what you wrote with a classmate and see how many of your reasons are the same or different.

Traditional Students: Making the Transition

If you are a traditional student, meaning that you just graduated from high school, the transition you are making means that you have to adjust to some distinct differences between high school and college. For instance, you will probably be part of a more diverse student body, not just in terms of race but also in terms of age, religion, political opinions, and life experiences. If you attend a large college or university, you might feel like a "number" and not as special as you felt in high school. You will have more potential friends to choose from, but familiar assumptions about people based on where they live, where they go to church, or what high school they attended might not apply to the new people you're meeting.

Because of the many competing opportunities you'll be faced with both in and out of class, managing your time is sure to be more complex than it was in high school. Your classes will meet on various days and times, and you will likely have additional commitments, including work, family, activities, and sports. Your college classes might meet for longer class periods than your high school classes. Tests are given less frequently in college—sometimes only twice a term—and you will most likely spend more time writing in college than you did in high school. You will be encouraged to do original research and to investigate differing points of view on a topic. You will be expected to study outside of class, prepare assignments, do assigned reading, and be ready for in-class discussions.

If any upper-level students work as peer leaders in your college success course, get to know them. Peer leaders are selected because of their knowledge, experience, and willingness to help new students. A peer leader can serve as an informal academic adviser, mentor, and friend.

As discussed throughout this chapter, college is also the time when you will begin making serious plans for your work life after college. Although you may have thought about potential careers in high school, determining a particular career direction takes on special urgency in college. The college success course and this textbook give you tools to help you identify and choose the right career path among the endless choices offered at many colleges and universities. We'll discuss college majors toward the end of this chapter.

your turn Work Together

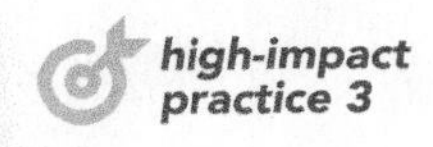

Are You Surprised?

Talk with a classmate to discover whether college life is what each of you thought it would be. Share what you have experienced and times when you have been pleasantly or unpleasantly surprised.

Challenges and Opportunities for Nontraditional Students

If you are a nontraditional or adult student, you might have experience in the job market, and you might have a spouse or partner and children.

techtip

E-MAIL WITH STYLE

As you planned for college, you probably heard about all the ways you'll use technology as a student. First, you need to activate your college e-mail as soon as possible to receive information regarding class cancellations, weather-related closings, student events, and other types of communication that your college or your instructors may send you. Many colleges require you to use your student e-mail account to send and receive official communications. It is a good idea to get in the habit of checking that account daily, or at least every other day.

Whether your class meets online or face-to-face, at some point you will need to communicate with your instructor via e-mail. Although you may prefer to use Facebook or Twitter, be sure to use e-mail to communicate with your instructors unless they tell you otherwise. Writing e-mails to your instructors is different from writing e-mails or sending texts to your friends.

The Problem

You need help with an assignment or you have a question about the syllabus and have to send your professor an e-mail, but you've never sent an e-mail to any kind of teacher before.

The Fix

Take a few minutes to figure out what exactly you need to ask, jot down your main points, and then construct a clear and concise e-mail.

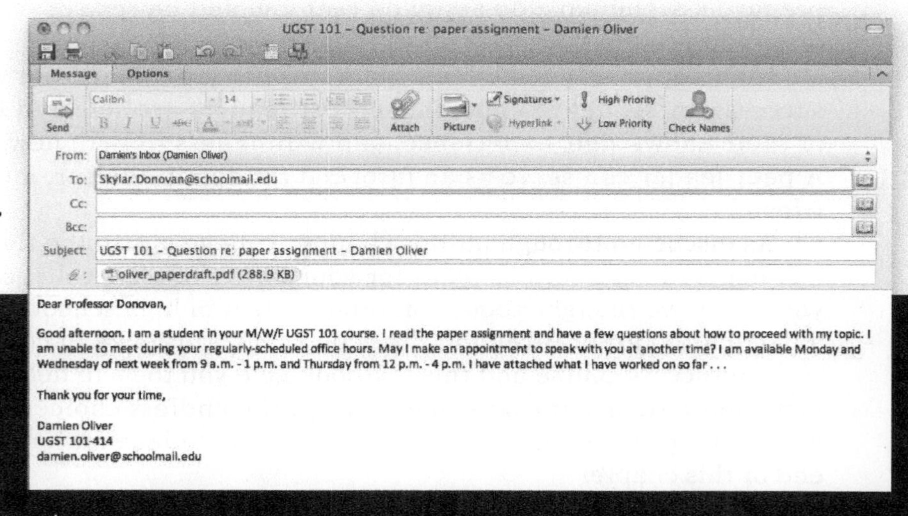

UGST 101 – Question re: paper assignment – Damien Oliver

From: Damien's Inbox (Damien Oliver)
To: Skylar.Donovan@schoolmail.edu
Cc:
Bcc:
Subject: UGST 101 – Question re: paper assignment – Damien Oliver
oliver_paperdraft.pdf (288.9 KB)

Dear Professor Donovan,

Good afternoon. I am a student in your M/W/F UGST 101 course. I read the paper assignment and have a few questions about how to proceed with my topic. I am unable to meet during your regularly-scheduled office hours. May I make an appointment to speak with you at another time? I am available Monday and Wednesday of next week from 9 a.m. - 1 p.m. and Thursday from 12 p.m. - 4 p.m. I have attached what I have worked on so far . . .

Thank you for your time,

Damien Oliver
UGST 101-414
damien.oliver@schoolmail.edu

How to Do It

Look at the example shown here and follow its format in your e-mail.

It's best to use your college e-mail address because it has your name and your college's e-mail address, which will help your professor immediately recognize that your message has been sent by a student. If you have to use another e-mail address, use a professional, simple address that includes your name.

- Make the subject line informative. Your instructor might receive hundreds of e-mails every day, and a relevant subject like the name of the course or the assignment will help him or her respond to your e-mail promptly. A subject line like "Class" or "Question" isn't helpful; a blank subject line usually goes to the instructor's spam folder.
- Address your instructor with respect. Think about how you address your instructor in class, or look at your syllabus to see his or her proper title. If an instructor uses Doctor, then you should use Doctor. If you don't know your instructor's title, you can never go wrong with Dear Professor, plus your instructor's last name.
- Sign every e-mail with your full name, course number, and e-mail address.
- When attaching files to your e-mail (a skill you should have), use widely accepted file formats like .doc, .docx, or .pdf. Also, be sure your last name is included in the file name. See the example shown.

EXTRA STYLE POINTS: Set your college e-mail to feed into your phone, tablet, or regular online account. Tie it into your regular e-mail, like Google or Outlook. Most of these services can be configured so that you can receive e-mail from multiple accounts. This way, you will have all of your e-mail in one place that you're sure to check.

**Note:* If you want to cut back on e-mails from Web sites that you visit, use a free service like UnRollMe (https://unroll.me) that condenses the blanket e-mails you get, but allows you to read them when you have time. You can list your instructors as "favorites" so you don't miss their e-mails.

You might be returning to college or beginning college for the first time. You will face a special set of challenges, such as trying to relate to younger students and juggling the responsibilities of work, caring for a family, and being in college. You will likely experience a challenging lack of freedom in dealing with so many important, competing responsibilities. Remember, though, that nontraditional students tend to have intrinsic motivation that comes with maturity and experience, and they appreciate the value of an education. You will have the advantage of approaching college work with a very clear purpose for why you are there.

No matter where you are on the age continuum—seventeen or eighteen or much older—you will bring certain strengths to your college experiences that will help both you and others. Older students have a lot of determination and a set of real-life experiences that they can relate to what they're learning. Eighteen- and nineteen-year-olds are comfortable with technology and social media, and they are pop-culture experts. These kinds of strengths are all important to the learning process.

is**this**you?

I Don't Know What I'm Doing Here

Is everyone in your family excited about your being in college–except you? Are you wondering why you've made this major commitment of time, energy, and money? You will read in this chapter that finding a sense of purpose is important if you want to make the most of college. But identifying that purpose doesn't always happen for everyone at the same time or in the same way. Don't give up. It could be that you are a bit homesick, fearful of the unknown, or feeling lost in a new environment. Find a counselor, a chaplain, an instructor, an older student, a peer leader, or a fellow first-year student you can talk to about the way you're feeling. It is very likely that others can relate to you because they either share these feelings, or did in the recent past. Ask how they overcame these feelings to get ideas on how you can, too. Connecting with others who have overcome the same challenges that you are facing can make all the difference.

Communicating with Your Instructors

In college, whether you're a nontraditional student adjusting to less freedom than you've been used to or a traditional student adjusting to more freedom, you will find that your instructors are not going to tell you what, how, or when to study. In addition, they will rarely monitor your progress. However you will have more freedom to express views that are different from theirs. They will usually have private offices and keep regular office hours when they can meet with you. Check with your instructors to find out if you need to make an appointment before coming to their office. (Read the Tech Tip: E-Mail with Style, which shows you how to communicate with your instructors appropriately via e-mail.) You might be able to ask your instructors a quick question before or after class, but you will be able to get far more help by actually visiting their offices. By taking advantage of office hours, you will also let the instructor know that you are serious about learning. You can ask the instructor for direct help with any question or misunderstanding that you have. You might also want to ask some questions about the instructor's educational career and particular research interests. Many students develop close relationships with their instructors, relationships that can be important both now and in the future.

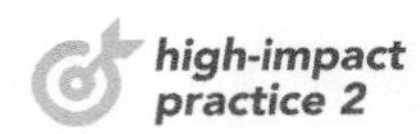

your turn Write and Reflect

What Does "The American Dream" Mean to You?

Using Google or another search engine, look up "American Dream" images. What images appear? Choose a few that resonate with you. Write a short essay describing these images and why you find them meaningful.

EXPLORING PURPOSE AND SETTING GOALS

You might think that you know exactly what you want to do with your life and where you want to go once you finish college. Or, like many students, you might be struggling to balance being in college, working, and having a satisfying personal life. You might be highly motivated to do your best in college, or you may be unsure about why you're in college at this time in your life. It is possible that as you discover more about yourself and your abilities, your purpose for coming to college will change.

Let's stop and think about what "purpose" means. A firefighter who enters a burning building with people trapped inside has a clear purpose: He has been trained to get those people out of the building safely. He is determined to fulfill the commitment of his job. The reason to go into the burning building is clear: to accomplish the objective of rescuing the people.

These words—determination, resolve, goal, reason, and objective—all relate to purpose. What will the training and education that you get in college teach you to do? How will succeeding in college help you succeed in the job and life that you envision for yourself? What do you feel determined to be, to have, and to accomplish? As you consider your answers to these questions, you'll get closer to understanding your purpose for being in college and setting the right goals to achieve this purpose. The more you keep the answers to these questions in the front of your mind, the more purposeful you will feel in what you do, and the more motivated you will be to do it. In this course and in this book, we'll help you answer questions about purpose, and we will equip you with strategies to help you achieve your goals.

Another concept that we stress in this book is "resilience," which is an ability to recover from or adjust easily to misfortune or change. Virtually every college student faces an occasional disappointment, whether it's a poor grade, an unsatisfactory performance on a stage or in an athletic arena, or the end of a relationship. Students who are resilient—who bounce back quickly from difficult situations—will be more successful in college and later in life. We encourage you to develop your own resilience as a tool you will use now and in the future.

Getting Started with Goal Setting

Think about how you define success. Is success about money, friendship, or power? Is it about achieving excellence in college and beyond, or is it about finding a sense of purpose in your life? For most people, success is a combination of all these factors and more. Although luck or "who you know" may play a role, first and foremost your success will be the result of intentional steps you take. So, in your quest for success, where do you start?

Identify Your Personal Strengths. Do you like to talk, deal with conflict, and stand up for yourself? Are you a good reader? If your answers to these questions are "yes," you may want to consider a career in the legal profession. Are you a good science student, and do you enjoy working with your hands? If so, you might want to think about dentistry. Your campus career center can help you discover your unique strengths—and weaknesses—which can influence your direction as you explore career choices.

Ask Yourself Tough Questions. Am I here to find out who I am and to study a subject that I am truly passionate about, regardless of whether it leads to a career? Am I here to engage in an academic program that provides an array of possibilities when I graduate? Am I here to prepare myself for a graduate program or for immediate employment? Am I here to obtain specific training in a field that I am committed to? Am I here to gain specific skills for a job I already have?

Establish Goals for Today, This Week, This Year, and Beyond. Although some students prefer to "go with the flow" and let life happen to them, those students are more likely to flounder and less likely to achieve success in college or in a career. So, instead of "going with the flow" and simply reacting to what college and life present, think instead about how you can take more control over the decisions and choices you make now, because these decisions and choices will lay the foundation for the achievement of future life goals. It is easy to make vague plans for the future, but you must determine which short-term steps are necessary if those plans are to become a reality.

College is an ideal time to begin setting and fulfilling short- and long-term goals. A short-term goal might be to read twenty pages from your history text twice a week to prepare for an exam that will cover the first hundred pages of the book. A long-term goal might be to begin predicting which elective college courses you could choose that would help you attain your career goals.

Thinking about a career might seem unrelated to some of the general education courses you are required to take in your first year. Sometimes it's hard to see the connection between a history or literature course and what you want to do with the rest of your life. If you're open to learning, however, you may discover potential areas of interest that you have never considered before, and these areas of interest may lead you to discover a new career path.

Setting SMART Goals

Follow these guidelines to set some short-term goals and consider how they fall within the framework of setting goals that are *specific, measurable, attainable, relevant,* and achievable within a given *time* (SMART).[2] (Figure 2 gives you a chance to practice.)

1. Be specific about what you want to achieve and when.
2. State your goal in measurable terms.
3. Be sure that the goal is attainable. If you don't have the necessary skills, strengths, and resources to achieve your goal, change it to one that is more appropriate for you. Be sure that you really want to reach the goal. Don't set out to work toward something only because you want to please others.
4. Know how the goal is relevant to your life and why the goal matters. Be sure that your goal helps your larger life plan and gives you a sense of moving forward.
5. Consider the time frame and whether the goal is achievable within the period you desire. Allow yourself enough time to pursue it considering any difficulties you might have. Plan for ways you might deal with problems. Decide which goal comes next. How will you begin? Create steps and a time line for reaching your next goal.

For instance, let's assume that after you graduate, you think that you might want to work in an underdeveloped country, perhaps spending some time in the Peace Corps. What are some short-term goals that would help you reach this long-term objective? One goal might be to take courses focused on different countries or cultures, but that goal isn't very specific and doesn't state a particular time period. A much more specific goal would be to take one course each year that helps you build a body of knowledge about other countries and cultures. An even more specific goal would be to review the course catalog, identify the courses you want to take, and list them on a personal time line.

Before working toward any long-term goal, it's important to be realistic and honest with yourself. Is it truly *your* goal—one that you yourself value and desire to pursue—or is it a goal that a parent or friend argued was right for you? Given your abilities and interests, is the goal realistic? Remember that dreaming up long-term goals is the easy part. To reach your goals, you need to be specific and systematic about the steps you will take today, this week, and throughout your college experience.

ACADEMIC PLANNING

If you have a goal to drive across the United States, you could, in theory, hop in a car that may need an oil change and travel without GPS or an itinerary and without a carefully packed bag or a planned

[2]T. Doran, "There's a S.M.A.R.T. Way to Write Management's Goals and Objectives," *Management Review* 70, no. 11 (1981): 35–36.

FIGURE 2 > Practice Setting SMART Goals

Using this chart, try to set one goal in each of the areas listed: academic, career, personal, and financial. Follow the goal through time, from immediate to long term. An example is provided for you.

Types of Goals	Immediate (this week)	Short Term (this term)	Long Term (this year)
Example: Academic	I will list all of my tests and project due dates on my academic calendar.	I will keep a file with my own test and exam grades in case of a discrepancy with my final grades.	I will research graduate programs in my field to determine if I have the grades and scores to be admitted.
Academic			
Career			
Personal			
Financial			

budget. You could simply follow the stars and road signs and hope for the best with weather, lodging, money, and the condition of the car. You might make it to your destination—which you didn't even narrow down beyond getting to the opposite coast—but what is likely to go wrong? How would some planning have improved the journey? Planning your college education is no different. Some preparation, a navigation system, and a clear destination will help you reach your goals, and smoothly.

Academic planning is a vital step in your college career, and it should be an ongoing process that starts on day one. Once you lay a foundation for your studies, you'll save time and money, avoid missing credits, and take ownership of your curriculum. You'll also stay motivated with a clear sense of how each step in your academic plan contributes to your overall purpose for being in college. It's no coincidence that students who engage in academic planning are more likely to stay in school. They are the people who know where they're going and how to get there. They have set their goals, and they know what it takes to achieve them.

Choosing a Major

Even before you have figured out your purpose for going to college, you might be required to select a program of study also referred to as a major, an area of study like psychology, engineering, education, or nursing. Selecting a major is one step in academic planning. In every major, students take a variety of courses; some are directly related to the area of study, whereas others are general education and elective courses. For example, all students should take college-level math and English courses as part of general education, but they can choose electives depending on their interests.

Many students change majors as they better understand their strengths and weaknesses, learn more about career options, and become interested in different areas of study. Some colleges and universities allow you to be undecided for a while or to select liberal arts as your major until you make a decision about what to study.

Although it's OK to be undecided, planning your major and your college curriculum as soon as possible saves valuable time and resources. Even if you're on financial aid, you're not going to have an unlimited amount of cash. If you randomly take courses without a specific goal in mind, your tuition funds could dry up before your plan takes shape. Therefore, it's essential to have a strategy for your program of study. Start by building a solid base of general courses that could qualify you for a few different majors, but leave time in your schedule to explore other subjects that grab your interest. Do you like math? Try an accounting or economics class. Love *CSI*? Sign up for Criminology 101 or the equivalent. An academic adviser or counselor can provide you with proper information and guidance to make a decision about your major.

Working with an Academic Adviser

Before you register for classes next term, sit down for a strategy session with your academic adviser. On most campuses, you'll be assigned an adviser, who is usually an instructor or a staff person in your chosen field of study. Some colleges offer special advisory centers run by professional advisers. A good adviser can help you choose courses, decide on a major, weigh career possibilities, and map out your degree and certificate requirements. Your adviser can also recommend instructors and help you simplify all aspects of your academic life, so it's important to meet with your adviser right away. Here are a few ways to make sure that your first meeting is a valuable experience.

- **Prepare for the meeting by looking at the course catalog, thinking about available majors, and familiarizing yourself with campus resources.** If you haven't decided on a major, investigate opportunities for taking an aptitude test or self-assessment to help you narrow down your options; ask your adviser about these tests during your meeting. The early days of college are critical; once classes start, you might not have time for in-depth research.
- **Prepare materials to bring to the meeting.** Even if you submitted one with your application, take along a copy of your academic transcript. The transcript, which contains your complete high school record, is an

important tool. It shows your academic adviser where you've been, what your academic strengths are, and where your interests lie.

- **Make a list of majors that appeal to you.** Academic advisers love it when students come prepared. It shows that you're passionate and serious about your future.
- **Map out your time frame and goals.** Do you plan to enroll full-time or part-time? If you're at a four-year college or university, when do you plan to graduate and with what degree? Are you planning to go to graduate school to finish your studies? If you are at a two-year college, do you want an associate's degree or a certificate? Do you plan to transfer to a four-year institution?
- **Know the right questions to ask.** Once you've chosen a major, you'll need to understand how to move forward in your academic program to meet the necessary requirements. Fortunately, the process is straightforward. You will have prerequisites, which are the core courses that you need to take before you can enroll in upper-level classes in your major. Your major may also have corequisites, courses that you have to take in conjunction with other courses during the same term, such as a chemistry lab alongside your chemistry class. With this knowledge under your belt, here is what you need to find out:

  1. How many credits must I take each term to graduate on time? (Note: If you are on financial aid, doing a work-study program, or are a college athlete, you may have to take a minimum number of credits per term to maintain your benefits.)
  2. What are the prerequisites for my major? Corequisites?
  3. If I've taken any advanced placement credits or exams, can I use them to fulfill some of my major's requirements?
  4. What career opportunities will I have once I graduate? What will the salary potential look like?

- **Know what to take away from your meeting.** By the end of the meeting, you should have a printout of your current course schedule and plans for classes that you might take in the next term and beyond. At many institutions, you and your adviser will set up a five- to seven-term plan online.
- **Know these rules of thumb about selecting your classes:**

  1. Most full-time students take four to six courses a term. Most classes don't meet every day. With that in mind, decide which classes you want to take, find out which days and times they meet, and make sure they don't overlap.
  2. To get the classes you want, make sure to register as early as possible, either in person or online.
  3. Resist the temptation to cram all your classes into one or two days. It's better to aim for a manageable workload, so spread your classes over the week.
  4. Go for a mix of hard and easy classes. Especially at the beginning, you might not realize how challenging college classes can be or how much outside work they entail. If you load up on organic chemistry, Russian 101, and advanced thermodynamics, your grades and general well-being could suffer.

- **Know what to do if your academic adviser isn't very helpful.** If you think that you and your adviser are not a good match, talk to your college success course instructor about what you need to do to be assigned to a different adviser. Alternately, drop by the campus counseling center for assistance. But whatever you do, be resilient. Don't throw in the towel. Academic planning is so critical to your success in college that it's worth persevering until you find an adviser with whom you feel comfortable.
- **Set up subsequent meetings with your academic adviser.** Touch base with your adviser at least once a term, if not more. It's important to stay connected and make sure that you're on a positive track. Programs change requirements occasionally, so it's smart to touch base to make any necessary adjustments. Here are some questions to ask your adviser as you check in:
  1. Have there been any changes to my program of study?
  2. If I want to officially withdraw from a class, will I be penalized at a later time?
  3. Am I still taking classes in the right order?
  4. What courses do I need to take to satisfy the major requirements at the institution where I plan to transfer?
  5. For those students who are considering graduate school: Am I meeting the criteria for graduate school, and will my grades qualify me for the program I'm interested in?

your turn Stay Motivated

Academic Planning

You have probably already met with an academic adviser, but if not, schedule a meeting right away. Think about this meeting and what you accomplished. Then write a short paper or journal entry about something you learned that increased your motivation to take academic planning seriously. Also, describe in writing at least three problems you might encounter when it comes to choosing your major or planning your program of study if you do not take academic planning seriously. How can these possible negative consequences increase your motivation to plan well for your next meeting with your adviser?

checklist for success

Welcome to Your College Experience

- **Know and appreciate the value of a college education, your college success course, and this textbook.** College is a major investment of both time and money, an investment that will pay rich dividends both now and in the future. This course and this textbook can help you make the right choices and increase your chances for success. Read the table of contents, skim the entire book, and access the information that you need now.

- **Meet with your instructors outside of class.** You can talk to your instructors before or after class, but the better option is to visit them during their office hours. You'll probably also have the opportunity to get to know your instructors in informal settings; some of them may even invite you and your classmates to their homes or to a local restaurant to share a meal and conversation.

- *high-impact practice* **Pursue high-impact practices.** Throughout this textbook, we have highlighted high-impact practices. These practices will begin in the first year and continue throughout your college experience. By taking every opportunity to participate in high-impact practices, you will increase your learning and overall success in college.

- **Meet the challenges of making the transition from high school to college or of being a nontraditional student returning to college.** Whatever your age or stage of life, beginning college is one of life's most significant transitions. This book will help you become more aware of the particular kinds of transition experiences you will encounter either as a student fresh out of high school or one who has been working or raising a family before beginning college.

- **Set both short-term and long-term goals.** You are far more likely to succeed in college if your goals for today, tomorrow, and four years from now are clear. For instance, if you plan to graduate from college in four years, what goals could you set for this week or this term that would help you reach this important long-term goal?

- **Find a competent and caring academic adviser or counselor.** Prepare thoroughly for your first meeting with your adviser, know what questions to ask, and keep in touch throughout each term. Doing so will lead to successful academic planning. Remember that if you are not comfortable with the person who has been assigned as your academic adviser, you can request a different one.

- **Have realistic expectations.** If you are disappointed in your grades, remember that college is a new experience and that your grades will probably improve if you continue to work hard and apply yourself. Be sure to take advantage of the services available through your campus's learning center.

build your experience

REFLECT ON CHOICES

high-impact practice 2

Reflect and write about what you have learned about college success in this chapter and how you are going to apply this information to the choices that you need to make this term. Select a few choices you need to make such as when to meet with an academic adviser and whether or when to visit instructors during their office hours. Write about these choices in a journal entry or readily accessible file. Revisit these questions throughout your first-year experience.

APPLY WHAT YOU'VE LEARNED

Now that you have read and discussed this chapter, consider how you can apply what you have learned to your academic and personal life. The following prompts will help you reflect on chapter material and its relevance to you, both now and in the future.

1. Why are you in college? Reflect on your decision to enter this college at this time in your life. Be honest about who or what influenced you to make this decision. What challenges do you face, and what strategies for success in this chapter can you use to overcome those challenges?
2. College students often feel the stress of trying to balance their personal and academic lives. The ups and downs of life are inevitable, but we can control our choices and attitudes. You will want to develop a personal strategy for being resilient—for bouncing back after a particularly difficult time.

USE YOUR RESOURCES

- **Academic Advising Center** Does your institution have an academic advising center, or is advising done by faculty? If you don't already know, find out this week where you can get help with selecting courses, learning how to get information on degree requirements, and deciding on a major.
- **Academic Skills Center** Whether you need help or not, explore this facility. Its services can include tutoring, help with study and memory skills, and help with studying for exams.
- **Adult Reentry Center** If you are an adult or returning student, visit this center to learn about special programs, make contacts with other adult students, and gather information about services such as child care.
- **Career Center** You may visit the career center as part of your college success course. If not, put it on your list of important campus services. Career centers usually feature a career library, interest assessments, counseling, and help in finding a major.
- **Commuter Services** Commuter students are the new majority. If you are a commuter student, find the campus office that provides lists of special services for you.
- **Counseling Center** Find out about your institution's counseling center and the services it offers, which will probably include stress-management programs and confidential counseling.
- **Financial Aid and Scholarship Office** Be sure to meet with someone in this office to learn about financial aid programs, scholarships, and grants.
- **Veterans Affairs Office** If you are a veteran, be sure to learn about the services of this office, including special financial aid.
- **Health Center** Don't wait until you need a doctor or a nurse. Locate your campus health center and learn about their services.
- **Math Center** If your math instructor hasn't already told you about help from the math center, ask whether your college or university has such a center.
- **Writing Center** As you write your first research paper, ask an expert in the writing center to read a first draft for help with proper grammar, syntax, and punctuation, as well as the appropriate method for citing and listing references.

LaunchPad

LaunchPad for *Your College Experience* is a great resource! Go online to master concepts using the LearningCurve study tool and much more. macmillanhighered.com/gardner12e

Michael Krinke/Getty Images

2 TIME MANAGEMENT

YOU WILL EXPLORE

Ways to manage your time

Time-management tools

Procrastination and how to overcome it

Setting priorities and achieving balance

The value of time and the importance of allocating your time wisely

High-impact practices 2 (writing) and 3 (collaboration)

John N. Gardner and Betsy O. Barefoot, "Time Management," from *Your College Experience: Strategies for Success*, Twelfth Edition, pages 23–44. Copyright © 2016 by Bedford/St. Martin's.

Abby York, 19

Economics major
California State University, Los Angeles

"It is difficult balancing school, volunteer work, and a job, but as long as you have everything scheduled and planned, it is easily achievable and very rewarding."

When Abby York started college, she had already begun to build a solid foundation in time-management skills. She was born in New York City and moved to Los Angeles, California, when she was three years old. During her senior year of high school, she participated in a college preparation program, which meant taking all her classes at a local college to gain transferable credits. The curriculum included a course that focused on learning how to manage time and set priorities. She credits that course with helping her learn how to manage time in her first year of college and beyond. But even with a solid foundation, Abby didn't make it through her first year of college without a few time-management roadblocks. "Sometimes I just got overwhelmed with school and just wanted to work or hang out with my friends and would put my schoolwork on the back burner. This had some bad side effects. Once I saw the drop in my grades, I knew that I had to reprioritize and get back on track."

One key to Abby's success with time management is organization. "I use both paper and electronic organizational tools. If my computer ever goes down, I still have all my information, plans, and due dates in my planner, and vice versa, if I lose my planner, I still have everything on my computer."

Abby recognizes that prioritizing is the key to maintaining her busy schedule and her sanity. "My first priority is school, second comes work, and then everything else—volunteering, exercising, friends, and family," she says. "I find places in my schedule to fit them in every week. All these things are important and essential for me to be successful and happy. It's like each piece of my life is a puzzle piece. If I don't keep making sure that each piece fits, or if there is any piece missing, the puzzle doesn't work and breaks apart."

Abby recently changed her major from psychology to economics. She just returned from a semester abroad in England and is looking into transferring to a school more geared toward her new major. After college, she hopes to move to the East Coast, find a job in market research or finance, and possibly continue her education in graduate school. Her advice to other first-year students: "Take a class on time management and balancing all your priorities. It definitely helped me ease into college life and balance my life."

To access the LearningCurve study tool, video activities, and more, go to LaunchPad for *Your College Experience*. macmillanhighered.com/gardner12e

Time management is a challenge for almost all first-year college students, many of whom misallocate their time at first. Soon they realize they will have to change their behavior to ensure that they have sufficient time to give to their coursework. How did Abby deal with the time-management roadblocks that she encountered? How do you deal with those you face? This chapter covers many challenges to time management, such as procrastination and distractions, and it offers techniques you can use to meet your obligations and use your time effectively.

assess your strengths

Time management is challenging for almost all college students. What time-management tools are you already using to manage your time? How do you set and manage your priorities? As you begin to read this chapter, consider the strengths you have in this area.

set goals

Think about challenges you have had in the past with managing your time. Use this chapter to help you understand some strategies and develop goals that relate to time management, such as developing an hour-by-hour record this week of how you spend your time.

MANAGING YOUR TIME

People approach the concept of time differently based on their personalities and backgrounds. Some people are always punctual, while others are almost always late. Some students enter all due dates for assignments on a calendar as soon as they receive the syllabus for each class. Other students take a more laid-back approach and prefer to go with the flow rather than follow a daily or weekly schedule. These students might deal well with the unexpected, but they might also leave everything to the last minute and be less successful than if they managed their time more effectively. Even if you prefer to go with the flow, improving your organizational skills can help you do better in college, work, and life. Think of it this way: If *you* were hiring someone for a job, wouldn't you choose an organized person who gets things done on time?

Taking Control of Your Time

The first step to effective time management is recognizing that you can be in control. Psychologists use the term *locus of control—locus* means "place"—to refer to a person's beliefs about how much control they have over the events that affect them. Being in control means that you make your own decisions and accept responsibility for the outcomes of those decisions.

Some people believe that their locus of control is internal, or within themselves; others believe that it is external, or beyond their power. If you frequently find yourself saying "I don't have time," you likely have an external locus of control. The next time you find yourself saying this, stop and ask yourself whether it is actually true. Do you *really* not have time, or have you made a choice not to make time for a particular task or activity? When we say we don't have time, we imply that we don't have a choice. We do have a choice because we have control over how we use our time and how many commitments and small decisions we choose to make every day. For example, we have control over when we get up in the morning; how much sleep we get; and how much time we spend studying, working, and exercising. All of these small decisions have a big impact on our success in college and in life.

Your Memory Cannot Be Your Only Planner

How you manage your time reflects what you value—what is most important to you and what consequences you are willing to accept when you make certain choices. For instance, if you value time with friends above everything else, your academic work likely takes a backseat to social activities. How you manage your time also corresponds to how successful you will be in college and throughout life. Almost all successful people use some sort of calendar or planner to help them keep up with their appointments, assignments, tasks, and other important activities. Using your memory as your only planner—trying to remember everything you have to do without recording it anywhere—means that you will probably forget important events and deadlines.

your turn Make Good Choices

Does Your Planner Work for You?

What kind of planner do you currently use, if any? Do you use a paper planner or mark the calendar on your phone? Do you think you have chosen the best kind of planner for you? Why or why not? Can you think of a different planner that might work even better?

USING TIME-MANAGEMENT TOOLS

Getting a bird's-eye view—or big picture—of each college term will allow you to plan ahead effectively. An **academic calendar** is a calendar that shows all the important dates that are specific to your campus: financial aid, registration, and add/drop deadlines; midterm and final exam dates; holidays; graduation deadlines; and so forth. You may have received an academic calendar when you registered for classes, or your campus bookstore may have one for sale.

Knowing your big-picture academic deadlines will be helpful as you add deadlines for specific assignments, papers, and exams into your calendar. It is important to refer to your college's academic calendar to add important dates and deadlines, such as when the registration period starts and ends and when you need to pay your tuition or file your application for financial aid or scholarships. Remember, also, that you have to keep track of important dates, not only in your own life, but also in the lives of those close to you—birthdays, doctor's appointments, work schedules, travel, visits from out-of-town guests, and so on. Different aspects of your life have different sorts of time requirements, and the goal is to stay on top of all of them.

You might prefer to use an electronic calendar on your phone, tablet, laptop, or desktop. (See the Tech Tip in this chapter for different options.) Regardless of whether you prefer a paper or electronic calendar, it's a good idea to begin the academic term by reviewing the syllabus for each of your courses and then completing a preview (Figure 1), recording all of your commitments for each day, and using different colors for each category:

- Classes
- Study time for each class you're taking
- Tests and assignment due dates
- Personal obligations such as work, family, friends
- Scheduled social events (including phone numbers in case you need to cancel)

FIGURE 1 › Monthly Calendar

Using the course syllabi provided by your instructors, create your own monthly calendars for your entire term. Provide details such as the number of hours you anticipate spending on each assignment or task.

MONTH: SEPTEMBER

MONDAY	TUESDAY	WEDNESDAY	THURSDAY	FRIDAY	SATURDAY	SUNDAY
					1	2
3 9–12 Work	4 First Day of Classes 9–12 Psychology 2–5 Work 8–9 Psychology: Read Ch. 1	5 9–12 Work 1–4 Math 8–10 Math HW1	6 10–1 English 2–5 Work 8–10 English: Read Ch. 1	7 10–12 Work 9–10 Psychology: Review Notes	8 10–4 Work 8–9 Math HW 1 9–10 English: Read Ch. 1	9 2–4 Review Math Notes 6–10 Party at Susan's
10 9–12 Work 1–5 Biology	11 9–12 Psychology 2–5 Work 8–10 Biology: Read Ch. 1	12 9–12 Work 1–4 Math 8–10 Psychology: Read Ch. 2	13 10–1 English 2–5 Work 7–8 Math HW 2 9–11 Biology: Read Ch. 1	14 10–12 Work 1–3 Lunch with Mary 6–7 Start English Summary Paper	15 10–4 Work 4–6 Shopping 9–10 Finish English Summary Paper	16 10–1 Study for Psychology Test 6–8 Review Math notes for Quiz 1
17 9–12 Work 1–5 Biology 7–10 Study for Psychology Test	18 9–12 Psychology Psychology Test 1 2–5 Work 8–9 Review Math notes for Quiz 1	19 Work 9–12 Math 1–4 Math Quiz 1 8–9 Revise English Summary Paper	20 10–1 English English Summary Paper due 2–5 Work 8–10 Biology: Read Ch. 2	21 10–12 Work 1–2 Attend Student Club Meeting 6–9 Math HW 3	22 10–4 Work 5–7 Psychology: Read Ch. 3 9–10 English: Read Ch. 2	23 10–12 Biology: Read Ch. 2 9–10 Biology: Lab Report 1
24 9–12 Work 1–5 Biology 6–8 Math Tutoring 10–11 Math HW 3	25 9–12 Psychology 2–5 Work 8–10 Biology: Read Ch. 3 10–11 Math HW 3	26 9–12 Work 1–4 Math 8–9 Psychology: Read Ch. 4 9–10 Prepare English Paper Outline	27 10–1 English 2–5 Work 7–9 Math HW 9–10 Review Biology Notes	28 10–12 Work 1–3 Meet with Biology Study Group 8–9 Biology: Lab report 2 9–11 English: Read Ch. 3	29 10–4 Work 8–9 English: Read Ch. 3	30 4–8 Nina's Birthday

Recording your daily commitments allows you to examine your toughest weeks during each month and each term. If research paper deadlines and test dates fall during the same week, find time to finish some assignments early to free up study time. If you use an electronic calendar, set reminders for these important deadlines and dates.

Overall, you should create monthly (Figure 1), weekly (Figure 2), and daily (Figure 3) views of your calendar. All three views are available in an

FIGURE 2 ❯ Weekly Timetable

Using your term calendar, create your own weekly timetable using a conventional template or one that uses an app such as LifeTopix. At the beginning of each term, track all of your activities for a full week by entering everything you do and how much time each task requires into your schedule. Use this record to help you estimate the time you will need for similar activities in the future.

SEPTEMBER

	MONDAY	TUESDAY	WEDNESDAY	THURSDAY	FRIDAY	SATURDAY	SUNDAY
Time	3	4 *First Day of Classes*	5	6	7	8	9
5 am							
6 am							
7 am							
8 am							
9 am	*Work*	*Psychology*	*Work*				
10 am				*English*	*Work*	*Work*	
11 am							
12 pm							
1 pm			*Math*				
2 pm		*Work*		*Work*	*Mom's Doctor's Appointment*		*Review Math Notes*
3 pm							
4 pm							
5 pm							
6 pm							*Party at Susan's*
7 pm							
8 pm		*Psychology: Read Ch. 1*	*Math HW1*	*English: Read Ch. 1*		*Math HW 1*	
9 pm					*Psychology: Review Notes*	*English: Read Ch. 1*	
10 pm							
11 pm							
12 am							

FIGURE 3 › Daily Planner
Notice how college, work, and personal activities are noted on this daily planner.

	FRIDAY, SEPTEMBER 14
5 am	
6 am	
7 am	
8 am	
9 am	
10 am	*Work*
11 am	
12 pm	
1 pm	*Lunch with Mary*
2 pm	
3 pm	
4 pm	
5 pm	
6 pm	*Start English Summary Paper*
7 pm	
8 pm	

electronic planner, but you can also create monthly, weekly, and daily calendars with paper planners.

Once you complete your monthly templates, you can put them together to preview your entire academic term. Remember to provide details such as the number of hours you anticipate spending on each assignment or task.

As you create your schedule, try to reserve study time for each class and for each assignment. Not all assignments will take an equal amount of time to complete. Estimate how much time you will need for each one, and begin your work well before the assignment is due. A good time manager frequently allows for emergencies by finishing assignments before actual due dates. If you are also working on or off campus, reconsider how many hours per week it will be reasonable for you to work on top of your academic commitments, and whether you need to reduce your credit load to ensure that you have enough time for both work and school.

Remember that managing your time effectively requires practice. You may have to rearrange your schedule a few times, rethink some priorities, and try to use your time differently. The more you apply time-management skills, the more time you can save.

Being a good student does not necessarily mean studying day and night and doing little else. Scheduling time for work and pleasure is important, too. After all, most students have to juggle a *lot* of responsibilities. You might have to work to help pay for college, and you probably want to spend time with family or friends to recharge your battery. And most people also need time to relax and unwind; that time can include getting some exercise, reading a book for pleasure, or seeing a movie. Note that the daily planner (Figure 3 on the previous page) includes time for other activities as well as time for classes and studying.

When using an electronic calendar, it's a good idea to print a backup copy in case you lose your phone, cannot access the Internet, experience a computer crash, or leave your charger at home or in your residence hall. Carry your calendar with you in a place where you're not likely to lose it. Checking your calendar regularly helps you keep track of commitments and maintain control of your schedule. This practice will become invaluable to you in your career. Check your calendar daily for both the current week and the coming week. It takes just a moment to be certain that you aren't forgetting something important, and it helps relieve stress. Consider setting regular times to check your calendar every day, perhaps right after eating breakfast and then again in the evening, to see what's coming in the days and weeks ahead.

Keep the following points in mind as you organize your day:

- **Set realistic goals for your study time.** Assess how long it takes to read a chapter in your different textbooks and how long it takes you to review your notes from different instructors.
- **Use waiting, commuting, and travel time to review.** Allow time to review your notes as soon as you can after class. You can review your notes if you have a break between classes or while you're waiting for or riding the bus or train. Consider formally budgeting this commuting time in your planner. If you have a long drive, consider listening to recorded notes or asking those riding with you to quiz you. Make a habit of using waiting time wisely, and it will become bonus study time to help compensate for unexpected events that might pop up in your day and throw off your schedule.
- **Limit distracting and time-consuming communications.** Check your phone, tablet, or computer for messages or updates at a set time, not whenever you're tempted to do so. Constant texting, browsing, or posting can keep you from achieving your academic goals. Remember that when time has passed, you cannot get it back.
- **Avoid multitasking.** Doing more than one thing at a time, referred to as multitasking, requires that you divide your attention among tasks. You might think that you are good at multitasking. However, the reality is (and research shows) that you can get tasks done faster and more accurately if you concentrate on one at a time.[1] Don't take our word for it: Try setting up your schedule to focus on one important task at a time. You'll probably find you do a better job on your assignment, test, or project.
- **Be flexible.** You cannot anticipate every disruption to your plans. Build extra time into your schedule so that unexpected events do not prevent you from meeting your goals.
- **Schedule breaks.** Relax, catch up with friends and family, or spend time in the cafeteria or student center.

[1]E. Ophir, C. Nass, and A. Wagner, "Cognitive Control in Media Multitaskers," *Proceedings of The National Academy of Sciences* 106, no. 37 (2009).

your turn Make Good Choices

Select Your Best Study Times

What times of day or night do you usually study? Have you selected times when you can concentrate and be productive, or do you just study whenever you can fit it in, even if you're really tired and distracted? For instance, have you already figured out that early morning is your best time to read and remember what you're reading, or that studying after 10:00 p.m. is a waste? Everyone is different, so based on your college experience so far, make a list of the best and worst times for you to study. Most instructors will expect you to study two hours out of class for every hour you spend in class. Using your list as a guide, be intentional about the times you set aside for studying.

PROCRASTINATION

Procrastination is the habit of delaying something that needs your immediate attention. Putting things off can become a serious problem for college students. Dr. Piers Steel, a leading researcher and speaker on the science of motivation and procrastination, writes that procrastination is on the rise, with 80–95 percent of students in college spending time procrastinating.[2] According to Steel, half of college students report that they procrastinate on a regular basis, spending as much as one-third of their time every day in activities solely related to procrastination. All this procrastination takes place even though most people, including researchers who study the negative consequences of procrastination, view procrastination as a significant problem. These numbers, plus the widespread acknowledgment of the negative effects of procrastination, provide evidence that it is a serious issue that trips up many otherwise capable people. Researchers at Carleton University in Canada have found that college students who procrastinate in their studies also avoid confronting other tasks and problems and are more likely to develop unhealthy habits, such as higher levels of alcohol consumption, smoking, insomnia, a poor diet, or lack of exercise.[3]

The good news is that, of those people who procrastinate on a regular basis, 95 percent want to change their behavior.[4] As a first step toward initiating change, it is important to understand why people procrastinate. According to Steel, some people who are highly motivated fear failure, and

---

[2]Piers Steel, "The Nature of Procrastination: A Meta-Analytic and Theoretical Review of Quintessential Self-Regulatory Failure," *Psychological Bulletin* 133, no. 1 (2007): 65–94.

[3]Timothy A. Pychyl and Fuschia M. Sirois, "*Procrastination:* Costs to Health and Well-Being," presentation at the American Psychological Association convention, Aug. 22, 2002, Chicago.

[4]Piers Steel, "The Nature of Procrastination: A Meta-Analytic and Theoretical Review of Quintessential Self-Regulatory Failure," *Psychological Bulletin* 133, no. 1 (2007): 65–94.

GET DIGITALLY ORGANIZED

Mapping out your schedule doesn't have to be a chore. Think of a well-appointed calendar as a compass for a college student. Besides being a guide for navigating your current term, it will also keep you pointed toward your long-term goals.

The Problem

You keep forgetting assignments and can't find the paper planner that your college provided.

The Fix

Replace the lost paper planner with your phone or computer by using a free electronic calendar or phone app.

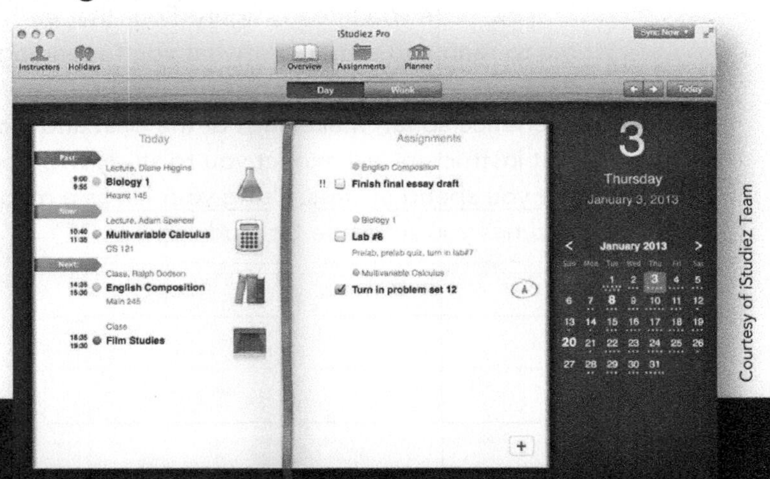

iStudiez Pro App for Android Devices

Courtesy of iStudiez Team

How to Do It

Select the device and platform you would be most likely to use. Don't make this complicated. You are trying to be more efficient.

- Would you check your phone, tablet, or computer?
- Do you have a Gmail or a Hotmail account already? (These will also allow you to share files with classmates for group projects using GoogleDrive or SkyDrive and will allow you to create and store files in the "cloud" using the Internet like a hard drive).
- Look at platforms like **iStudiez** (istudentpro.com) or **Studious** (studiousapp.com), which allow you to coordinate and sync your schedule across devices.

Collect schedule information. Depending on what system you are using, look at the syllabi you have gotten from your classes, especially if your instructors provided schedules for assignments, tests, quizzes, and projects. Also, go to your college's Web site and get a copy of the academic calendar, which will include dates that the college is closed, registration dates, and other important information.

Use the information you have collected. Set up your electronic calendar with important dates and your class schedule for the term. Your electronic calendar will allow you to repeat a weekly schedule so you won't have to type in each class meeting time individually. Set up alerts for major events (tests, registration deadlines, holiday closings, etc.) on your schedule so that your electronic calendar will send you text or e-mail reminders in advance. If you are confused about how to do this, go to YouTube and search "set up

Pick a time every week to review your schedule. Add things you need to accomplish to the list. Make a to-do list, and cross off tasks as you complete them.

Optional: Add your work schedule or other regular commitments and social events, so that you see them in real time next to your class schedule. Doing so will help you make time for the things you really want to do.

Remember: Setting up your schedule at the beginning of the term does take time, but fortunately, this is usually the time when fewer assignments are due. Having a schedule will pay you big dividends in fewer missed assignments and deadlines or worse, showing up for class on a day when there are no classes.

EXTRA STYLE POINTS: Sync your phone or tablet with your calendar so that if you make changes on your phone, they appear on your online system (Google Calendar, etc.), and if you make changes on your online system, they appear on your phone. Go to YouTube again, and search "Sync (your phone's name) with (the name of your online system)," and view some videos that show you exactly how to sync them. If you tied your Gmail or Outlook account to your campus e-mail, you should already be synced.

some people even fear success, although that might seem counterintuitive. Consequently, some students procrastinate because they are perfectionists; not doing a task might be easier than having to live up to your own very high expectations or those of your parents, teachers, or peers. Many procrastinate because they are easily distracted—a topic we'll explore below. Often they have difficulty organizing and regulating their lives, have difficulty following through on goals, view the assigned task as too far into the future, or find an assigned task boring or irrelevant[5] or consider it "busy work," believing they can learn the material just as effectively without doing the homework.

Overcoming Procrastination

Many of the traits most associated with people who chronically procrastinate can make change more difficult. Fortunately, though, there is hope. With certain changes in behaviors and mind-set, you can reduce procrastination and become more effective at managing your time. In college, changing how you think about and approach less enjoyable assignments is key to decreasing procrastination and increasing your success.

For instance, simply disliking an assignment is not a good reason to put it off; it's an *excuse*, not a valid *reason*. Throughout life you'll be faced with tasks you don't find interesting, and in many cases you won't have the option not to do them. Whether it is cleaning your house, filing your taxes, completing paperwork, or responding to hundreds of e-mails, tedious tasks will find you, and you will have to figure out strategies to complete them. College is a good time to practice and hone your skills at finishing uninteresting tasks in a timely manner. Perhaps counterintuitively, research indicates that making easier or less-interesting tasks more challenging can decrease boredom and increase your likelihood of completing the tasks on time.[6]

your turn Work Together

Staying on Task and on Time

With two or three other students, discuss ways to avoid procrastination. What works for you? Share examples from your experiences.

When you're in college, procrastinating can signal that it's time to reassess your goals and objectives; maybe you're not ready to make a commitment to academic priorities at this point in your life. Only you can decide, but an academic adviser can help you sort it out. If you cannot get procrastination under control, it is in your best interest to seek help at your campus counseling service before you begin to feel as though you are also losing control of other aspects of your life. Taking the Procrastination Self-Assessment in this chapter will help give you a sense of whether or not procrastination is a problem for you.

[5]Ibid.

[6]Ibid.

Procrastination Self-Assessment

Place a number from 1 to 5 before each statement. (For example, if you "agree" with a statement, place a 4 before the statement.)

1 = Strongly Disagree
2 = Disagree
3 = Mildly Disagree
4 = Agree
5 = Strongly Agree

____ I have a habit of putting off important tasks that I don't enjoy doing.

____ My standards are so high that I'm not usually satisfied enough with my work to turn it in on time.

____ I spend more time planning what I'm going to do than actually doing it.

____ The chaos in my study space makes it hard for me to get started.

____ The people I live with distract me from doing my class work.

____ I have more energy for a task if I wait until the last minute to do it.

____ I enjoy the excitement of living on the edge.

____ I have trouble prioritizing all my responsibilities.

____ Having to meet a deadline makes me really nervous.

____ My biggest problem is that I just don't know how to get started.

If you responded that you "agree" or "strongly agree" with two questions or fewer, then you may procrastinate from time to time, but it may not be a major problem for you. Reading this chapter will help you continue to stay focused and avoid procrastination in the future.

If you responded that you "agree" or "strongly agree" with three to five questions, then you may be having difficulties with procrastination. Revisit the questions to which you answered "agree" or "strongly agree" and look in the chapter for strategies that specifically address these issues to help you overcome obstacles. You *can* get a handle on your procrastination!

If you responded that you "agree" or "strongly agree" with six or more questions, then you may be having a significant problem with procrastination, and it could interfere with your success in college if you do not make a change. Revisit the questions to which you answered "agree" or "strongly agree" and look in the chapter for strategies that specifically address these issues. Also, if you are concerned about your pattern of procrastination and you aren't having success in dealing with it yourself, consider talking to a professional counselor in your campus counseling center. It's free and confidential, and counselors have extensive experience working with students who have problems with procrastination.

Here are some strategies for beating procrastination and staying motivated:

- Remind yourself of the possible consequences if you do not get down to work, and then get started. Also, remind yourself that simply not enjoying an assignment is not a good reason to put it off; it's an *excuse*, not a valid *reason*.
- Create a to-do list. Check off items as you get them done. Use the list to focus on the things that aren't getting done. Move them to the top of the next day's list, and make up your mind to do them. Working from a list will give you a feeling of accomplishment.

- Break big jobs into smaller steps. Tackle short, easy-to-accomplish tasks first.
- Avoid doing other things that might seem more fun, and promise yourself a reward for finishing the task, such as watching your favorite TV show or going out with friends. For completing larger tasks and assignments, give yourself bigger and better rewards.
- Find a place to study that's comfortable and doesn't allow for distractions and interruptions.
- Say *no* to friends and family members who want your attention; agree to spend time with them later, and schedule that time.
- Shut off and put away all electronic devices during planned study sessions. If you *need* to use an electronic device for studying, turn off all social media and any other applications that are not part of your studying—and *keep* them off.
- Consider asking those living with you to help keep you on track. If they see that you are not studying when you should be, ask them to remind you to get back to the books. If you study in your room, close your door.

Dealing with Distractions

Overcoming procrastination and planning your time effectively are closely associated with achieving your goals. What you do on a daily basis affects your outcomes for that week, that month, that year, and so on. Distractions may push you off course and away from your intended goals. A good first step is becoming aware of what distractions trip you up and considering how much control you have over them.

Table 1 lists possible distractions that may or may not be a problem for you. Choose Yes (a problem) or No (not a problem) for each one. Then note whether the distraction is controllable or uncontrollable and write down possible solutions.

TABLE 1

Distraction	Yes (Y) No (N)	Controllable (C) Uncontrollable (U)	Solutions
Texting/Messaging			
Social media			
Gaming/Videos/Music			
Sports/Hobbies			
Television/Streaming			
Lack of sleep			
Relationships			
Meals/Snacking			
Daydreaming			
Perfectionism			
Errands/Shopping			
Lost items			

(continued)

TABLE 1 *(continued)*

Distraction	Yes (Y) No (N)	Controllable (C) Uncontrollable (U)	Solutions
Worries/Stress			
Family			
Socializing/Friends			
Multitasking			
Illness, self or others			
Work schedule			
Pleasure reading			

What did you learn about yourself, the distractions that get in your way, and some ideas for taking control? What choices are you willing to make to maximize your time?

SETTING PRIORITIES

As you work to overcome procrastination and limit distractions, think about how to **prioritize**, which means putting your tasks, goals, and values in order of importance. (Below, we'll discuss strategies to avoid becoming overextended, which goes hand in hand with setting priorities.) Ask yourself which goals are most important, but also which ones are most urgent. For example, studying in order to get a good grade on tomorrow's test might have to take priority over attending a job fair today, or completing an assignment that is due tomorrow might have to take priority over driving your friend somewhere.

However, don't ignore long-term goals in order to meet short-term goals. With good time management, you can study during the week prior to the test so that you can attend the job fair, too. Skilled time managers often establish priorities by maintaining a term calendar and to-do lists on which they rank the items in order of importance to determine schedules and deadlines for each task.

From the beginning of the term, plan your work on term papers and major projects that might not be due for several weeks or even months. Consult with a tutor or a more experienced student to help you break large assignments down into smaller steps, such as choosing a topic, doing research, creating an outline, or writing a first draft. Once you have entered your future commitments in a term planner and

is **this** you?

Time Flies

Do you find yourself wondering where your time has gone at the end of a long day? Are you aware of how you spend your time when you're not in class, or does this time just seem to vanish? Of all the time-management strategies presented in this chapter, developing an awareness of how you spend your time might be the most important. Using a day planner or your smart phone, develop an "ideal" hour-by-hour schedule that covers the next week. At the end of each day, go back and check to see if you used your time as planned. If not, make sure your projections were realistic, adjust them if necessary, and then try some of the strategies presented in this chapter to improve your ability to control the way you spend your time.

Set Priorities Like the Pros

Professional coaches help their teams thrive by setting effective priorities, whether it's making a plan for the next play, for the whole game, or for an entire season. In setting your own priorities, take a lesson from these coaches: Prioritize your long-term plans while making sensible play-by-play decisions every day.

Jeff Gross/Getty Images

decided how your time will be spent each week, create your to-do list, which is especially handy for last-minute reminders. A to-do list helps you keep track of errands to run, appointments to make, and anything else you might forget. You can keep this list on your cell phone or tablet, in a notebook, or on a bulletin board in your room. Use your to-do list to keep track of all the tasks you need to remember, not just academics. Consider developing a system for prioritizing the items on your list: using different colors of ink for different groups of tasks; highlighting the most important assignments; marking items with one, two, or three stars; or adding letters A, B, C, and so on to indicate which tasks are most important (Figure 4).

FIGURE 4 › To-Do List

You can keep a to-do list on a mobile device, in a notebook, or on a bulletin board. Use it to keep track of all the tasks you need to remember, not just academics. Consider adding Saturday and Sunday as these are productive days for many busy people. As you complete a task, cross it off your list. Enjoy the satisfaction of each accomplishment.

THIS WEEK	COLLEGE	WORK	PERSONAL
Monday	*Schedule a math tutoring session*	*Meet with the department chair about my schedule*	*Make a haircut appointment*
Tuesday	*Make appointment with Prof. Velez to discuss paper topic*		*Order birthday gift for dad*
Wednesday	*Meet my history study group at 4:00 p.m.*	*Work in department, 9:00 a.m.–noon*	
Thursday	*Finish English essay*		*Pick up dry cleaning*
Friday		*Work in department, 9:00 a.m.–noon*	*Make eye appointment*

Find a Balance

Another aspect of setting priorities while in college is finding a way to balance your academic schedule with the rest of your life. Social and extracurricular activities (for instance, participating in a club, writing for the college newspaper, attending special lectures, concerts, athletic events, or theater performances) are important parts of the college experience. Time spent alone and time spent thinking are also essential to your overall well-being.

Don't Overextend Yourself

Being **overextended**, or having too much to do given the resources available to you, is a primary source of stress for college students. Determine what a realistic workload is for you, but note that this can vary significantly from one person to another, and only you can determine what is realistic. Although being involved in social and family life is very important, don't allow your academic work to take a backseat to other time commitments. Take on only what you can handle. Learn to say *no,* as this is an effective time-management strategy! Say no to requests that will prevent you from meeting your academic goals. Remember that even if you can find the time for extra tasks, you may not be able to find the energy.

If you are feeling stressed, assess your time commitments and let go of one or more. If you choose to drop a course, make sure you do so before the drop deadline so that you won't have a low grade on your permanent record. If you receive financial aid, keep in mind that you must be registered for a minimum number of credit hours to maintain your current level of financial aid. Read more about financial aid in the chapter on managing money.

Hang On

It's important to find a balance between your studies, work, family, exercise, and other responsibilities so you do not overextend yourself. Keep your goals and priorities in mind, and avoid an event like this one the day before an exam!

your turn Stay Motivated

The Predicament of Too Many Obligations

Are you trying to do too much, and is your crazy schedule reducing your motivation for college? Are you overinvolved in campus organizations? Are you working too many hours off campus? Are you feeling really stressed out? In a small group, discuss strategies for reducing your stress level and maintaining your motivation for being successful in your academic work.

Stay Focused

Many students of all ages question their decision to attend college and sometimes feel overwhelmed by the additional responsibilities it brings. Some first-year students, especially recent high school graduates, might temporarily forget their main purposes for coming to college and spend their first term of college engaging in a wide array of new experiences.

Allowing yourself a little time to adjust to college is OK within limits, but you don't want to spend the next four or five years trying to make up for poor decisions made early in your college career, such as skipping class and not taking your assignments seriously. Such decisions can lead to a low grade point average (GPA) and the threat of academic probation or, worse, academic dismissal.

A great way to focus and to keep your priorities on track is to finish what *needs* to be done before you move from work to pleasure. From time to time, you will have competing responsibilities; for example, you might have to work additional hours at your job when you need additional time to study

Work Study

Did you know that the majority of college students have jobs? If you need to work, try to find a job that is flexible and allows you to study during down-time. Use every available minute to stay up to date with your classwork.

Courtesy of Sue McDermott Barlow

for an exam. In cases like these, talk to the people involved, including your instructors and your employer, to see how you can manage the conflict.

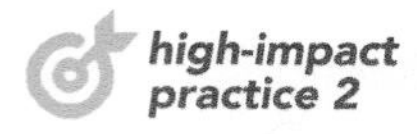
high-impact practice 2

your turn Write and Reflect

What Are Your Priorities?

List your current priorities, and assign a value to each on a scale of 1–5 with 1 as most important and 5 as least important. Write a short paper about why you consider some things more important than others. Think about whether your personal priorities support your goals for college success.

______________________________ ______________________________
______________________________ ______________________________
______________________________ ______________________________
______________________________ ______________________________
______________________________ ______________________________

APPRECIATING THE VALUE OF TIME

Time is a valuable resource, perhaps your most valuable resource. You've likely heard the expression "Time is money." Just as you don't want to waste your money, you shouldn't waste your time or the time of others. Did you ever make an appointment with someone who either forgot the

Getting from Here to There

College students have the responsibility to get themselves to class on time and must plan transportation carefully, whether walking, driving, bicycling, ride-sharing, taking public transportation, or using another method of getting from place to place. If you have an emergency situation that causes you to run late, talk to your instructor. He or she will understand a real emergency and help you make up work you missed.

wong yu liang/Shutterstock

appointment entirely or was very late? How did you feel? Were you upset or disappointed because the person wasted your time? Most of us have experienced the frustration of having someone else disrespect our time. In college, if you repeatedly arrive late for class or leave early, you are breaking the basic rules of politeness and showing a lack of respect for your instructors and your classmates.

Punctuality, or being on time, is expected in college, work, and elsewhere in our society. Being strictly on time may be a difficult adjustment for you if you grew up in a home or culture that is more flexible in its approach to time, but it is important to recognize the value of punctuality. Although you should not have to alter your cultural identity to succeed in college, you must be aware of the expectations that instructors typically have for students.

Here are a few basic guidelines for respectful behavior in class and in other interactions with instructors:

- Get to class on time. This means you need to get enough sleep at night so that you can wake up at a time that allows you to arrive in class early enough to take off your coat, shuffle through your backpack, and have your completed assignments and notebooks ready to go by the time the class starts.
- Be on time for scheduled appointments, such as during office hours.
- Avoid behaviors that show a lack of respect for both the instructor and other students, such as leaving class to answer your cell phone. Similarly, texting, doing homework for another class, falling asleep, or talking (even whispering) during a lecture are all considered rude.
- Make transportation plans in advance, and have a backup plan.

Not only is time management important for you, but it is also a way in which you show respect for your coworkers, friends, family, college instructors, and yourself. Can you think of the number of times you may have been late (one of the symptoms of procrastination) this week alone? Think back and then take the quiz shown here in Table 2:

TABLE 2

Situation	Number of Times This Week
How many times were you late to class?	
How many times were you late for appointments/ dates?	
How many times were you late for work, a car-pool, or another job and/or responsibility?	
How many times were you so late returning an e-mail, phone call, or text that a problem resulted from this lateness?	
How many times were you late paying a bill or mailing any important document?	
How many times were you late getting to bed or waking up?	
TOTAL	

Did the total number of times you were late surprise you? Two to five incidences of being late in a week is fairly normal. Everyone is late sometimes. Being late more than eight times this week might indicate that you are avoiding situations and tasks that are unpleasant for you. Or maybe you find it difficult to wait for other people, and so you would rather have others wait for you. Try and think of lateness from the other person's perspective. Getting more organized might help if you find that you don't have enough hours in the day to get everything done the way you think it should be. Position yourself for success and develop a reputation for being dependable!

Creating a Workable Class Schedule

Building your class schedule so that it works for you is part of using your valuable time wisely. If you live on campus, you might want to create a schedule that situates you near a dining hall at mealtimes or allows you to spend breaks between classes at the library. Alternatively, you might need breaks in your schedule for relaxation, catching up with friends, or spending time in a student lounge, college union, or campus center. You might want to avoid returning to your residence hall to take a nap between classes if the result is that you could feel lethargic or oversleep and miss later classes. Also, if you attend a large university, be sure to allow adequate time to get from one class to another.

Scheduling Your Classes in Blocks

One option for building a class schedule is using blocks of time when you can schedule several classes in a row, back-to-back, without any breaks. If you're a commuter student or if you must carry a heavy workload to afford going to school, you might prefer block scheduling, which allows you to cut travel time by attending school one or two days a week. Block scheduling might also provide more flexibility if you have to schedule a job or family commitments.

Scheduling classes in blocks, however, can also have significant drawbacks. When all your classes are scheduled in a block of time, you run several risks. If you become ill on a class day, you could fall behind in all your classes. You might also become fatigued from sitting in class after class. When one class immediately follows another, it will be difficult for you to have a last-minute study period immediately before a test because you will be attending another class and are likely to have no more than a 15-minute break in between. Finally, remember that if you take back-to-back classes, you might have several exams scheduled for the same day. Scheduling classes in blocks might work better if you have the option of attending lectures at alternative times in case you are absent, if you alternate classes with free periods, and if you seek out instructors who are flexible with due dates for assignments.

If your classes are offered at more than one time of day or more than one day a week, you will find it easier to design a schedule that works best for you. Often, however, you will be forced to take a class at an inconvenient time because that's the only time the class is offered. Remember that any schedule you develop will have pros and cons, but with advance planning, you can make the most of your in-class and out-of-class time.

your turn Work Together

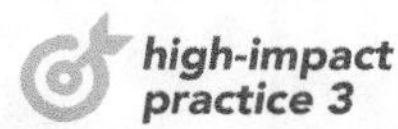

Scheduling Your Classes

In a small group or with a partner, share your current schedule and explain what you like or dislike about it. If your current schedule is not working well, discuss why that might be and identify changes you can make for the next term.

checklist for success

Time Management

- **Make sure that you set clear priorities for the way you spend your time.** All your time doesn't have to be spent studying, but remember that your instructors will expect you to study two hours out of class for each hour in class.
- **Get organized by using a calendar or planner.** Choose either an electronic or a paper calendar. Your campus bookstore will have a campus-specific version. Your calendar can help you allocate time in the present for completing large assignments that are due in the future.
- **Create and use daily paper or electronic to-do lists.** Crossing off those tasks you have completed will give you a real sense of satisfaction.
- **Quickly identify and address common time-management problems you are having before they spiral out of control.** Be aware of problems with procrastination, distractions, overscheduling, and motivation. As you notice them happening, take stock and make changes. If any of these issues becomes a serious problem, seek help from your campus counseling center.
- **Remember the relationship between time and respect.** Be aware of how others might perceive your behavior. If you disregard formal or informal appointments or if you are consistently late for class, you are showing a lack of respect for others even if that's not your intent.
- **Think about your course schedule.** As you plan for next term, try to schedule your classes in a way that works best for you, given your other obligations.

build your experience

REFLECT ON CHOICES

high-impact practice 2

College presents you with choices. One of them is whether you are going to pay close attention to how you spend your time. If you choose to neglect the issue of time management, you will risk losing a resource that you can never recover and sabotaging your chances for success in college. Did any of the time-management tips in this chapter appeal to you? If so, which ones? Do you still have questions about time management? If so, what are they? Write about these choices and questions in a journal entry or readily accessible file. Revisit these questions throughout your first-year experience.

APPLY WHAT YOU'VE LEARNED

Now that you have read and discussed this chapter, consider how you can apply what you have learned to your academic and personal life. The following prompts will help you reflect on chapter material and its relevance to you both now and in the future.

1. Review the procrastination section of this chapter. Think of one upcoming assignment in any of your current classes and describe how you can avoid waiting until the last minute to get it done. Break down the assignment and list each step it will take to complete the assignment. Give yourself a due date for each step and a due date for completing the assignment.
2. After reading about effective time-management strategies, consider how you manage your own time. If you were grading your current set of time-management skills, what grade (A, B, C, or lower) would you give yourself? Why? What is your biggest impediment to becoming a more effective time manager?

USE YOUR RESOURCES

- **Academic Skills Center** Your campus academic skills center offers more than just assistance in studying for exams. Head here for time-management advice specific to you. For instance, if you are struggling with managing the process of writing a paper, talk with a writing tutor about how to break the process into manageable steps, and create a timetable for those steps so you can meet course deadlines. If you are an online student, communicate with your instructors and other online students about how to manage time in an online environment.
- **Counseling Center** Make an appointment at your campus counseling office if your time-management problems involve emotional issues.
- **Your Academic Adviser or Counselor** If you have a good relationship with your academic adviser, ask him or her for time-management advice or for a referral to another person on campus.
- **Office for Commuter Students** If you commute back and forth to campus, visit the office for commuter students to see what kinds of suggestions they offer about transportation to and from campus. You may be able to reduce the amount of time you spend in transit.
- **Your Peer Leader** Peer leaders in college success classes are selected for their wisdom and experience. Talk to your peer leader about how he or she has developed time-management strategies.
- **A Fellow Student** Don't overlook your closest resources! If you feel your time slipping away, ask a friend who is a good student for advice.

LaunchPad

LaunchPad for *Your College Experience* is a great resource. Go online to master concepts using the LearningCurve study tool and much more. macmillanhighered.com/gardner12e

wavebreakmedia/Shutterstock

3 EMOTIONAL INTELLIGENCE

YOU WILL EXPLORE

What emotional intelligence is all about

Emotional intelligence in everyday life: motivation, resilience, establishing balance, prioritizing, and anger management

Developing emotional intelligence in college

How emotions influence success

Ways to improve your emotional intelligence

High-impact practices 2 (writing) and 3 (collaboration)

Gustavo Mejia, 20

Business Administration major
South Texas College

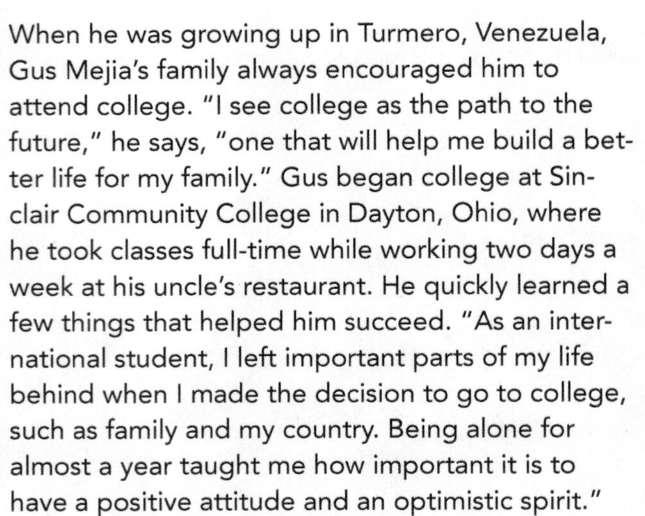

"Going to college is not only about enjoying success and accomplishments, but also about persevering when things get difficult or go wrong."

When he was growing up in Turmero, Venezuela, Gus Mejia's family always encouraged him to attend college. "I see college as the path to the future," he says, "one that will help me build a better life for my family." Gus began college at Sinclair Community College in Dayton, Ohio, where he took classes full-time while working two days a week at his uncle's restaurant. He quickly learned a few things that helped him succeed. "As an international student, I left important parts of my life behind when I made the decision to go to college, such as family and my country. Being alone for almost a year taught me how important it is to have a positive attitude and an optimistic spirit."

This realization didn't come without hard work and practice. One of the most important things Gus had to learn during his first year of college was how to deal with the stress of managing college, work, and living in a new environment, and Gus figured out that having a good sense of his own emotional intelligence helped. Being aware of how these stresses affected him emotionally helped him better understand how to deal with difficult situations and kept him from reacting negatively during times of stress. Emotional intelligence has also played a big role in Gus's favorite class (so far): organizational behavior, where he had to learn how to work with other students, no matter what their customs and beliefs. "I liked this class not only because it related directly to my major," he says, "but also because it taught me to communicate with others. Being able to work efficiently with different people from different backgrounds is very valuable."

Gus decided to begin the transfer process last year. Transferring to South Texas College represented a new beginning for him, one that came with its own fair share of challenges that he had to face with a clear head. Some of the credits for his classes—such as English literature, as well as courses on Microsoft Excel and PowerPoint—did not transfer because they weren't part of the business curriculum at his new college. Gus had to learn all the requirements for transferring, including admission tests, and be sure to meet them to make the transition as smooth as possible. His one piece of advice for other first-year students: Don't give up. "Going to college is not only about enjoying success and accomplishments, but also about persevering when things get difficult or go wrong," he says.

Gus had the ability to understand himself and others and to get along with people in a new environment. He was also able to manage time well, get things done, and anticipate potential problems before they occurred. Gus's problems with transferring to a new college are not uncommon, but he was able to deal with them without letting them become a barrier to his success. Why do some individuals struggle to handle stressful situations while others, like Gus, seem to handle them with ease? Although we tend to think of these abilities as inborn personality traits that can't be changed, social skills and stress-management skills really can be learned and improved.

assess your strengths

How well you understand and manage your emotions will affect your success in college. As you begin to read this chapter, think about your current strengths in managing emotions. How do your emotions regulate your behavior?

set goals

Think about challenges you have had in the past with understanding your emotions and managing your reactions to difficult situations. Perhaps you have been angry or frustrated about critical feedback you received from an instructor on a paper, or disappointed about your performance on an exam. How have you reacted in the past? Did your reaction make the situation better or worse? Describe a reaction that would lead to a positive outcome.

Particularly in the first year of college, some students who have the ability to succeed academically can have difficulty establishing positive relationships with others, dealing with pressure, or making wise decisions. Other students exude optimism and happiness and seem to adapt to their new environment without any trouble. The difference between the two types of students lies not in their academic talent but in their emotional intelligence (EI), or their ability to recognize and manage moods, feelings, and attitudes. A growing body of evidence shows a clear connection between students' EI and whether they stay in college.

LaunchPad

To access the LearningCurve study tool, video activities, and more, go to LaunchPad for *Your College Experience*. **macmillanhighered.com/gardner12e**

As you read this chapter, you will develop an understanding of EI, and you will learn how to use it to become a more successful student and person. You will begin to look at yourself and others through an EI lens, observe the behaviors that help people succeed, get to know yourself better, and learn to examine your feelings before you act. Then, as you read the other chapters in this book, try to apply what you have learned about EI and think about how it might relate to the behaviors of successful college students. You can't always control the challenges and frustrations of life, but with practice, you *can* control how you respond to them.

WHAT IS EMOTIONAL INTELLIGENCE?

Emotional intelligence is the ability to recognize, understand, use, and manage emotions—moods, feelings, and attitudes. There are many competing theories about EI, some of them complex. While experts vary in their definitions and models, all agree that emotions are real, can be changed for the better, and have a profound impact on whether a person is successful.

In the simplest terms, emotional intelligence consists of two general abilities:

1. *Understanding emotions* involves the capacity to monitor and label your feelings accurately (nervousness, happiness, anger, relief, and so forth) and to determine why you feel the way you do. It also involves predicting how others might feel in a given situation. Emotions contain information, and the ability to understand and think about that information plays an important role in behavior.
2. *Managing emotions* involves the ability to modify and even improve feelings. At times, you need to stay open to your feelings, learn from them, and use them to take appropriate action. At other times, it is better to disengage from an emotion and return to it later. Anger, for example, can lead you to act in negative or antisocial ways; used positively, however, anger can help you overcome adversity, bias, and injustice.

The first key step in learning to control your emotions and use them in productive ways is to understand that you and your emotions are not one

Emotional Intelligence Questionnaire

Your daily life gives you many opportunities to take a hard look at how you handle emotions. Here are some questions that can help you begin thinking about your own EI.

1. What do you do when you are under stress?
   a. I tend to deal with it calmly and rationally.
   b. I get upset, but it usually blows over quickly.
   c. I get upset but keep it to myself.
2. My friends would say that:
   a. I play, but only after I get my work done.
   b. I am ready for fun anytime.
   c. I hardly ever go out.
3. When something changes at the last minute:
   a. I easily adapt.
   b. I get frustrated.
   c. I don't care, since I don't really expect things to happen according to plan.
4. My friends would say that:
   a. I am sensitive to their concerns.
   b. I spend too much time worrying about other people's needs.
   c. I don't like to deal with other people's petty problems.
5. When I have a problem to solve, such as having too many assignments due at the end of the week:
   a. I write down a list of the tasks I must complete, come up with a plan indicating specifically what I can accomplish and what I cannot, and follow my plan.
   b. I am very optimistic about getting things done and just dig right in and get to work.
   c. I get a little frazzled. Usually I get a number of things done and then push aside the things I can't do.

Review your responses. **a** responses indicate that you probably have a good basis for strong EI. **b** responses indicate that you may have some strengths and some challenges in your EI. **c** responses indicate that your success in life and in school could be negatively affected by your EI.

and the same. You can stand apart from and observe your emotions; you are separate from them. Whatever your emotions at any given moment, you might be using them to filter your perception of a situation by magnifying all the negative details and filtering out all positive aspects—without realizing that you're doing this. You might even pick out a single pleasant or unpleasant detail and dwell on it exclusively so that your vision of reality becomes distorted. If you are feeling sad, you might view the world in a certain way, while if you are feeling happy, you are likely to interpret the same events differently.

Another important step in becoming more emotionally intelligent is developing an awareness of how your emotions affect you. When you start paying attention to emotions instead of ignoring them, you will have a better emotional understanding of different situations, and therefore be able to respond to these situations more appropriately. You can learn not only how to cope with life's pressures and demands, but also how to harness your knowledge of the way you feel, which can lead to more effective problem solving, reasoning, decision making, and creative endeavors.

A number of sophisticated tools can be used to assess emotional intelligence, or you can take the short questionnaire on the previous page to begin thinking about it. Even without a formal test, you can take a number of steps to get in touch with your own EI. You'll have to dig deep inside yourself and be willing to be honest about how you really think and how you really behave. This process can take time, and that's fine. Think of your EI as a work in progress.

your turn Stay Motivated

Overcoming Tough Challenges

Think about a challenge you have experienced in college that made you want to throw in the towel. How did that challenge affect your overall motivation for doing well in college? What lessons did you learn from the experience, and how can you use those lessons in the future to maintain your motivation?

EMOTIONAL INTELLIGENCE IN EVERYDAY LIFE

You have already used your emotional intelligence in your life experiences. For example, you graduated from high school and are making the transition to college. The decision to attend college might have involved evaluating the reputation and characteristics of different colleges or universities and the opportunities they offered. But if you had been planning to attend a particular college your whole life, you might have filtered your college-choice experience through your emotional attachment to one place. If you made campus visits, how did you react to hearing information that concerned or excited you, exploring the different buildings, or

Truth in Fiction

The 2012 film *Silver Linings Playbook*, which stars Bradley Cooper, Jennifer Lawrence, and Robert DeNiro, explores issues of mental illness, anger management, family, and new beginnings. If you have seen the film, discuss how the characters attempt to handle their emotions. What works? What doesn't work? What other movies, TV shows, or novels can you think of that feature characters with emotional issues? What can you learn from such fictional accounts?

meeting staff, faculty, or other students? What impact did your emotions have on your final decision?

Naming and labeling emotions, in addition to focusing on related experiences, strengthens emotional intelligence skills. For instance, new college students often face the fear of social rejection. You might feel ignored or rejected by students you have met before. The feeling of rejection can even cause a physical reaction—your face might feel hot and you might even feel slightly sick to your stomach. If you can acknowledge and name what you are feeling, you will be less likely to be controlled by it. You will be in a better place to confront the fear by walking up to the students, introducing yourself again, and perhaps asking to join them.

Hearing something emotional often triggers our own emotional reaction. For instance, how would you react if a close friend said she had been sexually assaulted? Could you be empathetic and helpful, or would your own emotional reaction cause you to barrage her with questions about where she had been, what she had been wearing, and whether she had been drinking? These accusations could impede your friend's recovery and make her even more vulnerable. As you work to develop your emotional intelligence, you'll need to consider how to use logic rather than your own emotional reactions to evaluate a situation and be helpful to others.

Motivation

Most college students have many responsibilities, and it can be hard to stay motivated when you have too much to do. Positive feedback can help, and it's important to realize that this can come from within—motivating yourself is a big part of being emotionally intelligent. Draw from past positive experiences to propel yourself through a current challenge. Consider how conquering a challenge provides an example to others. What positive outcomes will result? Being emotionally intelligent also means knowing when you need some distance from a challenge or project. Identify the experiences that have motivated you in the past and call on them when you do not feel motivated to persevere.

Resilience

Resilience is another important component of emotional intelligence. Being resilient means that you are optimistic and tough in the face of adversity. You remain positive even when you are faced with negative circumstances. While you're in college, you might receive an "F" on a paper, have trouble making connections with others in class, or lose a student government election. Such experiences might cause you to question whether you should be in college at all. Resilient students, though, look past negative experiences, learn from them, and try again. What can you do to improve your grade on your next paper? Perhaps you didn't allow yourself enough time to do the proper research. How can you feel more comfortable in your classes? Maybe it would help to join a study group. Why were you passed over for the student government office that you wanted? Consider the possibility that you may need to show a greater commitment to campus governance issues. Developing coping mechanisms and life skills leads to resilience. You were born with the ability to be resilient—it's up to you to let your resilience emerge and to embrace it.

Balance and Priority Management

You will find that it is difficult to balance the many, and often competing, aspects of your life when you are in college. Finding balance goes beyond taking care of obligations—it extends to your mental and physical health, which relates directly to wellness, a topic we'll discuss later in this book. Using healthy emotional intelligence to prioritize involves applying time-management techniques to how you handle your obligations. For instance, create a to-do list and review it regularly. If you know that packing your lunch and workout clothes in the evening will save you time in the morning, make that a priority and pack the night before. And schedule your day to make time for everything that is important to you, such as exercise, eating a healthy diet, talking to your friends, and studying. With more balance in your day comes greater confidence. Consider what happens when you fail to prioritize or use your time-management strategies. Does the stress lead to emotional reactions that then lead to negative consequences? Paying attention to these kinds of issues and making changes when needed are all part of developing a stronger emotional intelligence.

Anger Management

Humans experience a wide range of emotions and moods. On one hand, we can be very generous and positive, and on the other hand, we can lash out in anger. Anger management is an EI skill that is important to develop. Anger can hurt others and can harm your mental and physical health. You may even know someone who uses their anger to manipulate and control others.

Upside of Anger

Since the 1960s, college students have used their anger about political, social, and campus-specific issues (like tuition increases) in positive ways through organized demonstrations. Such demonstrations have influenced major actions in U.S. history, such as President Richard Nixon's decision to resign, and President Lyndon B. Johnson's decision to end the Vietnam War. What issues would "bring students to the barricades" today?

AP Photo/Cathleen Allison

In spite of the problems it creates, anger does not always result in negative consequences. Psychologists see anger as a primary, natural, and mature emotion that has value for human survival because it can mobilize us to take corrective action or to stand up for what is right.

How do you use anger? Are you in control of how you express this emotion, or does your anger occasionally control you?

is **this** you?

Older than Average

Are you an older student, maybe in your thirties or forties, who is back in college? As an adult, you probably have a great deal of life experience in dealing with tough times. You might have real strengths in emotional intelligence that you have developed at work, at home, or with your family, but you may also have some areas that you need to improve. How are you using your skills to stand up for yourself and negotiate with others as you face the challenges of college? Using your existing strengths and skills in college could allow you to be a role model for others. You might want to give some advice to younger students who seem to be struggling with the day-to-day interactions that are part of college life and help those students find ways to be more adaptable, resilient, and assertive.

DEVELOPING EMOTIONAL INTELLIGENCE

As you get to know yourself, you might find that engaging in deep personal reflection makes you feel vulnerable. But as you reflect more on your own attitudes and behavior and learn why you have the emotions that you do, you'll improve your emotional intelligence. Living on your own, studying unfamiliar subjects, and interacting with new and diverse people all challenge your EI skills and force you to step outside of your comfort zone. Your first year of college is especially critical and affords you a significant opportunity to grow as a person.

Identifying Competencies: Looking at the Research

Emotional intelligence includes many capabilities and skills that influence a person's ability to cope with life's pressures and demands. Reuven Bar-On, a professor at the University of Texas at Austin and a world-renowned EI expert, developed a model that demonstrates how categories of emotional intelligence directly affect general mood and lead to effective performance (see Figure 1).

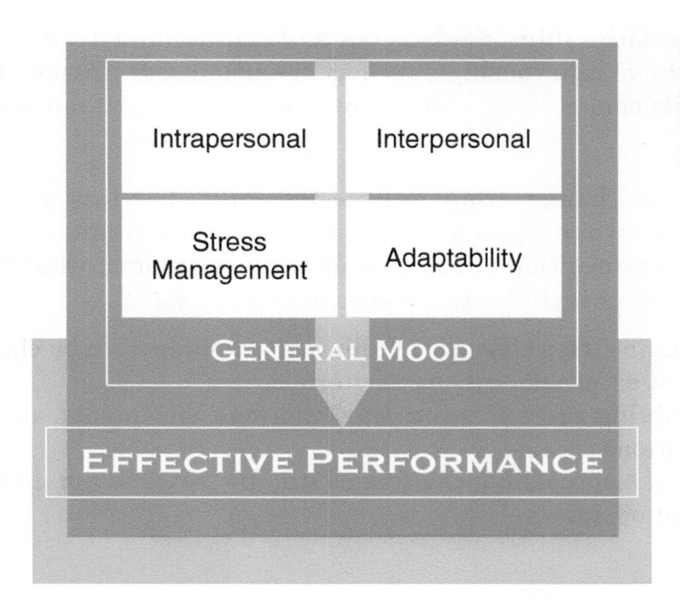

FIGURE 1 › Bar-On Model of Emotional Intelligence

Let's look more closely at the fifteen specific skills and competencies that Bar-On has identified as the pieces that make up a person's emotional intelligence.[1] They are similar to the pieces of a jigsaw puzzle—once you've put them all together, you will begin to see yourself and others more clearly.

Intrapersonal Skills. This first category relates to both how well you know and like yourself, and how effectively you can do the things you need to do to stay happy. Understanding yourself and why you think and act as you do is the glue that holds all of the EI competencies together. This category is made up of five specific competencies:

1. **Emotional self-awareness.** Knowing how and why you feel the way you do.
2. **Assertiveness.** Standing up for yourself when necessary without being too aggressive.
3. **Independence.** Making important decisions on your own without having to get everyone's opinion.
4. **Self-regard.** Liking yourself in spite of your flaws (and we all have them).
5. **Self-actualization.** Being satisfied and comfortable with your achievements.

[1] Adapted from Bar-On EQ-i Technical Manual © 1997, 1999, 2000 Multi-Health Systems, Inc. Toronto, Canada.

Interpersonal Skills. Recent studies have shown that people with extensive support networks are generally happier and tend to enjoy longer, healthier lives. Your ability to build relationships and get along with other people depends on the competencies that form the basis for the interpersonal skills category:

- **Empathy.** Making an effort to understand another person's situation or point of view.
- **Social responsibility.** Establishing a personal link with a group or community and cooperating with its other members in working toward shared goals.
- **Interpersonal relationships.** Seeking out and maintaining healthy and mutually beneficial relationships, such as friendships, professional networks, family connections, mentoring relationships, and romantic partnerships.

Adaptability. Things change. Adaptability—the ability to adjust your thinking and behavior when faced with new or unexpected situations—helps you cope and ensures that you'll do well in life, no matter what the challenges. This category includes three key competencies:

- **Reality testing.** Ensuring that your feelings are appropriate by checking them against external, objective criteria.
- **Flexibility.** Adapting and adjusting your emotions, viewpoints, and actions as situations change.
- **Problem solving.** Approaching challenges step by step and not giving up in the face of obstacles.

your turn Work Together

Observing Emotional Intelligence

Working with one or two other students, agree to watch at least one TV show during the coming week—a situation comedy, drama, or even a cable news program. Each group member can watch the same show or a different show. Take brief notes on how the fictional or nonfictional characters handle their emotions, especially in stressful situations. How many of the fifteen EI competencies were represented—either positively or negatively—in the shows you watched? During next week's class, discuss what you saw and what you learned.

Stress Management. In college, at work, and at home, now and in the future, you'll face what can seem like never-ending pressures and demands. Managing the resulting stress depends on two skills:

- **Stress tolerance.** Recognizing the causes of stress and responding in appropriate ways, so you can stay strong under pressure.
- **Impulse control.** Thinking carefully about potential consequences before you act, and delaying gratification for the sake of achieving long-term goals.

"The key to stress management is knowing how to vent your frustration."

Don't Blow Your Top

There are good ways and bad ways to vent frustration. Having it out with another person or eating a gallon of ice cream are poor strategies. Going for a walk or run, doing yoga, or "talking it out" with someone you trust, however, will help you deal with the frustrations that are common to college life without making things worse.

Overall Mood. It might sound sappy, but having a positive attitude really does improve your chances of doing well. Bar-On emphasizes the importance of two emotions in particular:

- **Optimism.** Looking on the bright side of any problem or difficulty and being confident that things will work out for the best.
- **Happiness.** Being satisfied with yourself, with others, and with your situation in general. It makes sense: If you feel good about yourself and manage your emotions, you can expect to get along with others and enjoy a happy, successful life.

Knowledge of self is strongly connected to respect for others and their way of life. If you don't understand yourself and why you do the things you do, it can be difficult for you to understand others. What's more, if you don't like yourself, you can hardly expect others to like you.

your turn Make Good Choices

Act Instead of React

Your emotional reactions, whether positive or negative, affect your interactions with other people. Pretend that you are your own therapist. In what kinds of situations have you had "knee-jerk" reactions when you've reacted with defensiveness, anger, sadness, annoyance, resentment, or humiliation? Take a step back and "process" these reactions. Think about what you said or did in response to your feelings, and why. Then talk with a trusted friend or classmate about how you reacted and whether you could have chosen to act differently. What can you do to take control and make good choices the next time you are faced with a potentially volatile situation?

Accentuate the Positive

You probably know people who always find the negative in any situation. Constantly focusing on what's missing or what's not perfect will likely make you the kind of person whom others avoid. Practice looking on the bright side.

marekuliasz/Shutterstock

HOW EMOTIONS INFLUENCE SUCCESS

Emotions are strongly tied to physical and psychological well-being. For example, some studies have suggested that cancer patients who have strong EI live longer than those with weak EI. People who are aware of the needs of others tend to be happier than people who are not. An extensive study done at the University of Pennsylvania found that the best athletes succeed in part because they're extremely optimistic. A number of studies link strong EI skills to college success in particular. Studies indicate that emotionally intelligent students get higher grades. Researchers looked at students' grade point averages at the end of their first year of college. Students who had tested high for intrapersonal skills, stress tolerance, and adaptability when they entered in the fall did better academically than those who had lower overall EI test scores. Here are a few other highlights of those studies:

- **Motivation:** Motivation is one of the most important attributes that college students can have. Figuring out what actually does motivate anyone is complex, but striving to find out and nurture these motivations is the goal.
- **Resilience:** We discussed resilience above—stronger emotional intelligence leads to greater resilience. Students with healthy emotional intelligence might act proactively by asking instructors for feedback on projects, papers, and tests, participating in classroom discussions, and joining study groups. Students with unhealthy EI are likely to struggle academically, panic before taking tests, have trouble concentrating on coursework, and engage in risky behaviors such as alcohol and drug abuse in an effort to cope. Dr. Richard Kadison, a former director of mental health services at Harvard University, noted that "the emotional well-being of students goes hand in hand with their academic development. If they're not doing well emotionally, they are not going to reach their academic potential."[2]
- **Persistence:** Some college students develop persistence in spite of the obstacles and challenges during their college experience. Persistent students make forward progress through challenging situations, even if progress is slow.
- **Delaying gratification:** Research has shown that students who can delay gratification tend to do better overall. Impulse control leads to achievement. A study conducted in the 1970s looked at the case of willpower in children. It is referred to as the Stanford Marshmallow Study.[3] The study observed children's behavior when they were left alone at a table with a marshmallow. They were told that they could have a second marshmallow if they waited 15 minutes before eating

[2]Richard Kadison and Theresa Foy DiGeronimo, *College of the Overwhelmed: The Campus Mental Health Crisis and What to Do about It* (San Francisco: Jossey-Bass, 2004), 156.

[3]Walter Mischel, et al., "Delay of Gratification in Children," *Science,* 244, no. 4907 (1989): 933–38.

the first one. Fourteen years later, the children who had immediately eaten their marshmallow were more likely to experience significant stress, irritability, and an inability to focus on goals. The children who had waited to eat their marshmallow scored an average of 210 points higher on the SAT; had more confidence, better concentration, and reliability; held better-paying jobs; and reported being more satisfied with life.

Healthy EI and the First-Year Seminar

Healthy EI contributes to overall academic success, positive professional and romantic relationships, and overall career development and satisfaction. EI skills can be enhanced in a first-year seminar. In one study conducted in Australia and another conducted separately in the United States, researchers found that college students enrolled in a first-year seminar who demonstrated good EI skills were more likely to do better in college than students who did not exhibit those skills.

You can get by in college without strong EI, but you might miss out on the full range and depth of competencies and skills that can help you succeed in your chosen field and have a fulfilling and meaningful life.

HOW TO IMPROVE YOUR EMOTIONAL INTELLIGENCE

Developing your EI is an important step toward getting the full benefit of a college education. Think about how you cope with emotional stress. Do you often give up because something is just too hard or because you can't figure it out? Do you take responsibility for what you do, or do you blame others if you fail? How can you communicate effectively if you are not assertive or if you are overly aggressive? If you're inflexible, how can you solve problems, get along with coworkers and family members, or learn from other people's points of view?

The good news is that you *can* improve your EI. It might not be easy—old habits are hard to change—but it can definitely be done. Here are some suggestions:

1. **Identify your strengths and weaknesses.** Take a hard look at yourself, and consider how you respond to situations. Most people have trouble evaluating their own behaviors realistically, so ask someone you trust and respect for insight.
2. **Set realistic goals.** As you identify areas of emotional intelligence that you would like to improve, be as specific as possible. Instead of deciding to be more assertive, for example, focus on a specific issue that is giving you trouble.
3. **Formulate a plan.** With a particular goal in mind, identify a series of steps you could take to achieve the goal, and define the results that would indicate success.
4. **Check your progress on a regular basis.** Continually re-evaluate whether or not you have met your goals, and adjust your strategy as needed.

techtip

USE BLOGS AND TWITTER

Everyone is an expert at something. Web sites like WordPress, Twitter, and Blogger give people space to write about or otherwise produce information that they know something about. Many of the most frequently used news Web sites and social networking sites get information that is sent—or "fed"—to them from someone's blog.

Twitter is a microblogging site. It's called "microblogging" because you can only write a maximum of 140 characters per message, or "tweet." Get off the sidelines and into the world of microblogging. It doesn't take much time to post to Twitter because of its 140-character limit. Twitter also allows you to follow the tweets of people, events, and organizations that interest you.

The Problem

You've heard people talk about blogs and Twitter, but you don't know why you'd join or what you'd do with them.

The Fix

Dive in!

How to Do It

Research areas that you find interesting on blogging sites like wordpress.com, blogger.com, technorati.com, or alltop.com, or create a Twitter account.

Add the WordPress, Blogger, or Twitter app to your phone or tablet. This will allow you to keep up-to-date on information you find interesting and will get you in the habit of commenting, liking, responding, and posting so that you develop your "digital self" as a professional.

Participate in a network of people who share your interests. While you are in college, connect with people who are experts in your professional or personal areas of interest. Follow their posts to get advice and understand what people are talking about. You can also create a blog yourself and have other people follow your journey.

Sports/Entertainment: You can use Twitter or a blog to keep up with your favorite actors, bands, and sports teams. Some tweet about projects they're working on, some tweet political commentary, and others just share great jokes.

Education: Authors tweet or blog about their books and often engage in conversations with their readers. Professionals and scholars in many fields share links to news articles, book reviews, Web sites, and videos related to their careers and areas of study.

Job-hunting: Many career Web sites have Twitter accounts and blogs. Following the official Twitter feed of a company you want to work for can lead to instant notifications of new job opportunities and give you the chance to get your résumé ready.

Community involvement: One amazing feature of Twitter is that it allows for real-time global conversations on important issues. Twitter was a key component in the Arab Spring of 2011–2012, a period that saw dozens of political demonstrations and revolutionary movements across the Arab world.

EXTRA STYLE POINTS: Create an online professional self that shows how fun or interesting or creative or compassionate you really are. A word of caution: Think about what you reveal about your emotional intelligence by what you post, and think about what you can tell about others' emotional intelligence by their posts.

It's important not to try to improve everything at once. Instead, identify specific EI competencies that you can define and describe, and then set measurable goals for change. Don't expect success overnight. Remember that it took you a while to develop your specific approach to life, and changing it will take commitment and practice.

your turn Write and Reflect

Thinking Ahead

Write a description of yourself as a successful person ten years after you graduate. What kinds of skills will you have? Don't just focus on your degree or a job description; include the EI competencies that help explain why you have become successful.

checklist for success

Emotional Intelligence

- **What is emotional intelligence?** Define the most significant abilities of EI and reflect on your connection to those abilities.
- **Be aware of how your emotions affect the way you react to difficult or frustrating situations.** Some key aspects of EI include motivation, resilience, balance, and anger management. Use your awareness to try to control your negative reactions before you get into a potentially frustrating situation.
- **Identify how you develop EI in college.** What can you learn from other students? Think about the most significant ways you have developed since you started college.
- **Evaluate your EI skills through assessment.** As a student, use assessments as tools to gauge where you are in terms of your development. This is how you improve.
- **Learn and then practice EI improvement strategies such as** identifying your strengths and weaknesses, setting realistic goals, formulating a plan, and checking your progress on a regular basis.
- **If you aren't satisfied with your emotional reactions, make an appointment at the campus counseling center to discuss your feelings and get help.** Counselors can help you monitor and understand your emotional responses in a confidential setting.

build your experience

REFLECT ON CHOICES

high-impact practice 2

This chapter offers several opportunities for self-reflection and writing in an effort to encourage you to identify and improve your EI skills. What goals can you set to improve your emotional intelligence, and what strategies did you get from this chapter that can help? Consider situations that you will confront in the coming weeks and months. What choices can you make that involve emotional intelligence? What skills will you use? Reflect on these choices and questions in a journal entry or readily accessible file. Revisit these questions throughout your first-year experience.

APPLY WHAT YOU'VE LEARNED

Now that you have read and discussed this chapter, consider how you can apply what you have learned to your everyday life, both academically and personally. The following prompts will help you reflect on the chapter material and its relevance to you, both now and in the future.

1. Managing stress is an important skill in college, and balancing priorities is a component of emotional intelligence. Take a look through your course syllabi and make a list of assignments, exams, and important dates. Do any of your assignments or exams seem to cluster around the same time in the term? Can you anticipate times when you might be especially likely to get stressed? What can you do in advance to avoid becoming overwhelmed and overstressed?
2. College life offers many opportunities to meet new people and develop a new support network, but finding friends and mentors you can trust is not always easy. What steps have you taken so far to meet new people and build a network of support in college? How can these experiences help you develop your emotional intelligence?

USE YOUR RESOURCES

Academic Advising Center
Academic advisers are trained to help you deal with the stress of taking certain courses or planning your degree program.

Your College Counseling Center
Counselors who work in these centers have special training in stress management, anger management, conflict resolution, and other behavioral issues.

Health or Wellness Center
If personal problems are affecting your overall health—your sleep, diet, or ability to concentrate—visit your campus health center and talk to a health professional about strategies to deal with these issues.

Special Workshops that Focus on Personal Emotional Issues Be alert for any workshops offered at your institution or in the local community that would help you improve your overall emotional intelligence.

Disability Services
If you are a student with a physical or learning disability that causes additional emotional problems for you, the office of disability services may be your best source of support.

Adult Student Services
Professionals in this office have special training in helping nontraditional students manage the social, personal, and emotional challenges that often arise when adults return to college.

Your Peer Leader
Your peer leader can be a sounding board for you if you are having problems with relationships, stress, anger, or any other personal issues. He or she can also refer you to an appropriate office for additional support.

LaunchPad

LaunchPad for *Your College Experience* is a great resource. Go online to master concepts using the LearningCurve study tool and much more. macmillanhighered.com/gardner12e

wavebreakmedia/Shutterstock

4 HOW YOU LEARN

YOU WILL EXPLORE

Tools for measuring your learning style

Strategies for handling a mismatch between how you learn best and how you are being taught

How to understand and recognize a learning disability

High-impact practices 2 (writing), 3 (collaboration), and 6 (learning communities)

Daniel Graham, 24

Computer Science major
Northeastern Illinois University

> **"Apply your learning style to your everyday life. Eventually you will learn in a different, smarter, and more efficient way."**

Although he tells us, "I didn't have much knowledge of learning styles before I started college," Daniel Graham from Northeastern Illinois University in Chicago enrolled in the college success seminar in his first term. There, he took a learning-styles inventory called the VARK and learned that he's both a kinesthetic learner, which means that he learns by doing, and a read/write learner, which means that he learns by reading and writing down material from class. Since then, he has been able to employ numerous strategies that apply specifically to his form of multimodal learning to help him succeed in class. He does things like rewriting terms and concepts in his own words so that he better understands what they mean, and he uses note cards to help him memorize. He says that knowing his learning style has improved his performance. "When I take notes, I read them silently on note cards and continue to return to them so I can memorize the meaning," he says.

It's not surprising that Daniel is also a kinesthetic learner, as he spends ten to fifteen hours a week working in his family home-remodeling business. "A hands-on approach has my name written all over it. I like being able to use my hands and express myself, and I like being able to figure things out just by playing with them for a bit." He translates this hands-on approach to learning by using tactics like taking practice exams until he feels ready for the real exam.

Daniel chose to begin higher education at Northeastern because it was close to home and because he learned from former Northeastern students that he would receive lots of one-on-one attention there. When Daniel enrolled, he took advantage of the TRiO program, which helps prepare students for college success through advising services and extra tutoring. All that work paid off: After completing his bachelor's degree, Daniel plans to transfer to the University of Illinois at Chicago to pursue a master's degree in computer information systems. Daniel plans to finish his master's and then explore job opportunities. He ultimately hopes to be working in computer science or finance, and he plans to continue to rely on his learning styles: "Apply your learning style to your everyday life. Eventually you will learn in a different, smarter, and more efficient way."

To access the LearningCurve study tool, video activities, and more, go to LaunchPad for *Your College Experience*. macmillanhighered.com/gardner12e

Have you ever thought about how you learn? If not, it would probably help to think about this topic now that you are in college. People learn differently. This is hardly a new idea, but if you want to do well in college, it is important that you become aware of how you learn. Maybe you have trouble paying attention to a long lecture, or maybe listening is the way you learn best. You might love classroom discussion, or you might consider hearing what other students have to say in class a big waste of time. You have developed your learning style or preference over time because of your personal characteristics and experiences. Even if you didn't exactly choose your preference for the way you learn best, you can choose to learn how to adapt to multiple styles of classroom instruction.

assess your strengths

Understanding your own preferred style of learning will help you study and earn good grades. Do you know how you learn best? Were your learning styles evaluated in high school? As you begin to read this chapter, consider the insights you already have about your own learning styles.

set goals

Think about challenges you have had with relating to the way some instructors teach and expect you to learn. Use this chapter to help develop strategies and goals that link your preferred style of learning to what you are experiencing in the classroom such as thinking about your favorite and least favorite classes and how your preferences might relate to how you prefer to learn.

Perhaps you have not thought about it, but college instructors have their own styles of teaching and communicating. Those different styles will be evident in the way that courses are organized and taught. Your preferred style of learning might not match up with the teaching methods in some of your courses. Many instructors lecture almost exclusively; others use lots of visual aids, such as PowerPoint or Prezi presentations, charts, graphs, and pictures. In science courses, you will conduct experiments or go on field trips where you can observe or touch what you are studying. In dance, theater, or physical education courses, learning takes place in both your body and your mind. And in almost all courses, you'll learn by reading both textbooks and other materials. Some instructors are friendly, warm, and obviously enjoy all aspects of teaching; others seem to want little interaction with students.

This chapter will first help you understand how you learn best, and then help you think of ways in which you can create a link between your learning style and the expectations of each of your courses and instructors. This chapter will also explore learning disabilities, which are common among college students. You will learn how to recognize them and what to do if you or someone you know has a learning disability.

While the concept of learning may seem simple, educational researchers have discovered that not everyone learns in the same way. Not only do we have different learning styles, we also have unique preferences for the speed at which we learn, the mode of learning (online or face to face), and whether we learn better alone or in a group. Your college or university may offer courses that run four to six weeks or "flipped" classes in which you learn material on your own before class and spend class time in discussion groups or working problems.

If your college success course is linked with one or more other courses so that you share other classes with the same group of students, you are in a learning community. About 50 percent of U.S. colleges and universities offer learning communities in the first year. Being in a learning community will help you learn in a different way by emphasizing the connections between different courses. This experience will also help you develop stronger relationships with other students in the linked classes.

LEARNING STYLES AND THE TOOLS USED FOR MEASURING THEM

Learning styles are particular preferences for learning that are unique to each individual. For example, one person might prefer to read instructional materials to understand how something works, whereas another might prefer to use a "hands-on" approach. There are many ways of thinking about and describing learning styles. Some learning styles will make a lot of sense to you; others might seem confusing at first. Some learning style theories are very simple, and some are complex. You will notice at least a little overlap between the different theories and tools; using more than one of them might help you do a better job of discovering your own learning style. If you are interested in reading more about learning styles, the library and your campus learning center will have many resources on this topic.

Learning happens all the time, especially in a college or university setting. Some, but not all, of what students learn happens in the classroom, organized by an instructor or other students. If you had been a student in the Middle Ages (500 AD–1500 AD), your instructor, most likely a monk, would have taught you entirely through lecture. Only a few handwritten books existed at that time, and if you wanted a book, you would most likely have had to write it yourself, if you even knew how to write. The invention of the printing press (credited to Johannes Gutenberg in 1440) and the availability of books made reading another option for learning. Even today, listening and reading remain the primary learning methods students are expected to use in college.

Over time, however, instructors have realized that not all students learn best through listening and reading. New technology offers visual tools such as PowerPoint, graphics, video, and online resources that help many students learn. And we also know that powerful learning results when students take charge of their own learning through "experiential," kinesthetic, or hands-on methods.

is this you?

Disappointed in My Classes

Have you found that some of your classes aren't as interesting and engaging as you expected? Is one of the problems a mismatch between the way you like to learn and the instructor's teaching method? Perhaps you're a visual learner but are forced to sit through mostly lecture classes, or perhaps you really don't enjoy working with others even though your chemistry course requires you to complete lab assignments with a partner. This chapter will help you understand your own learning style and adapt it to any classroom situation.

The VARK Learning-Styles Inventory

The VARK is a sixteen-item questionnaire that focuses on how learners prefer to use their senses (hearing, seeing, writing, reading, experiencing) to learn. The acronym VARK stands for "Visual," "Aural," "Read/Write," and "Kinesthetic." As you read through the following descriptions, see which ones ring true to how you learn.

- **Visual** learners prefer to learn information through charts, graphs, symbols, and

Bodies in Motion

As you'll learn in the next section, the theater arts have strong appeal for kinesthetic learners who prefer to learn through experience and practice.

Hill Street Studios/Getty Images

other visual means. If you can most easily remember data that is presented in graphic form or in a picture, map, or video, you are a visual learner.

- **Aural** learners prefer to hear information and discuss it with friends, classmates, or instructors. If talking about information from lectures or textbooks helps you remember it, you are an aural learner.
- **Read/Write** learners prefer to learn information through words on a printed page. During a test, if you can sometimes visualize where information appears in the textbook, you are a read/write learner.
- **Kinesthetic** learners prefer to learn through experience and practice, whether simulated or real. They often learn through their sense of touch. Recopying or typing notes helps them remember the material. They also learn better when their bodies are in motion, whether participating in sports, dancing, or working out. If you are a kinesthetic learner, you may find that even your sense of taste or smell contributes to your learning process.

Two or three of these modes probably describe your preferred ways of learning better than the others. At the college level, faculty members tend to share information primarily via lecture and the textbook, but many students like to learn through visual and interactive means. This difference creates a mismatch between learning and teaching styles. Is this a problem? Not necessarily, if you know how to handle such a mismatch. Later in this chapter you'll learn strategies to adapt lecture material and the text to your preferred modes of learning. First, though, to determine your learning style(s) according to the VARK, respond to the questionnaire.

The VARK Questionnaire, Version 7.1

This questionnaire is designed to tell you about your preferences for how you work with information. Choose answers that explain your preference(s). Check the box next to those items. For each question, select *as many boxes as apply to you.* If none of the response options applies to you, leave the item blank. (You can also take the VARK questionnaire online at **vark-learn.com/english/page.asp?p=questionnaire.**)

1. You are helping someone who wants to go to your airport, the center of town, or railway station. You would:

☐ a. go with her.
☐ b. tell her the directions.
☐ c. write down the directions.
☐ d. draw, or show her a map, or give her a map.

2. A Web site has a video showing how to make a special graph. There is a person speaking, some lists and words describing what to do, and some diagrams. You would learn most from:

☐ a. seeing the diagrams.
☐ b. listening.
☐ c. reading the words.
☐ d. watching the actions.

3. You are planning a vacation for a group. You want some feedback from them about the plan. You would:

☐ a. describe some of the highlights they will experience.
☐ b. use a map to show them the places.
☐ c. give them a copy of the printed itinerary.
☐ d. phone, text, or e-mail them.

4. You are going to cook something as a special treat. You would:

☐ a. cook something you know without the need for instructions.
☐ b. ask friends for suggestions.
☐ c. look on the Internet or in some cookbooks for ideas from the pictures.
☐ d. use a good recipe.

5. A group of tourists wants to learn about the parks or wildlife reserves in your area. You would:

☐ a. talk about, or arrange a talk for them, about parks or wildlife reserves.
☐ b. show them maps and Internet pictures.
☐ c. take them to a park or wildlife reserve and walk with them.
☐ d. give them a book or pamphlets about the parks or wildlife reserves.

6. You are about to purchase a digital camera or mobile phone. Other than price, what would most influence your decision?

☐ a. trying or testing it
☐ b. reading the details or checking its features online
☐ c. it is a modern design and looks good
☐ d. the salesperson talking about its features

7. Remember a time when you learned how to do something new. Avoid choosing a physical skill (e.g., riding a bike). You learned best by:

☐ a. watching a demonstration.
☐ b. listening to somebody explaining it and asking questions.
☐ c. diagrams, maps, and charts—visual clues.
☐ d. written instructions (e.g., a manual or book).

8. You have a problem with your heart. You would prefer that the doctor:

☐ a. give you something to read to explain what was wrong.
☐ b. use a plastic model to show what was wrong.
☐ c. describe what was wrong.
☐ d. show you a diagram of what was wrong.

9. You want to learn a new program, skill, or game on a computer. You would:

☐ a. read the written instructions that came with the program.

☐ b. talk with people who know about the program.
☐ c. use the controls or keyboard.
☐ d. follow the diagrams in the book that came with it.

10. You like Web sites that have:

☐ a. things you can click on, shift, or try.
☐ b. interesting design and visual features.
☐ c. interesting written descriptions, lists, and explanations.
☐ d. audio channels where you can hear music, radio programs, or interviews.

11. Other than price, what would most influence your decision to buy a new nonfiction book?

☐ a. the way it looks is appealing
☐ b. quickly reading parts of it
☐ c. a friend talks about it and recommends it
☐ d. it has real-life stories, experiences, and examples

12. You are using a book, CD, or Web site to learn how to take photos with your new digital camera. You would like to have:

☐ a. a chance to ask questions and talk about the camera and its features.
☐ b. clear written instructions with lists and bullet points about what to do.
☐ c. diagrams showing the camera and what each part does.
☐ d. many examples of good and poor photos and how to improve them.

13. You prefer a teacher or a presenter who uses:

☐ a. demonstrations, models, or practical sessions.
☐ b. questions and answers, talk, group discussion, or guest speakers.
☐ c. handouts, books, or readings.
☐ d. diagrams, charts, or graphs.

14. You have finished a competition or test and would like some feedback:

☐ a. using examples from what you have done.
☐ b. using a written description of your results.
☐ c. from somebody who talks it through with you.
☐ d. using graphs showing what you achieved.

15. You are going to order food at a restaurant or café. You would:

☐ a. choose something that you have had there before.
☐ b. listen to the waiter or ask friends to recommend choices.
☐ c. choose from the descriptions in the menu.
☐ d. look at what others are eating or look at pictures of each dish.

16. You have to make an important speech at a conference or special occasion. You would:

☐ a. make diagrams or get graphs to help explain things.
☐ b. write a few key words and practice saying your speech over and over.
☐ c. write out your speech and learn from reading it over several times.
☐ d. gather many examples and stories to make the talk real and practical.

Scoring the VARK. Now you will match up each one of the boxes you selected with a category from the VARK Questionnaire using the following scoring chart. Circle the letter (V, A, R, or K) that corresponds to each one of your responses (A, B, C, or D). For example, if you marked both B and C for question 3, circle both the V and R in the third row.

Responses to Question 3:	A	B	C	D
VARK letter	K	(V)	(R)	A

Count the number of each of the VARK letters you have circled to get your score for each VARK.

Scoring Chart

Question	A Category	B Category	C Category	D Category
1	K	A	R	V
2	V	A	R	K
3	K	V	R	A
4	K	A	V	R
5	A	V	K	R
6	K	R	V	A
7	K	A	V	R
8	R	K	A	V
9	R	A	K	V
10	K	V	R	A
11	V	R	A	K
12	A	R	V	K
13	K	A	R	V
14	K	R	A	V
15	K	A	R	V
16	V	A	R	K

Total number of **V**s circled = ____ Total number of **A**s circled = ____
Total number of **R**s circled = ____ Total number of **K**s circled = ____

Because you could choose more than one answer for each question, the scoring is not a simple matter of counting. It's like four stepping stones across water. Enter your scores **from highest to lowest** on the stones in the figure, with their V, A, R, and K labels.

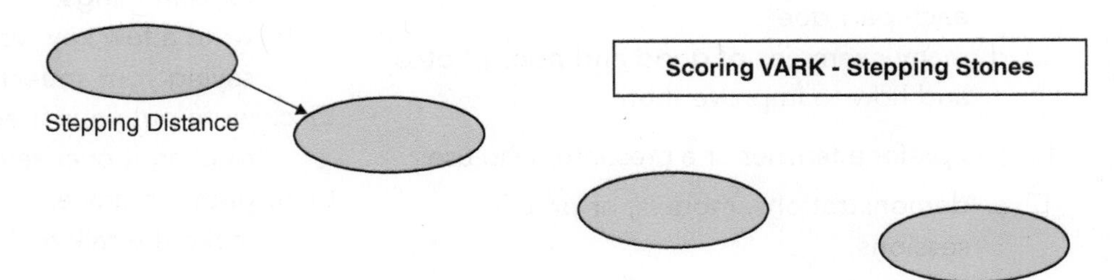

Your stepping distance comes from this table:

The total of my four VARK scores is	My stepping distance is
16–21	1
22–27	2
28–32	3
More than 32	4

Follow these steps to establish your preferences:

1. Your first preference is always your highest score. Check that first stone as one of your preferences.

2. Now subtract your second highest score from your first. If that figure is larger than your stepping distance, you have a single preference. Otherwise, check this stone as another preference and continue with step 3.
3. Subtract your third score from your second one. If that figure is larger than your stepping distance, you have a strong preference for two learning styles (bimodal). If not, check your third stone as a preference and continue with step 4.
4. Last, subtract your fourth score from your third one. If that figure is larger than your stepping distance, you have a strong preference for three learning styles (trimodal). Otherwise, check your fourth stone as a preference, and you have all four modes as your preferences! You may also find that you prefer the four learning styles equally.

Note: If you are bimodal or trimodal or you have checked all four modes as your preferences, you are *multimodal* in your VARK preferences.

your turn Work Together

Sharing Different Approaches to Learning

Did you know what type of learner you were before taking the VARK? Find one or two other students in your class with different learning styles. Share thoughts on strategies you are using to study in all your classes, referring to the examples in Table 1. What strategies are working for everyone in the group?

Use VARK Results to Study More Effectively

How can knowing your VARK score help you do better in your college classes? The following table offers suggestions for using learning styles to

TABLE 1 › Study Strategies by Learning Style

Visual	Aural	Read/Write	Kinesthetic
Underline or highlight your notes.	Talk with others to verify the accuracy of your lecture notes.	Write and rewrite your notes.	Use all your senses in learning: sight, touch, taste, smell, and hearing.
Use symbols, charts, or graphs to display your notes.	Put your notes on audiotape, or audiotape class lectures.	Read your notes silently.	Supplement your notes with real-world examples.
Use color to highlight important concepts.	Read your notes out loud; ask yourself questions and speak your answers.	Organize diagrams or flowcharts into statements.	Move and gesture while you are reading or speaking your notes.
Create a graphic representation of your notes (e.g., a mind map) and redraw it from memory.		Write imaginary exam questions and respond in writing.	

develop your own study strategies. Consider also how online course management systems (see this chapter's Tech Tip) provide opportunities for different types of learners to connect with the material they are studying.

The Kolb Inventory of Learning Styles

The Kolb Inventory of Learning Styles is a widely used and referenced learning model that is more complex than the VARK Inventory. While the VARK Inventory investigates how learners prefer to use their senses in learning, the Kolb Inventory focuses on the abilities we need to develop so we can learn. This inventory, developed in the 1980s by David Kolb, is based on a four-stage cycle of learning (see Figure 1 below).

According to Kolb, effective learners need four kinds of abilities:

1. *Concrete experience* abilities, which allow them to be receptive to others and open to other people's feelings and specific experiences. An example of this type of ability is learning from and empathizing with others.
2. *Reflective observation* abilities, which help learners reflect on their experiences from many perspectives. An example of this type of ability is remaining impartial while considering a situation from a number of different points of view.
3. *Abstract conceptualization* abilities, which help learners integrate observations into logically sound theories. An example of this type of ability is analyzing ideas intellectually and systematically.
4. *Active experimentation* abilities, which enable learners to make decisions, solve problems, and test what they have learned in new situations. An example of this type of ability is being ready to move quickly from thinking to action.

Kolb's Inventory of Learning Styles measures differences along two basic dimensions that represent opposite styles of learning. The first dimension is *abstract-concrete,* and the second is *active-reflective.* See Figure 1 below to visualize how these opposing characteristics combine to create four discrete groups of learners: *divergers, assimilators, convergers,* and *accommodators.*

Doing well in college will require you to adopt some behaviors that are characteristic of each of these four learning styles. Some of them might be uncomfortable for you, but that discomfort will indicate that

FIGURE 1 › Kolb's Four-Stage Cycle of Learning

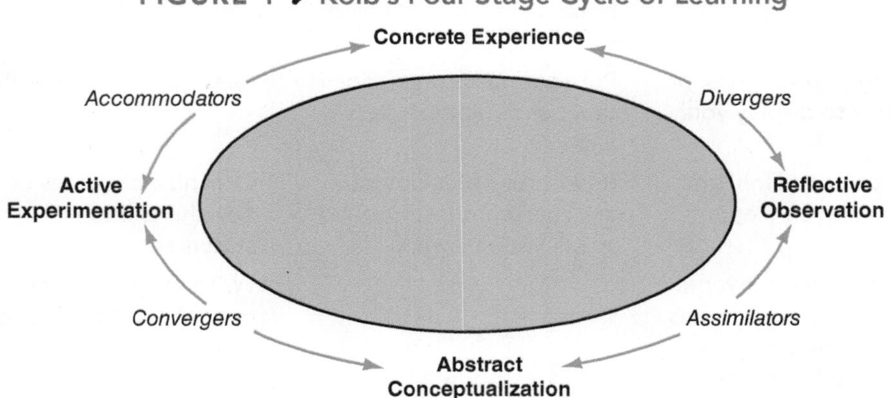

you're growing, stretching, and not relying on the learning style that might be easiest or most natural for you.

If you are a diverger, you are adept at reflecting on situations from many viewpoints. You excel at brainstorming, and you're imaginative, people-oriented, and sometimes emotional. On the downside, you sometimes have difficulty making decisions. Divergers tend to major in the humanities or social sciences.

If you are an assimilator, you like to think about abstract concepts. You are comfortable in classes where the instructor lectures about theoretical ideas without relating the lectures to real-world situations. Assimilators often major in math, physics, or chemistry.

If you are a converger, you like the world of ideas and theories, but you are also good at thinking about how to apply those theories to real-world, practical situations. You differ from divergers in your preference for tasks and problems rather than social and interpersonal issues. Convergers tend to choose health-related and engineering majors.

If you are an accommodator, you prefer hands-on learning. You are skilled at making things happen, and you rely on your intuition. You like people, but you can be pushy and impatient at times, and you might use trial and error, rather than logic, to solve problems. Accommodators often major in business, especially in marketing or sales.[1]

your turn Stay Motivated

Where Are You on the Cycle of Learning?

On the basis of the descriptions we have provided here, where do you see yourself in the Kolb Inventory? Are you more like a diverger, assimilator, converger, or accommodator? Do you sometimes feel forced to engage in behaviors that are uncomfortable for you? Is it hard to be motivated when you want hands-on experience but find that some courses require you to consider abstract theories, or when you want to use your imagination but find you must come up with concrete answers? Choose to adopt behaviors that are characteristic of each of Kolb's learning styles. Don't let some initial discomfort hamper your motivation.

The Myers-Briggs Type Indicator

One of the best-known and most widely used personality inventories that can also be used to describe learning styles is the Myers-Briggs Type Indicator, or MBTI.[2] Whereas the VARK measures your preferences for using your senses to learn and the Kolb Inventory focuses on learning abilities, the MBTI investigates basic personality characteristics and how they relate to human interaction and learning. The MBTI was created by Isabel Briggs Myers and her mother, Katharine Cook Briggs. The inventory identifies and measures psychological types as developed in the personality theory of Carl Gustav Jung, the great twentieth-century psychoanalyst. The MBTI

[1]Adapted from *The Modern American College: Responding to the New Realities of Diverse Students and a Changing Society*/Chickering. Copyright © 1981. Reprinted with permission of John Wiley & Sons, Inc.

[2]Isabel Briggs Myers, *Introduction to Type*, 6th ed. (Mountain View, CA: CPP, 1998).

Take a Time-Out

Do you find that you need some occasional time by yourself? Although introverts are more likely to enjoy time alone, even extraverts can benefit from private time to relax or escape from the hustle and bustle of daily life.
Jonathan Stark

is given to several million people around the world each year. Employers often use this test to give employees insight into how they perceive the world, make decisions, and get along with other people. Many first-year seminar or college success courses also include a focus on the MBTI because it provides a good way to begin a dialogue about human interaction and how personality types affect learning.

All the psychological types described by the MBTI are normal and healthy. There is no good or bad or right or wrong; people are simply different. When you complete the MBTI, your score represents your "psychological type," or the combination of your preferences on four different scales. These scales measure how you take in information and how you then make decisions or come to conclusions about that information. Each preference has a one-letter abbreviation. The four letters together make up your type. Although this book doesn't include the actual survey, you will find a description of the basic MBTI types below. Based on these scales, you can be any combination of these eight types.

high-impact practice 2

your turn Write and Reflect

Discerning the Extraverts from the Introverts in Your Life

Read the following descriptions of extraverts and introverts. Make a list of your friends and family members, and indicate with an "E" or an "I" which are extraverts and which are introverts. How about you? Which type describes you best? Would you like to be different from the way you are? Reflect on these questions in a journal entry.

Extraversion (E) versus Introversion (I): The Inner or Outer World. The E-I preference indicates whether you direct your energy and attention primarily toward the outer world of people, events, and things or the inner world of thoughts, feelings, and reflections. Personality characteristics of extraverts and introverts are summarized here:

Extraverts	Introverts
Outgoing, gregarious, talkative (may talk too much)	Shy, reflective; careful listeners
People of action (may act before they think)	Consider actions deeply (may think too long before acting or neglect to act at all)
Energized by people and activity	Refreshed by quiet and privacy
Good communicators and leaders	Less likely to voice their opinions; often viewed as unaware of people and situations around them

Sensing (S) versus Intuition (N): Facts or Ideas. The S-N preference indicates how you perceive the world and take in information: directly, through your five senses, or indirectly, by using your intuition. Personality characteristics of sensing and intuitive types are summarized here:

Sensing Types	Intuitive Types
Interested above all in the facts, what they can be sure of; dislike unnecessary complication; prefer practicing skills they already know	Fascinated by concepts and big ideas; prefer learning new skills over those already mastered
Relatively traditional and conventional	Original, creative, and nontraditional
Practical, factual, realistic, and down-to-earth	Innovative but sometimes impractical; need inspiration and meaning; prefer to look to the future rather than at the present
Accurate, precise, and effective with routine and details; sometimes miss the "forest" for the "trees"	May exaggerate facts unknowingly; dislike routine and details; work in bursts of energy

Thinking (T) versus Feeling (F): Logic or Values. The T-F preference indicates how you prefer to make your decisions: through logical, rational analysis or through your subjective values, likes, and dislikes. Personality characteristics of thinking types and feeling types are summarized here:

Thinking Types	Feeling Types
Logical, rational, analytical, and critical	Warm, empathetic, and sympathetic
Relatively impersonal and objective in making decisions, less swayed by feelings and emotions; sometimes surprised and puzzled by others' feelings	Need and value harmony; often distressed or distracted by argument and conflict; reluctant to tackle unpleasant interpersonal tasks
Need and value fairness; can deal with interpersonal disharmony	Need and value kindness and harmony
Fair, logical, and just; firm and assertive	Facilitate cooperation and goodwill in others; sometimes unable to be assertive when appropriate
May seem cold, insensitive, and overly blunt and hurtful in their criticisms	Occasionally illogical, emotionally demanding, and unaffected by objective reason and evidence

Judging (J) versus Perceiving (P): Organization or Adaptability. The J-P preference indicates how you characteristically approach the outside world: by making decisions and judgments or by observing and perceiving instead. Personality characteristics of judging and perceiving types are summarized here:

Judging Types	Perceiving Types
Orderly, organized, punctual, and tidy	Spontaneous and flexible
In control of their own world and sphere of influence	Adapt to their world rather than try to control it; comfortable dealing with changes and unexpected developments
Quick decision makers; like to make and follow plans	Slow to make decisions; prefer a wait-and-see approach
Sometimes judgmental and prone to jump to conclusions or make decisions without enough information; have trouble changing plans	Tendency toward serious procrastination and juggling too many things at once without finishing anything; sometimes messy and disorganized

To learn more about these personality types and to access a questionnaire to find out more about your type, visit the Myers & Briggs Foundation at **myersbriggs.org/my-mbti-personality-type/take-the-mbti-instrument.** Remember that while some Myers-Briggs personality types may be particularly advantageous in certain situations, no one type is inherently superior to another. Be alert to both the positive and negative effects your type might have on your success in college.

Multiple Intelligences

Another way of measuring how we learn is the theory of **multiple intelligences**, which suggests that all human beings have at least eight different types of intelligence. This theory was developed in 1983 by Dr. Howard Gardner, a professor of education at Harvard University. Gardner's theory is based on the idea that the traditional definition of human intelligence is very limited. Gardner argues that students should be encouraged to develop the abilities they have, and that evaluation should measure all forms of intelligence.

your turn Write and Reflect

Is There Really More than One Type of Intelligence?

Do a Google search for the phrase *multiple intelligences debate.* Write a one-page paper that describes different opinions about Howard Gardner's theory. Do you agree with the theory? Why or why not?

Gardner's work is controversial because it questions our traditional definitions of intelligence. According to Gardner's theory,

A Knack for Music

Consider the checkmarks you made under musical/rhythmic intelligence in the Multiple Intelligences Inventory in this chapter. Do you play an instrument? Do you find yourself tapping out rhythms? Can you listen to a song and then play it "by ear"? If music comes naturally to you, you probably have a strong musical/rhythmic intelligence.
Blend Images-Hill Street Studios/Getty Images

all human beings have at least eight different types of intelligence, as follows:

1. A **verbal/linguistic** learner likes to read, write, and tell stories, and is good at memorizing information.
2. A **logical/mathematical** learner likes to work with numbers and is good at problem solving and logical processes.
3. A **visual/spatial** learner likes to draw and play with machines and is good at puzzles and reading maps and charts.
4. A **bodily/kinesthetic** learner likes to move around and is good at sports, dance, and acting.
5. A **musical/rhythmic** learner likes to sing and play an instrument and is good at remembering melodies and noticing pitches and rhythms.
6. An **interpersonal** learner likes to have many friends and is good at understanding people, leading others, and mediating conflicts.
7. **Intrapersonal** learners like to work alone, understand themselves well, and are original thinkers.
8. A **naturalistic** learner likes to be outside and is good at preservation, conservation, and organizing a living area.

Where do you think you see yourself? In your opinion, which of these eight intelligences best describes you? As you think of your friends and family, what kinds of intelligences do you think they have? Verify your assumptions about the intelligences of friends and family members by taking the Multiple Intelligences Inventory together. Were there any surprises or were your assumptions confirmed?

Multiple Intelligences Inventory

Put a check mark next to all the items within each intelligence that apply to you.

Verbal/Linguistic Intelligence

____ I enjoy telling stories and jokes.

____ I enjoy word games (e.g., Scrabble and puzzles).

____ I am a good speller (most of the time).

____ I like talking and writing about my ideas.

____ If something breaks and won't work, I read the instruction book before I try to fix it.

____ When I work with others in a group presentation, I prefer to do the writing and library research.

Logical/Mathematical Intelligence

____ I really enjoy my math class.

____ I like to find out how things work.

____ I enjoy computer and math games.

____ I love playing chess, checkers, or Monopoly.

____ If something breaks and won't work, I look at the pieces and try to figure out how it works.

Visual/Spatial Intelligence

____ I prefer a map to written directions.

____ I enjoy hobbies such as photography.

____ I like to doodle on paper whenever I can.

____ In a magazine, I prefer looking at the pictures rather than reading the text.

____ If something breaks and won't work, I tend to study the diagram of how it works.

Bodily/Kinesthetic Intelligence

____ My favorite class is gym because I like sports.

____ When looking at things, I like touching them.

____ I use a lot of body movements when talking.

____ I tend to tap my fingers or play with my pencil during class.

____ If something breaks and won't work, I tend to play with the pieces to try to fit them together.

Musical/Rhythmic Intelligence

____ I enjoy listening to CDs and the radio.

____ I like to sing.

____ I like to have music playing when doing homework or studying.

____ I can remember the melodies of many songs.

____ If something breaks and won't work, I tend to tap my fingers to a beat while I figure it out.

Interpersonal Intelligence

____ I get along well with others.

____ I have several very close friends.

____ I like working with others in groups.

____ Friends ask my advice because I seem to be a natural leader.

____ If something breaks and won't work, I try to find someone who can help me.

Intrapersonal Intelligence

____ I like to work alone without anyone bothering me.

____ I don't like crowds.

____ I know my own strengths and weaknesses.

____ I find that I am strong-willed, independent, and don't follow the crowd.

____ If something breaks and won't work, I wonder whether it's worth fixing.

Naturalist Intelligence

____ I am keenly aware of my surroundings and of what goes on around me.

____ I like to collect things like rocks, sports cards, and stamps.

____ I like to get away from the city and enjoy nature.

____ I enjoy learning the names of living things in the environment, such as flowers and trees.

____ If something breaks and won't work, I look around me to see what I can find to fix the problem.

Review your responses. Now, count up the check marks for each intelligence, and write the total for each intelligence here. Your score for each intelligence will be a number between 1 and 6:

TOTAL SCORE

____ Verbal/Linguistic

____ Logical/Mathematical

____ Visual/Spatial

____ Bodily/Kinesthetic

____ Musical/Rhythmic

____ Interpersonal

____ Intrapersonal

____ Naturalist

Your scores of 3 or more will help you to get a sense of your own multiple intelligences.

Depending on your background and age, some intelligences are likely to be more developed than others. Now that you know where your intelligences are, you can work to strengthen the other intelligences that you do not use as often. How do college courses measure ways in which you are intelligent? Where do they fall short? Looking to the future, you can use your intelligences to help you choose a major, choose activities, and investigate career options. This information will help you appreciate your own unique abilities, and also those of others.

Source: Greg Gay and Gary Hams, "The Multiple Intelligences Inventory." Copyright © Learning Disabilities Resource Community, www.ldrc.ca. Reprinted by permission of the authors.

WHEN LEARNING STYLES AND TEACHING STYLES CONFLICT

Do you enjoy listening to lectures, or do you find yourself gazing out the window or dozing? When your instructor assigns a group discussion, what is your immediate reaction? Do you dislike talking with other students, or is that the way you learn best? How do you react to lab sessions when you have to conduct an actual experiment? Is it an activity you look forward to, or one you dread? Each of these learning situations appeals to some students more than others, but each is inevitably going to be part of your college experience. Your college or university has intentionally designed courses for you to have the opportunity to listen to professors who are experts in their field, to interact with other students in structured groups, and to learn through doing. Because they are all important components of your college education, it's important for you to make the most of each situation.

Instructors tend to teach in ways that fit their *own* particular styles of learning, which might surprise you. So an instructor who learns best in a read/write mode or aural mode will probably just lecture and give the class little opportunity for either interaction or visual and kinesthetic learning. But an instructor who prefers a more interactive, hands-on environment will likely involve students in discussion and learning through experience.

When you recognize a mismatch between how you best learn and how you are being taught, it is important that you take control of your

techtip

CORRELATE ONLINE LEARNING WITH YOUR LEARNING STYLE

Do you like the idea of taking an online class? Maybe that would be a good fit for your work or family schedule. Maybe it would be easier than looking for a parking space on campus. But would you still learn, even if you don't go to a class meeting?

First, consider your learning style:

- If you like the thought of a two-hour lecture where you mostly listen to someone talking, chances are you're an **auditory learner**.
- If you're a **visual learner**, you want to see charts, graphs, and videos.
- If you are a **hands-on learner**, you thrive when engaged in an activity and working with others.

Many colleges and universities use an online learning management system (LMS) for online learning. An LMS is a Web site that helps you connect with the material you're studying—as well as with your instructors and classmates. There is something for every learning style in the LMS environment.

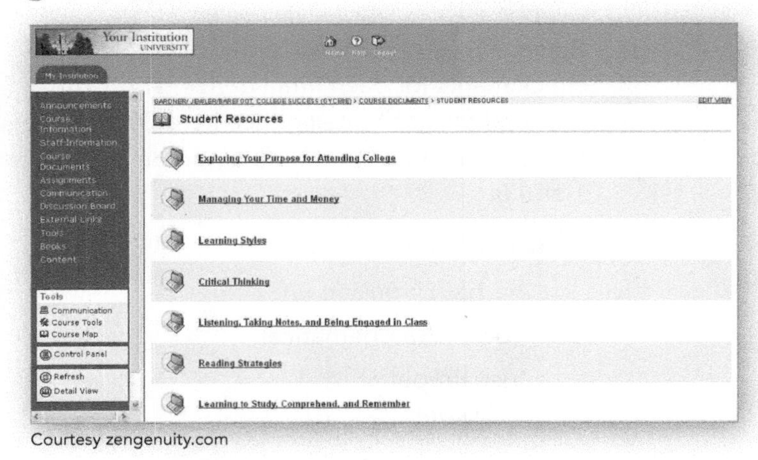

Courtesy zengenuity.com

The Problem

You have some idea about how you learn best, but you don't really understand what an LMS is or how to use one.

The Fix

Understand your learning style and what kind of learning environment will work best for you.

How to Do It

Explore your school's LMS. Be open-minded and patient with yourself. Find out if there is an orientation seminar or video you can watch; you can ask your instructors or visit the student learning center.

- Take online surveys to understand your learning style. Here are two sites to try: edutopia.org/multiple-intelligences-learning-styles-quiz and vark-learn.com.

An LMS offers lots of ways to connect with your instructors, classmates, and material. It lets you keep track of your grades and assignments, and offers a digital drop box where you can submit your work. It can also offer a lot of fun things, such as online discussion forums and interactive group projects where you can sketch ideas on whiteboards that other students can view, or even collaborate on written assignments in real time. Some platforms have videos, recorded lectures, or even your instructor's lecture notes.

1. If you're an auditory learner, you'll love audio recordings. Read your notes and textbook aloud back to yourself.) Consider listening to audiobooks and joining a study group for discussions. Another tip: Listen to videos once and then play them back with your eyes closed.
2. If you're a visual learner, you'll love videos, pictures, maps, and graphs. Whenever you take notes, illustrate them, playing up key points with colored highlighters, pictures, or symbols. You can also create your own graphs or charts.
3. If you're a hands-on learner, you'll love labs, group projects, and fieldwork. Be sure to take notes and read things aloud as you study. Build models or spreadsheets. Take a field trip with others or even by yourself.

IS IT FOR YOU?

Now that you know what kind of learner you are and something about your college's LMS:

- Are you disciplined enough to work independently?
- Would you miss interacting with your instructor or classmates if you didn't attend classes?

You need to know yourself because learning is really

learning process. Use Table 2 as a guide to identify these mismatches and discover strategies for how to handle them. Don't depend on the instructor or the classroom environment to give you everything you need to maximize your learning. Employ your own preferences, talents, and abilities to develop many different ways to study and retain information. For instance, if you don't like listening to a lecture, you will want to sit close to the front of the classroom to reduce distractions. You might also want to record the lecture (with the instructor's permission) so that you can listen to it again. Look back through this chapter to remind yourself of the ways that you can use your own learning styles to be more successful in any class you take.

TABLE 2 › Using the VARK to Adapt

Try to use the VARK to figure out how your instructors teach their classes. List your classes, your instructors' teaching styles, and then your learning style. Do they match? If not, list a strategy you can use to adapt.

My Classes	Teaching Style	My Learning Style	Match: Yes or No?
Example: *Psychology*	*Uses PowerPoints with her lecture so: Visual and Auditory*	*I am kinesthetic and visual.*	*No, but I can ride a stationary bike while looking over my notes.*

LEARNING DISABILITIES

While everyone has a learning style, some people have a **learning disability,** a general term that covers a wide variety of specific learning problems resulting from neurological disorders that can make it difficult to acquire certain academic and social skills. Learning disabilities are very common in students of all ages.

Learning disabilities are usually recognized and diagnosed in grade school, but some students can successfully compensate for a learning problem, perhaps without realizing that's what it is, and reach the first year of college without having been properly diagnosed or assisted. Learning disabilities can show up as specific difficulties with spoken and written language, coordination, self-control, or attention. Such difficulties can impede the ability to read, write, or do math. The term *learning disability* covers a

Learn to Adapt

In college you will find that some instructors may have teaching styles that are challenging for you. It's okay to choose the kinds of classes that conform to the way you like to learn whenever you can, but you'll also need to develop your adaptive strategies to make the most of any classroom setting.
William G. Browning, Minneapolis, MN

"As we start a new school year, Mr. Smith, I just want you to know that I'm an Abstract-Sequential learner and trust that you'll conduct yourself accordingly!"

broad range of possible causes, symptoms, treatments, and outcomes. Therefore, it is difficult to diagnose a learning disability or pinpoint its cause. The types of learning disabilities that most commonly affect college students are attention disorders that affect the development of academic skills, including reading, writing, and mathematics.

You might know someone who has been diagnosed with a learning disability, such as dyslexia, which is a reading disability that occurs when the brain does not properly recognize and process certain symbols, or attention deficit disorder, which affects concentration and focus. It is also possible that you have a special learning need and are not aware of it. This section seeks to increase your self-awareness and your knowledge about such challenges to learning. You will learn more about common types of learning disabilities, how to recognize them, and what to do if you or someone you know has a learning disability.

Attention Disorders

Attention disorders are common in children, adolescents, and adults. Some students who have attention disorders appear to daydream excessively, and once you do get their attention, they can be easily distracted. Individuals with attention deficit disorder (ADD) or attention deficit hyperactivity disorder (ADHD) often have trouble organizing tasks or completing their work. They don't seem to listen to or follow directions, and their work might be messy or appear careless. Although they are not strictly classified as learning disabilities, ADD and ADHD can seriously interfere with academic performance, leading some educators to classify them with other learning disabilities.[4]

---

[4]Adapted from Sharyn Neuwirth, *Learning Disabilities* (Darby, PA: National Institute of Mental Health, 1993), 9–10.

If you have trouble paying attention or getting organized, you won't really know whether you have ADD or ADHD until you are evaluated. Check out resources on campus or in the community. After you have been evaluated, follow the advice you get, which might or might not mean taking medication. If you receive a prescription for medication, be sure to take it according to your physician's directions. You can also improve your focus through your own behavioral choices, whether or not you have an attention disorder. The Web site for the National Institute of Mental Health offers the following suggestions for adults with attention disorders:

> A professional counselor or therapist can help an adult with ADHD learn how to organize his or her life with tools such as a large calendar or date book, lists, reminder notes, and by assigning a special place for keys, bills, and paperwork. Large tasks can be broken down into smaller, more manageable steps so that completing each part of the task provides a sense of accomplishment.[5]

Cognitive Learning Disabilities

Other learning disabilities are related to cognitive skills. Dyslexia, for example, is a common developmental reading disorder. Though a person can have problems with any of the tasks involved in reading, scientists have found that a significant number of people with dyslexia share an inability to distinguish or separate the sounds in spoken words. For instance, people with dyslexia sometimes have difficulty assigning the appropriate sounds to individual letters or to letters that have been combined to form words. Reading is more than recognizing words, however. If the brain is unable to form images or relate new ideas to those stored in memory, the reader can't understand or remember the new concepts. So other types of reading disabilities can appear when the focus of reading shifts from word identification to comprehension.[6]

Writing involves several brain areas and functions as well. The brain networks for vocabulary, grammar, hand movement, and memory must all be in good working order. A developmental writing disorder might result from problems in any of these areas. Someone who can't distinguish the sequence of sounds in a word will often have problems with spelling. People with writing disabilities, particularly expressive language disorders (the inability to express oneself using accurate language or sentence structure), are often unable to write complete, grammatical sentences.[7]

A student with a developmental arithmetic disorder will have difficulty recognizing numbers and symbols, memorizing facts such as multiplication tables, and understanding abstract concepts such as place value and fractions.[8]

---

[5]"Attention Deficit Hyperactivity Disorder." U.S. Department of Health and Human Services, National Institutes of Health, NIH Publication No. 12-3572, p. 17 (Revised 2012). www.nimh.nih.gov/health/publications/attention-deficit-hyperactivity-disorder/index.shtml, accessed September 3, 2014.

[6]Ibid.

[7]Ibid.

[8]Ibid.

The following questions may help you determine whether you or someone you know should be screened for a possible learning disability:

Do you perform poorly on tests, even when you feel that you have studied and are capable of performing better?
Do you have trouble spelling words?
Do you work harder than your classmates at basic reading and writing?
Do your instructors point out inconsistencies in your classroom performance, such as answering questions correctly in class but incorrectly on a written test?
Do you have a really short attention span, or do your family members or instructors say that you do things without thinking?

Although responding *yes* to any of these questions does not mean that you have a disability, your campus learning center or the office for student disability services can help you address any potential problems and devise ways for you to learn more effectively.

If you have a documented learning disability, make sure to notify the office of student disability services at your college or university to receive reasonable accommodations, as required by law. Reasonable accommodations might include use of a computer during some exams, readers for tests, in-class note-takers, extra time for assignments and tests, or the use of audio textbooks, depending on your needs and the type of disability you have.

Anyone who is diagnosed with a learning disability is in good company. According to national data, between 15 and 20 percent of Americans have a learning disability. Pop star Jewel, National Football League host and former player Terry Bradshaw, actor Patrick Dempsey, and CNN news anchor Anderson Cooper are just a few of the famous and successful people who have diagnosed learning disabilities. Here is a final important message: A learning disability is a learning *difference*, but is in no way related to intelligence. Having a learning disability is not a sign that you are stupid. In fact, some of the most intelligent individuals in human history have had a learning disability.

your turn Make Good Choices

Accept the Challenge to Do Your Best, No Matter What!

Although you generally won't be able to select courses and instructors based on your learning style, you can choose how to handle yourself in each class. Think about your courses this term and look at how you filled in Table 2. Which classes are challenging you because of the way the instructors teach? If you are using an instructor's teaching style as an excuse for your poor performance, you are making a choice that may affect your overall college success. Your college or university has plenty of resources available to help you. Seek them out and choose to get the assistance you need to do your best.

checklist for success

How You Learn

- **Take a learning-styles inventory, either in this chapter or at your campus learning or counseling center(s).** See if the results might explain, at least in part, your level of performance in each class you are taking this term.

- **Learn about and accept your unique learning preferences.** Make a special note of your strengths, in terms of those things you learn well and easily. See if those skills could be applied to other learning situations.

- **Adapt your learning style to the teaching styles of your professors.** Consider talking to your professors about how you might best be able to adapt to their teaching strategies.

- **Use your learning style to develop study strategies that work best for you.** You can walk, talk, read, listen, or even dance while you are learning.

- **If you need help with making the best use of your learning style, visit your learning center.** Consider taking some courses in the social and behavioral sciences, which could help you better understand how people learn.

- **If you think you might have a learning disability, go to your campus learning center and ask for a diagnostic assessment so that you can develop successful coping strategies.** Make sure to ask for a personal interpretation and follow-up counseling or tutoring.

build your experience

REFLECT ON CHOICES

high-impact practice 2

This chapter has introduced you to the ways people prefer to learn from their environment. The choice of what to do with that information is up to you. Successful college students learn to adapt to teaching styles that they may not prefer. They know what they have to do to be successful learners, they set goals, and they monitor their progress toward their goals. In a journal entry or readily accessible file, reflect on and write about what you have learned about learning styles and learning disabilities in this chapter and how you can apply the chapter information and strategies in college and in your career. Revisit and build upon your observations throughout your first-year experience.

APPLY WHAT YOU'VE LEARNED

Now that you have read and discussed this chapter, consider how you can apply what you have learned to your academic life and your personal life. The following prompts will help you reflect on chapter material and its relevance to you both now and in the future.

1. It is almost certain that you will find yourself in a class where your learning style conflicts with your instructor's preferred style of teaching. After reading this chapter, describe what you can do to take control and make the most of your strongest learning preferences.
2. It is important to understand various learning styles in the context of education, but it is also important to understand how learning preferences affect career choices. Considering your own learning styles, what might be the best careers for you? Why?

USE YOUR RESOURCES

Campus Learning Center or Center for Students with Disabilities
Whether you are an online or on-campus student, a recent high school graduate, or someone who is older, your college or university will have resources to help students learn more about learning styles or to diagnose a learning disability.

Your Instructors or Your Peer Leader
To gather information about the support services your campus has to offer, talk to your first-year seminar instructor or instructors in education or psychology, who have a strong interest in the processes of learning. You'll find that your peer leader can also steer you in the right direction. If you *are* a peer leader, make sure you have a working knowledge of the learning styles covered in this chapter.

Campus Library
A great deal of published information is available that describes how we learn. A campus librarian can help you locate books and online resources on learning styles and learning disabilities.

Social Media
You will find groups on Facebook (**facebook.com**) that were created by students who have learning disabilities or ADHD. Connect with other students with learning disabilities at your college or university or at other institutions. If you have been diagnosed with a learning disability, the members of these groups can offer support and help you seek out appropriate resources to be successful in college.

LaunchPad for *Your College Experience* is a great resource. Go online to master concepts using the LearningCurve study tool and much more. macmillanhighered.com/gardner12e

Phase4Studios/Shutterstock

5 THINKING IN COLLEGE

YOU WILL EXPLORE

What college-level thinking involves

How to become a critical thinker

Bloom's taxonomy and how it relates to critical thinking

High-impact practices 2 (writing), 3 (collaboration), and 4 (diversity)

Alyssa Manning, 18

Psychology major
The University of North Carolina at Charlotte

David Aaron Troy/Getty Images. Licensed Material is being used for illustrative purposes only, person depicted in the Licensed Material is a model.

"Thinking for ourselves and coming up with new conclusions will be really helpful when we enter the workforce."

As a psychology student at the University of North Carolina at Charlotte (UNC Charlotte), Alyssa Manning understands the importance of thinking skills both inside and outside the classroom. When Alyssa arrived on campus last fall, she learned that she would be living in the international residence hall with students from all over the world. She quickly learned that interacting with people who don't know anyone else in the United States and who have different customs, study habits, and food presented some welcome challenges and tested her thinking skills. "Some of the questions the international students ask about America make me think in a different way because I never think about my own country in that way." One way she has been able to reach out to the students she lives with is by joining an international student organization, which helps bring new international students to campus and get them settled into campus life.

Alyssa grew up in Philadelphia and decided to attend UNC Charlotte because she was interested in the research opportunities available to her as an undergraduate psychology major. The beautiful campus and location in Charlotte didn't hurt either! So far, her favorite class has been social psychology. She has found good thinking skills to be essential to succeeding in all her classes. "Professors will give you a lot of facts and general information, but they expect you to be able to relate all the information and come up with your own conclusions. Thinking for ourselves and coming up with new conclusions will be really helpful when we enter the workforce," she says.

After Alyssa graduates, she's open to new experiences and opportunities, but she hopes to continue on to graduate school. As an aspiring psychiatrist, she says that "thinking skills will help a lot when dealing with cases and needing to diagnose disorders and develop treatment plans. They will also be helpful in clinical settings." Her advice to other first-year students? Look for ways to recognize problems and come up with unique solutions.

To access the LearningCurve study tool, video activities, and more, go to LaunchPad for *Your College Experience*. macmillanhighered.com/gardner12e

Learning to think—using the mind to produce ideas, opinions, decisions, and memories—is part of normal human development. Just as our bodies grow, so does our ability to think logically and rationally about abstract concepts. The Nobel-prize-winning economist, Daniel Kahneman, describes two types of thinking: "fast thinking" and "slow thinking." He characterizes fast thinking as automatic, emotional, stereotypic, and subconscious; this type of thinking is certainly appropriate in some circumstances. Slow thinking takes more effort, more conscious attention, and is more logical, rational, and deep.[1] By improving your slower and more logical thinking abilities and strategies, you will become a better learner and problem solver.

[1]Daniel Kahneman, *Thinking, Fast and Slow*, (New York: Farrar, Straus and Giroux, 2013).

assess your strengths

Thinking is one of the most valuable skills you can practice for success in college and in the workplace. What strengths do you currently have in solving problems and making decisions? How do you approach such issues? Do you make quick decisions, or are you more deliberate and thoughtful? Think of a couple of issues you have dealt with in the recent past. How has your approach helped or hurt each situation?

set goals

What are your most important objectives in learning the material in this chapter? Do you think deeply before making decisions? Consider an issue that you are currently dealing with. Are you investigating all sides of it rather than making a snap decision? Use this chapter to help you develop strategies and goals that relate to thinking.

The concept of "critical thinking" might not be new to you; you have probably heard the term before. Here we define **critical thinking** as the thoughtful consideration of the information, ideas, observations, and arguments that you encounter. In essence, critical thinking is a search for truth. It is similar to slow thinking as described by Kahneman, but it also emphasizes the importance of analyzing and evaluating information to guide belief and action—this is the kind of thinking you will do in college, and it's what this chapter is all about. We will explain how developing and applying your critical-thinking skills can make the search for answers a worthwhile and stimulating adventure.

COLLEGE-LEVEL THINKING: HIGHER AND DEEPER

In college, the level of thinking that your instructors expect from you exceeds that which you did in high school, both in terms of the questions that are asked and the answers that are expected. For instance, if a high school teacher asked, "What are the three branches of the U.S. government?" he or she would ask you to give the one right answer: "legislative, executive, and judicial." A college instructor, on the other hand, might ask, "Under what circumstances might conflicts arise among the three branches of government, and what do the circumstances and the conflicts reveal about the democratic process?" There is no simple, quick, or single acceptable answer to the second question—that's the point of higher education. Questions that suggest complex answers engage you in the process of deep thinking. The shift to this higher or deeper level of thinking can be an adjustment—it might even catch you off guard and cause you some stress.

One step toward deep and critical thinking is becoming comfortable with uncertainty. In college, it's important to challenge assumptions and conclusions, even those presented by so-called experts. Rather than just taking in information, studying it, and then recalling it for a test, in college you'll go far beyond these skills and gain the ability and the confidence to arrive at your own conclusions—to think for yourself. Educational researchers describe this process as "constructing" knowledge for yourself rather than merely "receiving" knowledge from others. Courses in every discipline will encourage you to ask questions, sort through competing information and ideas, form well-reasoned opinions, and defend them.

It is natural to feel frustrated by answers that are neither entirely wrong nor right, yet the complicated questions are usually the ones that are the most interesting and worthy of study. Working out the answers can be both intellectually exciting and personally rewarding.

Problem Solving in and out of Class

College will give you experience in decision making and problem solving—processes that are linked to your abilities to use logical thinking processes, to weigh evidence, and to formulate conclusions. Your success both in college and in your future life will depend on how well you make decisions and solve problems. Here are some examples of situations commonly encountered in college that will call upon these skills:

- Deciding how to allocate your research and writing time when you have two papers due on the same day
- Finding a way to ask your roommate to compromise on a suitable lights-out time because you're not getting the sleep you need
- Mapping out how to incorporate time for exercising into your busy schedule in order to maintain a healthy fitness level and avoid weight gain
- Deciding whether to go home on the weekends or stay on campus to study and participate in campus events
- Understanding the advantages and disadvantages of the variety of readily available information sources, including Facebook, Twitter feeds, CNN, *USA Today*, *The New York Times*, the *Onion*, and your school newspaper.

In addition to these situations, which provide opportunities for you to flex your problem-solving muscles on a more personal level, the college years also represent a time in your life when you get to know yourself. You will begin to develop your own positions on societal and political issues, learn more about what is important to you, and develop into a contributing citizen of your country and also the world.

In college, you'll be exposed to ideas and often-conflicting opinions about contemporary issues such as same-sex marriage, U.S. military operations, global human rights, animal rights, comprehensive sex education, food safety, the state of public education in the U.S., student loan debt and loan forgiveness, and economic inequality. The list goes on and on. Before accepting any opinion on any issue as "the truth," look for evidence that supports different positions on these debates. In fact, look for opportunities to participate in such debates. In most colleges, these opportunities abound.

Making a Choice between Slow and Fast Thinking

At the start of the chapter, we introduced the concepts of slow and fast thinking. While fast thinking has its place, improving your slower and more logical thinking abilities will allow you to become a better learner. But you might notice that some people seem to do no real thinking at all, or at least no thinking of their own.

People who do not develop their thinking skills often make spur-of-the-moment decisions based on what seems easiest, results in the least conflict, or conforms to preconceived notions. You probably know a lot of people like that—who do not think critically, depend on others to think for them, and assume that what they believe is true simply because they wish, hope, or feel that it is true. You might also know people who like things just because they are popular, and still others whose beliefs may be based on what they heard growing up, without ever examining the underlying assumptions that support those beliefs. As you might have noticed, the followers, the wishful believers, and the rigid thinkers tend not to have much control over their lives or to have any real power in business or society.

The slow thinkers, those who use critical-thinking skills, are different. They examine problems, ask questions, suggest new answers that challenge the existing situation, discover new information, question authorities and traditional beliefs, make independent judgments, and develop creative solutions. Being a good critical thinker does not mean that you are "critical" or negative in your dealings with others. Rather, the term refers to thoughtful consideration of the information, ideas, and arguments that you encounter. When employers say they want workers who can find reliable information, analyze it, organize it, draw conclusions from it, and present it convincingly to others, that means they want employees who are good critical thinkers.

Whatever else you do in college, make it a point to develop and sharpen your critical-thinking skills. You won't become a great critical thinker overnight. With practice, however, you can learn how to tell if information is truthful and accurate. Thinking critically—mastering slow thinking—will help you make better decisions, come up with fresh solutions to difficult problems, and communicate your ideas effectively.

your turn Make Good Choices

If You Had a "Do-Over"

Think about a past problem or difficult situation you were unsuccessful in solving. If you could go back in time, how would you choose to solve the problem to get the outcome you desire? What would you do differently? What different choices would you make? Could you more deliberately use slow thinking in approaching the situation?

Rate Your Critical-Thinking Skills

It will be interesting to see how your critical-thinking skills change over the next few weeks and months. Given where you are currently, rate yourself as a "critical" thinker. At the end of the term, return to this table, and see how much you've changed.

Circle the number that best fits you in each of the critical situations described below.

Critical Situations	Never				Sometimes					Always
In class, I ask lots of questions when I don't understand.	1	2	3	4	5	6	7	8	9	10
If I don't agree with what the group decides is the correct answer, I challenge the group opinion.	1	2	3	4	5	6	7	8	9	10
I believe there are many solutions to a problem.	1	2	3	4	5	6	7	8	9	10
I admire those people in history who challenged what was believed at the time, such as "the earth is flat."	1	2	3	4	5	6	7	8	9	10
I make an effort to listen to both sides of an argument before deciding which way I will go.	1	2	3	4	5	6	7	8	9	10
I ask lots of people's opinions about a political candidate before making up my mind.	1	2	3	4	5	6	7	8	9	10
I am not afraid to change my belief system if I learn something new.	1	2	3	4	5	6	7	8	9	10
Authority figures do not intimidate me.	1	2	3	4	5	6	7	8	9	10

The more 7–10 scores you have circled, the more likely it is that you use your critical-thinking skills often. The lower scores indicate that you may not use critical-thinking skills very often, or that you use them only during certain activities.

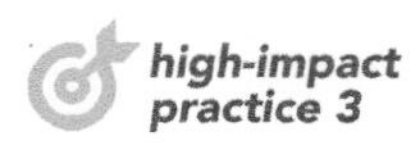

Collaboration

One way to become a better critical thinker is to practice with other people. By getting feedback from others, you can see the possible flaws in your own position or approach. Whether debating an issue in a political science class or making a dress in a fashion design class, appreciate how people bring their own life experiences, personal taste, knowledge, and expertise to the table. Most questions do not have clear-cut answers, and there are often several ways of approaching any task. Getting input from others can help make your finished product a masterpiece.

Researchers who study thinking of elementary school students, high school students, and college students find that critical thinking and collaboration go hand in hand. Students at all levels are more likely to exercise their critical-thinking abilities when they are confronted by the experiences and opinions of others. Having more than one student involved in the learning process generates a greater number of ideas than one person can generate alone. People think more clearly when they talk as well as listen, which is a very good reason to participate actively in your classes. Creative brainstorming and group discussion encourage original thought. These habits also teach participants to consider alternative points of view carefully and to express and defend their own ideas clearly. As a group negotiates ideas and learns to agree on the most reliable concepts, it moves closer to a conclusive solution.

As you leave college and enter the working world, you will find that collaboration—not only with people in your work setting but also with others around the globe—is essential to almost any career you may pursue. Whether in person or through electronic communication, teamwork improves your ability to think critically.

Creativity

Our society is full of creative individuals who think outside the box, challenge the status quo, or simply ask questions that others are not asking. Many have achieved fame by using their thinking skills and actions to change our world. Even a single thought can have a ripple effect that leads to major progress. As you move through your other first-year courses such as sociology, psychology, history, or technology, you will learn about people who have used their creative-thinking abilities to become world changers in their academic areas.

Below are some critical thinkers of our past and present. Some might surprise you. What contributions to our world did each of these individuals make, and how do these contributions continue to affect our lives?

- **Abraham Lincoln** When we think of great leaders, Lincoln often comes to mind. Lincoln was able to think about the relationship between national policy and human rights in new and different ways. By working slowly and deliberately, Lincoln changed American laws and began a long process toward guaranteeing equal rights for all U.S. citizens—a journey that culminated in the civil rights legislation of the 1960s.
- **Martin Luther King Jr.** King could be considered one of the greatest activists of all time. When segregation ruled in the South, he contributed to the civil rights movement by voicing his concerns and presenting his dream of a different world. He created opportunities for change in many unfair societal policies and practices.
- **Twitter creators Jack Dorsey, Evan Williams, Biz Stone, and Noah Glass** Twitter was created in 2006 as a social networking and microblogging site to enhance communication around the world through hashtag statements that are limited to 140 characters each. In spite of early public resistance, the site quickly gained popularity and changed our way of communicating in times of national and international crisis due to its ability to disseminate information to millions of people instantly.
- **Steve Jobs** As an innovative and dynamic thinker, Jobs shaped the way our society viewed technology and digital capabilities. He persevered with passion, even through tough times, such as when he was ousted from his position as the head of Apple.

- **Lady Gaga** Pushing her artistic expression through fashion and activism, Lady Gaga projects an androgynous identity that challenges gender expectations and voices her belief in equality for all individuals.
- **Your instructors** You may not know it yet, but many of your instructors have conducted and written about cutting-edge research in their respective fields. Some may have even written textbooks that you are currently using in class!

your turn Stay Motivated

Follow the Examples of Others

People who make a difference in their communities, nation, or the world stay motivated. They don't quit, even when they experience tough times. What other people in our world today—religious leaders, politicians, scientists, athletes, or entrepreneurs—have maintained their motivation and achieved major successes within their spheres of influence? What can you learn from them about what it means to stay motivated?

BECOMING A CRITICAL THINKER

As you've read, a high-priority goal in college is to develop strong thinking and decision-making skills. Not only will you develop your own competence and confidence, you will contribute to the larger society by helping solve community and national problems.

Asking Questions

The first step of thinking at a deeper level, of true critical thinking, is to be curious. This involves asking questions. Instead of accepting statements and claims at face value, question them. Here are a few suggestions:

- When you come across an idea or a statement that you consider interesting, confusing, or suspicious, first ask yourself what it means.
- Do you fully understand what is being said, or do you need to pause and think to make sense of the idea?
- Do you agree with the statement? Why or why not?
- Can the statement or idea be interpreted in more than one way?

Don't stop there.

- Ask whether you can trust the person or group making a particular claim, and ask whether there is enough evidence to back up that claim (more on this later).
- Ask who might agree or disagree and why.
- Ask how a new concept relates to what you already know.
- Think about where you might find more information about the subject, and what you could do with what you learn.

- Ask yourself about the effects of accepting a new idea as truth.
  - Will you have to change or give up what you have believed in for a long time?
  - Will it require you to do something differently?
  - Will it be necessary to examine the issue further?
  - Should you try to bring other people around to a new way of thinking?

Comparison Shopping

Use your critical-thinking abilities to practice healthy skepticism in your life. Shopping is a great opportunity to practice. What questions do you need to ask to find out if what seems like a good deal really is a good deal? Can you think of a time when you had to think hard about a purchase to make sure it was a wise choice?

Considering Multiple Points of View and Drawing Conclusions

Before you draw any conclusions about the validity of information or opinions, it's important to consider more than one point of view. College reading assignments might deliberately expose you to conflicting arguments and theories about a subject, or you might encounter differences of opinion as you do research for a project. Your own belief system will influence how you interpret information, just as others' belief systems and points of view might influence how they present information. For example, consider your own ideas about the issue of K–12 education in the United States. American citizens, politicians, and others often voice opinions on options such as charter, private, and public schools. What kind of pre-college education do *you* think is best, and *why* do you hold this viewpoint?

The more ideas you consider, the more sophisticated your thinking will become. Ultimately, you will discover not only that it is okay to change your mind but also that a willingness to do so is the mark of a reasonable, educated person. Considering multiple points of view means synthesizing material, evaluating information and resources that might contradict each other or offer multiple points of view on a topic, and then honoring those differences. After considering multiple viewpoints and drawing conclusions, the next step is to develop your own viewpoint based on credible evidence and facts, while staying true to your values and beliefs. Critical thinking is the process you go through in deciding how to align your experience and value system with your viewpoint.

This process isn't necessarily a matter of figuring out the right idea. Depending on the goals of the activity, the "right" idea might simply be the one that you think is the most fun or the most practical, or it might be a new idea of your own creation.

Drawing conclusions based on your consideration of many opinions and other types of evidence involves looking at the outcome of your inquiry in a more demanding, critical way. If you are looking for solutions to a problem, which ones seem most promising after you have conducted an exhaustive search for materials? If you have found new evidence, what does that new evidence show? Do your original beliefs hold up in the face of new evidence? Do they need to be modified? Which notions should be abandoned? Most important, consider what you would need to do or say to persuade someone else that your ideas are valid. Thoughtful conclusions are the most useful when you can share them with others.

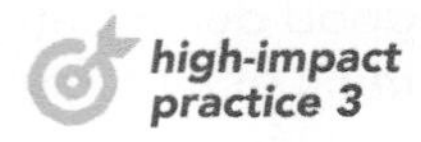

your turn Work Together

Moving from Opinion to Logical Conclusion

Imagine that your state has just approved a license plate design incorporating a cross and the slogan, "I Believe." Almost immediately, a number of organizations begin protesting that this license plate is a violation of the First Amendment of the U.S. Constitution. Work with a small group of other students in your class and decide whether you agree or disagree with the state's action. Ask all members of the group to set aside their personal opinions and try to reach the best conclusion using solid evidence.

Making Arguments

What does the word *argument* mean to you? If you're like most people, the first image it conjures up might be an ugly fight you had with a friend, a yelling match you witnessed on the street, or a heated disagreement between family members. True, such unpleasant confrontations are arguments, but the word also refers to a calm, reasoned effort to persuade someone of the value of an idea.

When you think of it this way, you'll quickly recognize that arguments are central to academic study, work, and life in general. Scholarly articles, business memos, and requests for spending money all have something in common: The effective ones make a general claim, provide reasons to support it, and back up those reasons with evidence. That's what argument is.

It's important to consider multiple points of view, or arguments, in tackling new ideas and complex questions, but arguments are not all equally valid. Good critical thinking involves analyzing assumptions that might have been omitted and scrutinizing the quality of the evidence used to support a claim. Whether examining an argument or making one, a good critical thinker is careful to ensure that ideas are presented in an understandable, logical way.

Challenging Assumptions and Beliefs

To some extent, it's unavoidable to have beliefs based on gut feelings or blind acceptance of something you've heard or read. However, some assumptions should be examined more thoughtfully, especially if they will influence an important decision or serve as the foundation for an argument.

We develop an understanding of information based on our value systems and how we view the world. Our family backgrounds influence these views, opinions, and assumptions. College is a time to challenge those assumptions and beliefs and to think critically about ideas we have always had.

Well-meaning people will often disagree. It's important to listen to both sides of an argument before making up your mind. If you follow the guidelines in this chapter, we can't promise that your classes will be easier or that you'll solve major problems, but you will be better equipped to handle them. You will have the skills to use critical thinking to figure things out instead of depending purely on how you feel or what you've heard. As you listen to a lecture, debate, or political argument about what is in the public's best interest, try to predict where it is heading and why. Ask yourself whether you have enough information to justify your own position.

is**this**you?

When New Knowledge and Old Beliefs Collide

Are you having conversations in class or with your friends about topics or ideas that go against what you have been taught? Do you feel anxious that these new ideas don't align with what your family has taught you? Ideas presented by college instructors are almost always supported by evidence and research, much of which is derived from data and cutting-edge technology. It is important to keep an open mind, even if it makes you uncomfortable. Develop a relationship with a mentor or colleague who can help you process some of the more sensitive information you hear.

Examining Evidence

Another important part of thinking critically is checking that the evidence supporting an argument—whether someone else's or your own—is of the highest possible quality. To do that, simply ask a few questions about the argument as you consider it:

- What general idea am I being asked to accept?
- Are good and sufficient reasons given to support the overall claim?
- Are those reasons backed up with evidence in the form of facts, statistics, and quotations?
- Does the evidence support the conclusions?
- Is the argument based on logical reasoning, or does it appeal mainly to emotions?
- Do I recognize any questionable assumptions?

- Can I think of any counterarguments, and if so, what facts can I muster as proof?
- What do I know about the person or organization making the argument?
- What credible sources can I find to support the information?

If you have evaluated the evidence used in support of a claim and are still not certain of its quality, it's best to keep looking for more evidence. Drawing on questionable evidence for an argument has a tendency to backfire. In most cases, a little persistence will help you find better sources.

Recognizing and Avoiding Faulty Reasoning

Although logical reasoning is essential to solving any problem, whether simple or complex, you need to go one step further to make sure that an argument hasn't been compromised by faulty reasoning. Here are some of the most common missteps—referred to as logical fallacies or flaws in reasoning—that people make in their use of logic:

- **Attacking the person.** Arguing against other people's positions or attacking their arguments is perfectly acceptable. Going after their

Logic That Just Doesn't Fly

This cartoon presents an obvious example of faulty reasoning. Some conversations or arguments tend to include reasoning like this. Can you think of a similarly illogical leap that someone used in an argument with you? Did you use critical thinking to counter it, or did your emotions get the best of you?

personalities, however, is not OK. Any argument that resorts to personal attack ("Why should we believe a cheater?") is unworthy of consideration.

- **Begging.** "Please, officer, don't give me a ticket! If you do, I'll lose my license, and I have five little children to feed, and I won't be able to feed them if I can't drive my truck." None of the driver's statements offer any evidence, in any legal sense, as to why she shouldn't be given a ticket. Pleading *might* work if the officer is feeling generous, but an appeal to facts and reason would be more effective: "I fed the meter, but it didn't register the coins. Since the machine is broken, I'm sure you'll agree that I don't deserve a ticket."
- **Appealing to false authority.** Citing authorities, such as experts in a field or the opinions of qualified researchers, can offer valuable support for an argument. However, a claim based on the authority of someone whose expertise is questionable relies on the appearance of authority rather than on real evidence. We see examples of false authority all the time in advertising: Sports stars who are not doctors, dieticians, or nutritionists urge us to eat a certain brand of food; famous actors and singers who are not dermatologists extol the medical benefits of a costly remedy for acne.
- **Jumping on a bandwagon.** Sometimes we are more likely to believe something that many others also believe. Even the most widely accepted truths can turn out to be wrong, however. At one time, nearly everyone believed that the world was flat, until someone came up with evidence to the contrary.
- **Assuming that something is true because it hasn't been proven false.** If you go to a bookstore or look online, you'll find dozens of books detailing close encounters with flying saucers and extraterrestrial beings. These books describe the people who had such encounters as beyond reproach in their integrity and sanity. Because critics could not disprove the claims of the witnesses, the events are said to have actually occurred. Even in science, few things are ever proved completely false, but evidence can be discredited.
- **Falling victim to false cause.** Frequently, we make the assumption that just because one event followed another, the first event must have caused the second. This reasoning is the basis for many superstitions. The ancient Chinese once believed that they could make the sun reappear after an eclipse by striking a large gong, because they knew that on a previous occasion the sun had reappeared after a large gong had been struck. Most effects, however, are usually the result of a complex web of causes. Don't be satisfied with easy before-and-after claims; they are rarely correct.
- **Making hasty generalizations.** If someone selected a green marble from a barrel containing a hundred marbles, you wouldn't assume that the next marble drawn from the barrel would also be green. After all, you know nothing about the colors of the ninety-nine marbles still in the barrel. However, if you were given fifty draws from the barrel, and each draw produced a green marble after the barrel had been shaken thoroughly, you would be more willing to conclude that the next marble drawn would be green, too. Reaching a conclusion based

on the opinion of one source is like assuming that all the marbles in the barrel are green after pulling out only one marble.

- **Slippery slope.** "If we allow tuition to increase, the next thing we know, it will be $20,000 per term." Such an argument is an example of "slippery slope" thinking. Fallacies like these can slip into even the most careful reasoning. One false claim can derail an entire argument, so be on the lookout for weak logic in what you read and write. Never forget that accurate reasoning is a key factor in succeeding in college and in life.

your turn Write and Reflect

Tempted to Use a Logical Fallacy?

Have you ever used a logical fallacy to justify decisions you have made? In looking back, did your flawed argument convince anyone that you were right? Why or why not? Describe your experiences in a journal entry.

APPLYING BLOOM'S TAXONOMY

Benjamin Bloom, a professor of education at the University of Chicago during the second half of the twentieth century, worked with a group of other researchers to design a system of classifying goals for the learning process. This system is known as Bloom's taxonomy, and it is now used at all levels of education to define and describe the process that students use to understand and think critically about what they are learning.

Bloom's Six Levels of Learning

Bloom identified six levels of learning, as represented in Figure 1. The higher the level, the more critical thinking it requires. Bloom's taxonomy is used in developing curricula, textbooks, learning management systems, and other academic work. You have been using the levels of Bloom's taxonomy throughout your education, perhaps without being aware of it.

Bloom's Taxonomy and the First Year of College

As you progress through your first year of college, you will notice that your level of comprehension and reflection begin to deepen as you engage with material and apply it to your experience in order to retain and synthesize it. If you pay close attention, you will discover that Bloom's taxonomy is often the framework that college instructors use to design classroom activities and out-of-class assignments. No matter what the topic is, this framework will help move you to deeper understanding and an ability to apply what you learn to other situations and concepts. Now we'll take a closer look at Bloom's taxonomy and then we'll take a concept you're likely to encounter in your first year of college—diversity—and match your cognitive development of the concept to Bloom's taxonomy.

FIGURE 1 > The Six Levels of Learning of Bloom's Taxonomy

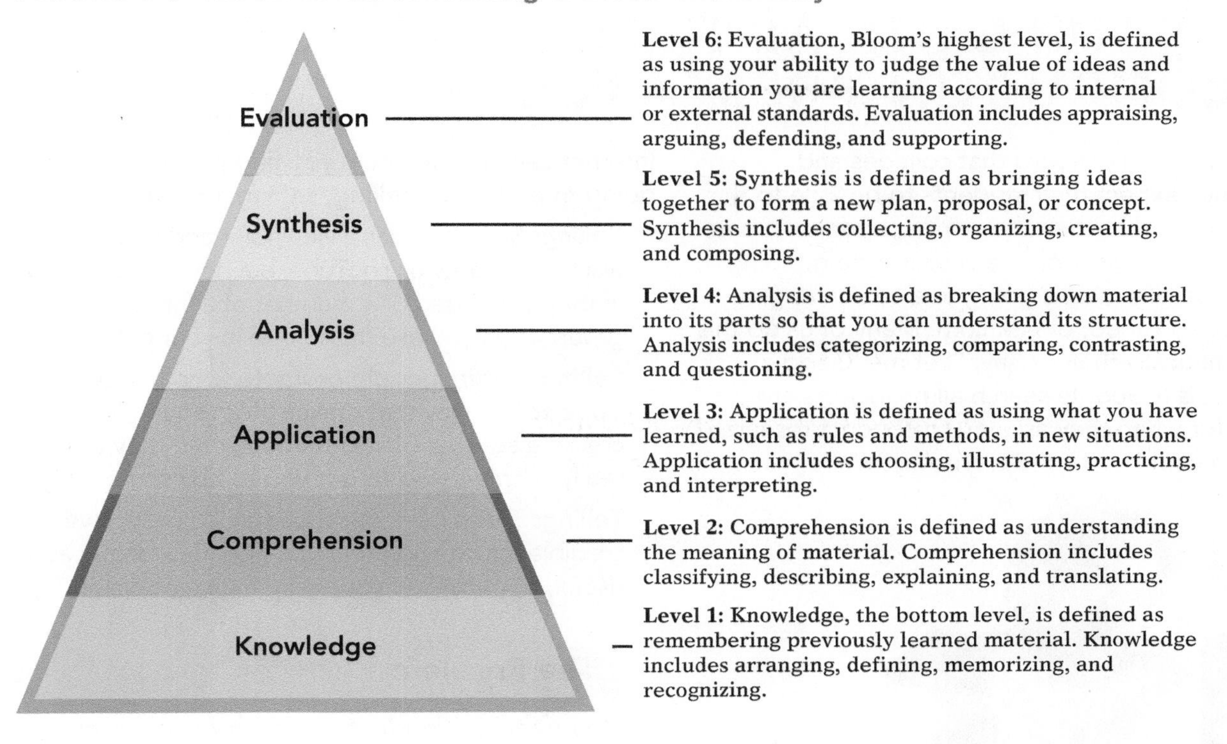

Concept: Diversity

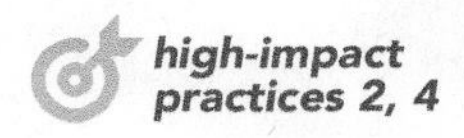

Level 1 (Knowledge) Read a dictionary definition of the word *diversity*.

Level 2 (Comprehension) Explain the concept of diversity to another student without reading the dictionary definition.

Level 3 (Application) Write about all the types of human diversity that exist within the student body at your college or university and possible categories of human diversity that are not represented there.

Level 4 (Analysis) Conduct two separate analyses. The first analysis will be why your institution has large numbers of certain types of students. The second analysis will be why your institution has small numbers of other types of students.

Level 5 (Synthesis) Write a paper that combines your findings in Level 4 and hypothesizes what components of your college or university culture either attract or repel certain students.

Level 6 (Evaluation) In your paper, evaluate the institution's "diversity profile" and argue for or against change in the way your campus supports diversity.

techtip

USE YOUR CRITICAL-THINKING SKILLS IN CONDUCTING RESEARCH

You have probably heard that colleges and universities expect their students to be able to conduct research when they write papers or create projects. In high school or a casual setting, doing research usually means going to a search engine like Google, Yahoo, or Ask.com. Many of us do this so automatically that we say, "Let me 'Google' that." But is a Google search all professors are looking for when they ask you to conduct research? How else could you conduct research?

Internet searches will help you find people basically doing three things: **yelling**, **selling**, or **telling**.

Yelling: Someone has a viewpoint and puts it forward on Blogger or YouTube, but how do you know if they are biased or a member of a fringe or hate group when you use their video in your project?

Selling: Often, people promote products or services in a way that makes them sound like credible sources of information when they are really simply trying to get you to buy something.

Telling: These places and people actually have credible information that you find informative and useful, but how can you verify their credibility?

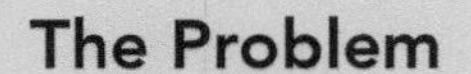

The Problem

You need to conduct research for a paper, but you're not sure how to evaluate the types of information found on the Internet.

The Fix

Use a critical-thinking system to conduct your research.

Rommel Canlas/Shutterstock

How to Do It

Start with good questions. If you are researching a topic, such as "marijuana legalization," generate some questions you have about that subject rather than just going to Google and typing "marijuana" into the search box:

- What is the history of marijuana use in the U.S.
- Why was it made illegal in the first place?
- Where has it been legalized and why?
- What have been some of the positive and negative outcomes of making it legal?

Generating questions will save you time by clarifying what you need to know, so you will recognize useful results and ignore the ones that won't help you.

Go to the library. Show the reference librarians your list of questions. They can help you fine-tune them and will recommend good places to find answers.

Use databases. Your school pays for research databases, which collect a variety of credible, scholarly research. When you use research databases, you can be sure that the information is reliable, and you can refine your search terms to produce 20 or 30 returns, as opposed to 20 or 30 million. Most databases are available online with login information that your college can provide, so you can use them anytime from home or on your laptop.

Use a variety of locations to confirm information. When you see the same information in a variety of credible sources, you can start to trust its accuracy. *Remember that there are still good sources of information in print form that are not available online.*

Consider the quality of the information. Where did it come from? Who said it and why? How current is it? Has anything major happened in this area since this information was published?

EXTRA STYLE POINTS: Get in the habit of reading (not just watching) a variety of information sources. If you get news only from TV or links on Facebook, you will miss important stories. Remember this: Professionals need to be up to date in their areas of expertise, but they also must understand larger current events happening in the world around them. You must have broad knowledge in order to place your professional knowledge in context.

checklist for success

Thinking in College

- **Make sure that you understand what kind of thinking you will develop in college.** If you are not clear, discuss it with the instructor of this course, another instructor, or a staff member in the learning center.
- **Find ways to express your imagination and curiosity, and practice asking questions.** If you have the impulse to raise a question, don't stifle yourself. College is the perfect venue for self-expression and exploration.
- **Challenge your own and others' assumptions that are not supported by evidence.** To help you better understand someone's position on a given issue, practice asking for additional information in a calm, polite manner that does not reject his or her ideas.
- **During class lectures, presentations, and discussions, practice thinking about the subjects being discussed from multiple points of view.** Start with the view that you would most naturally take toward the matter at hand. Then, force yourself to imagine what questions might be raised by someone who doesn't see the issue the same way you do.
- **Draw your own conclusions and explain to others what evidence you considered that led you to these positions.** Don't assume that anyone automatically understands why you reached your conclusions.
- **Seek out opportunities for collaboration.** Join study groups or class project teams so you can collaborate with other students. When you are a member of a team, volunteer for roles that challenge you. That is how you will really experience significant gains in learning and development.
- **Learn to identify false claims in commercials and political arguments.** Then look for the same faulty reasoning in people's comments you hear each day.
- **Practice critical thinking, not only in your academic work, but also in your everyday interactions with friends and family.** Your environment both in and out of college will give you lots of opportunities to become a better critical thinker.

build your experience

REFLECT ON CHOICES

high-impact practice 2

This chapter has introduced you to critical thinking—the kind of thinking you will be expected to do in college. Reflect on what you have learned and how you would explain college-level thinking to someone else. Create a written summary of your ideas.

APPLY WHAT YOU'VE LEARNED

Consider how you can apply what you have learned to your academic and personal life. The following prompts will help you reflect on chapter material and its relevance to you both now and in the future.

1. After reading this chapter, think of professions (for example, health care, engineering, marketing) for which problem solving and thinking outside the box are necessary. Choose one career and describe why you think critical thinking is a necessary and valuable skill for that job.
2. In your opinion, is it harder to think critically than to base your arguments on how you feel about a topic? Why or why not? What are the advantages of finding answers based on your feelings versus based on problem solving and evidence? How might you use both approaches in seeking answers to questions?

USE YOUR RESOURCES

Logic Courses
If you are interested in learning more about critical thinking and how to apply critical-thinking skills, check out the introductory course in logic offered by your college's philosophy department. It might be the single best course designed to teach you critical-thinking skills, and nearly all colleges and universities offer such a course. Also, talk with a philosophy or logic instructor about in-class and out-of-class opportunities on your campus. A major in either area might be right for you.

Argument Courses and Critical-Thinking Courses
Does your institution offer either an argument or a critical-thinking course? Check your campus catalog to see what you can find. Such courses will help you develop the ability to formulate logical arguments and avoid such pitfalls as logical fallacies.

Debating Skills
Some of the very best thinkers developed debating skills during college. Go to either your student activities office or your department of speech and drama to find out whether your campus has a debate club or team. Debating can be fun, and chances are you will meet some interesting student thinkers that way.

***12 Angry Men* by Reginald Rose (New York: Penguin Classics, 2006)**
This reprint of the original teleplay, which was written in 1954, was made into a film in 1958. Read the teleplay or watch the movie version of this stirring courtroom drama that pits twelve jurors against one another as they argue the outcome of a murder trial in which the defendant is a teenage boy. Although critical thinking is needed to arrive at the truth, all the jurors except one use noncritical arguments to arrive at a guilty verdict. The analysis of that one holdout, however, produces a remarkable change in their attitudes.

Bloom's Taxonomy
Florida International University provides a helpful resource about understanding and using Bloom's taxonomy at **online.fiu.edu/faculty/resources/bloomstaxonomy**.

Evaluating Resources
Ithaca College provides a guide to using critical-thinking skills to evaluate resources you'll encounter when doing research in college at **ithacalibrary.com/sp/subjects/evalres.**

LaunchPad

LaunchPad for *Your College Experience* is a great resource. Go online to master concepts using the LearningCurve study tool and much more. macmillanhighered.com/gardner12e

Chris Schmidt/Getty Images

6 READING TO LEARN

YOU WILL EXPLORE

The four steps in active reading: previewing, marking, reading with concentration, and reviewing

How to apply strategies for reading textbooks across different subject areas

Ways to improve and monitor your reading

High-impact practices 2 (writing) and 3 (collaboration)

Keira Sharma, 18

Communications major
Sam Houston State University

> **While my habits have worked well for me, students should get to know their own learning habits and find a reading method that works best for them.**

Keira Sharma was born in Texas and then spent most of her childhood in Baton Rouge, Louisiana, where she learned study habits that have helped throughout her education. Just before high school, her family moved back to Texas. She decided to go to Sam Houston State University after visiting the campus and speaking with faculty and current students in the communications program. In addition, she thought that the campus was beautiful, and she liked the community. Last, it put her only an hour away from her family.

As someone who loves to learn, Keira came to college with some strategies in place. "There is definitely a lot more reading involved in college than in high school," she says. "However, the good thing is that professors give out syllabi that detail when readings will be due, so you can plan accordingly." Like many first-year students, she also had to learn to balance the amount of reading required. "I had to get used to measuring how long it took to read, and then manage my time accordingly."

Many of the other strategies Keira employs revolve around good time management and organization. "Learning how to juggle all other coursework, meals, a social life, and sleep can be difficult, but it is possible. I mostly organize my time in order of priorities, usually based on due dates and how much time it takes to do [the assignment]," she says. Keira explains that once she starts reading, "I usually write down headings within the chapter as I go to keep me guided in the right direction and so that I know what the main point of upcoming sections will be. I then read through and write down any important dates, names, words, or anything that better explains the concept or explains it in a different way. This way I have multiple views on the subject that further enhance my understanding. It also doesn't hurt to reread sections and go over notes." She adds an important note: "While my habits have worked well for me, students should get to know their own learning habits and find a reading method that works best for them."

Keira also has some simple advice for other first-year students: "As much work as college is and as overwhelming as it can feel sometimes, *don't stress too much.* College is one of the best times of life. Enjoy it!"

To access the LearningCurve study tool, video activities, and more, go to LaunchPad for *Your College Experience.* macmillanhighered.com/gardner12e

As Keira mentions, reading college textbooks is more challenging than reading high school texts or reading for pleasure. College texts are loaded with concepts, terms, and complex information that you are expected to learn on your own in a short period of time. To accomplish it all, you will find it helpful to learn and use the active reading strategies in this chapter. They

assess your strengths

Are you a good reader? Do you make it a practice to do all the assigned reading for each of your classes, and do you have strategies for highlighting, annotating, or taking notes on what you read? Do you understand what you read so that you can explain it to others? As you read this chapter, consider your strengths in reading college textbooks and other academic materials.

set goals

What are your most important objectives in learning the material in this chapter? How can you improve your reading abilities and strategies? Use this chapter to help you develop strategies and goals for improving your reading of college texts. Check your course syllabi regularly to make sure you're up-to-date with all your assigned reading. Set a goal to catch up when you get a little behind.

are intended to help you get the most out of your college reading. This chapter will also explore different strategies you can use when reading textbooks across the academic disciplines. These strategies include building your overall vocabulary and increasing your familiarity with terms that are unique to your particular field of study. Choose to make your textbook reading something you do every day. Reading in small chunks will help you concentrate and will increase your comprehension.

Depending on how much reading you did before coming to college—reading for pleasure, for your classes, or for work—you might find that reading is your favorite or least favorite way to learn. Even if reading *isn't* your favorite thing to do, it is absolutely essential to doing well in college and at work—no matter your major or profession.

A PLAN FOR ACTIVE READING

Active reading involves using strategies, such as highlighting and taking notes, that help you stay focused. Active reading is different from reading for pleasure, which doesn't require you to do anything while you are reading. By choosing active rather than passive reading, you will increase your focus and concentration, understand more of what you read, and prepare more effectively for tests and exams.

These are the four active reading steps designed to help you read college textbooks:

1. Previewing
2. Marking
3. Reading with concentration
4. Reviewing

your turn Work Together

Comparing Textbook Reading Strategies

With a group of your classmates, share which of these four steps you always, sometimes, or never do. Have one member of the group keep a tally and report results to the class. Are there steps that almost everyone avoids? If so, discuss the reasons why.

Previewing

Previewing involves taking a first look at your assigned reading before you really tackle the content. Think of previewing as browsing in a newly remodeled store. You locate the pharmacy and grocery areas. You get a feel for the locations of the men's, women's, and children's clothing departments; housewares; and electronics. You pinpoint the restrooms and checkout areas. You get a sense for where things are in relation to each other and compared to where they used to be. You identify where to find the items that you buy most often, whether they are diapers, milk, school supplies, or prescriptions. You get oriented.

Previewing a chapter in your textbook or other assigned reading is similar. The purpose is to get the big picture, to understand the main ideas covered in what you are about to read and how those ideas connect both with what you already know and with the material the instructor covers in class. Here's how you do it:

- Begin by reading the title of the chapter. Ask yourself: What do I already know about this subject?
- Next, quickly read through the learning objectives, if the chapter has them, or the introductory paragraphs. **Learning objectives** are the main ideas or skills that students are expected to learn from reading the chapter.
- Then turn to the end of the chapter and read the summary, if there is one. A **summary** highlights the most important ideas in the chapter.
- Finally, take a few minutes to skim the chapter, looking at the headings, subheadings, key terms, tables, and figures. You should also look at the end-of-chapter exercises.

As you preview, note how many pages the chapter contains. It's a good idea to decide in advance how many pages you can reasonably expect to cover in your first study session. This can help build your concentration as you work toward your goal of reading a specific number of pages. Before long, you'll know how many pages are practical for you to read in one sitting.

Previewing might require some time up front, but it will save you time later. As you preview the text material, look for connections between the text and the related lecture material. Remember the related terms and concepts in your notes from the lecture. Use these strategies to warm up. Ask yourself: Why am I reading this? What do I want to know?

Keep in mind that different types of textbooks can require more or less time to read. For example, depending on your interests and previous knowledge, you might be able to read a psychology text more quickly than a biology text that includes many scientific words that might be unfamiliar to you. Ask for help from your instructor, another student, or a tutor at your institution's learning assistance center.

Mapping. **Mapping** is a preview strategy in which you draw a wheel or branching structure to show relationships between main ideas and secondary ideas and how different concepts and terms fit together; it also helps you make connections to what you already know about the subject (see Figure 1). Mapping the chapter during the previewing process provides a visual guide for how different chapter ideas work together. Because many students identify themselves as visual learners, visual mapping is an excellent learning tool, not only for reading, but also for test preparation.

In the wheel structure, place the central idea of the chapter in the circle. The central idea should be in the chapter introduction; it might even be in the chapter title. Place secondary ideas on the lines connected to the circle, and place offshoots of those ideas on the lines attached to the main lines. In the branching map, the main idea goes at the top, followed by supporting ideas on the second tier, and so forth. Fill in the title first. Then, as you skim the chapter, use the headings and subheadings to fill in the key ideas.

FIGURE 1 › Wheel and Branching Maps

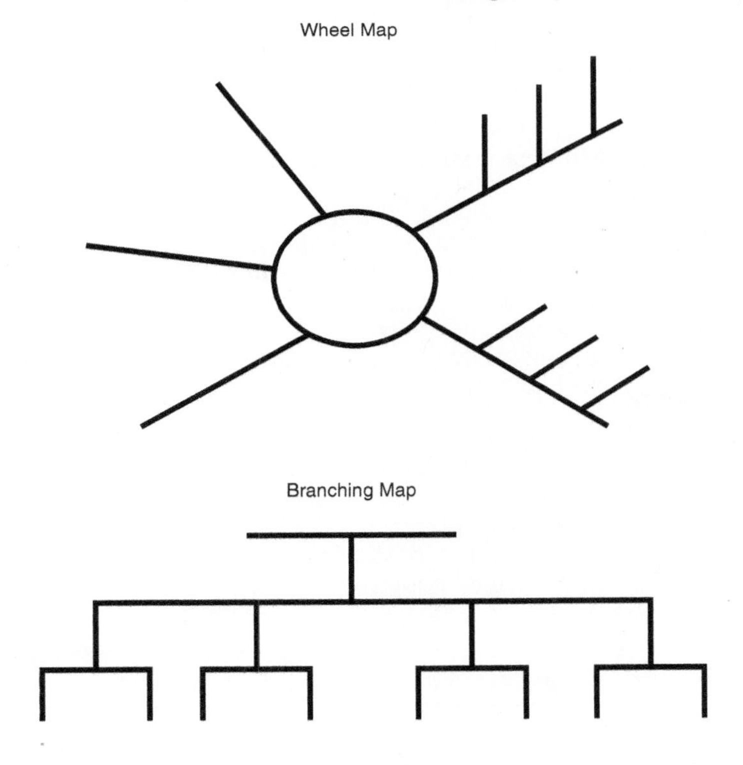

Outlining or Listing. Perhaps you are more of a read/write learner than a visual learner and prefer a more step-by-step visual image. If so, consider making an outline of the headings and subheadings in the chapter. You can usually identify the text's main topics, subtopics, and specific terms within each subtopic by the size of the print. Notice, also, that the different levels of headings in a textbook look different. In a textbook, headings are designed to show relationships among topics and subtopics covered within a section. Flip through this textbook to see how the headings are designed. See a sample outline of this chapter in Figure 2 below.

To save time when you are outlining, don't write full sentences. Rather, include clear explanations of new technical terms and symbols. Pay special attention to topics that the instructor covered in class. If you aren't sure whether your outlines contain too much or too little detail, compare them with the outlines your classmates or members of your study group have made. You can also ask your instructor to check your outlines

FIGURE 2 › Sample Outline

Here is how an outline of the first section of this chapter might look.

I. Active Reading
  A. Previewing
    1. Mapping
    2. Alternatives to Mapping
      a. Outlines
      b. Lists
      c. Chunking
      d. Flash cards
  B. Marking textbooks—Read and think BEFORE
    1. Underlining
    2. Highlighting
    3. Annotating (Margin notes)
  C. Reviewing—Each week, review
    1. Notes
    2. Study questions
    3. Annotations
    4. Flash cards
    5. Visual maps
    6. Outlines
  D. Reading with concentration—Use suggestions like
    1. Find proper location
    2. Turn off electronic devices
    3. Set aside blocks of time with breaks
    4. Set study goals

during office hours. In preparing for a test, review your chapter outlines so you can see how everything fits together.

Another previewing technique is listing. A list can be effective when you are dealing with a text that introduces many new terms and their definitions. Set up the list with the terms in the left column, and fill in definitions, descriptions, and examples on the right as you read or reread. Divide the terms on your list into groups of five, seven, or nine, and leave white space between the clusters so that you can visualize each group in your mind. This practice is known as **chunking**. Research has shown that we learn material best when it is presented in chunks of five, seven, or nine.

Creating Flash Cards.

Flash cards are like portable test questions—you write a question or term on the front of a small card and the answer or definition on the back. In a course that requires you to memorize dates, like American history, you might write a key date on one side of the card and the event that correlates to that date on the other. To study chemistry, you would write a chemical formula on one side and the ionic compound on the other. You might use flash cards to learn vocabulary words or practice simple sentences for a language course. (See Figure 3.) Creating the cards from your readings and using them to prepare for exams are great ways to retain information, and they are especially helpful for visual and kinesthetic learners. Some apps, such as Flashcardlet and Chegg Flashcards, enable you to create flash cards on your electronic devices.

FIGURE 3 › Examples of Flash Cards

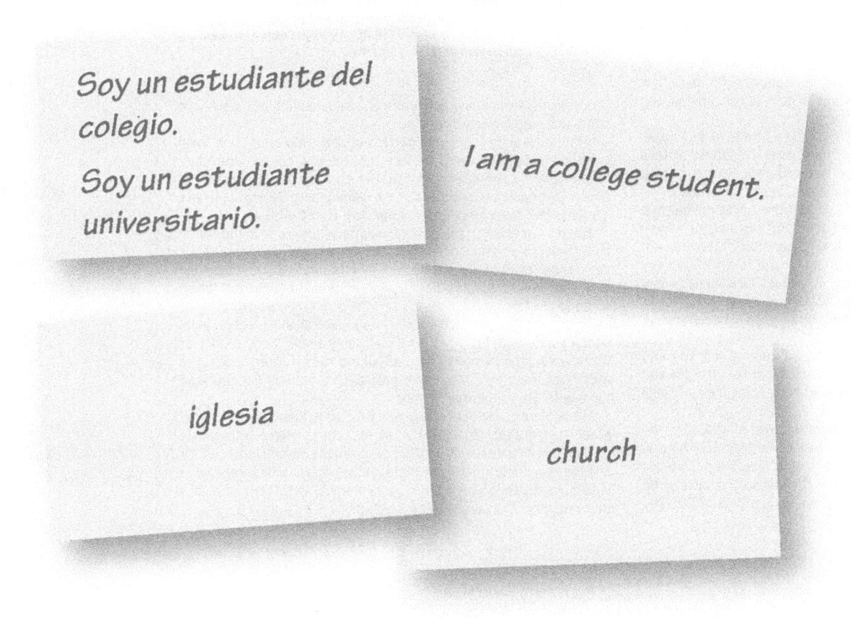

Strategies for Marking Your Textbook

After completing your preview, you are ready to read the text actively. With your map, outline, list, or flash cards to guide you, mark the sections that are most important. To avoid marking too much or marking the wrong information, first read without using your pencil or highlighter. This means you should read the text *at least* twice.

Marking is an active reading strategy that helps you focus and concentrate as you read. When you mark your textbook, you underline, highlight, or make margin notes or annotations. **Annotations** are notes or remarks about a piece of writing. Figure 4 provides an example of each method:

FIGURE 4 › Examples of Marking

Using a combination of highlighting, underlining, and margin notes, the reader has made the content of this page easy to review. Without reading the text, review the highlighted words and phrases and the margin notes to see how much information you can gather from them. Then read the text itself. Does the markup serve as a study aid? Does it cover the essential points? Would you have marked this page any differently? Why or why not? Source: Adapted from *Discovering Psychology*, 6th ed., p. 534, by D. H. Hockenbury and S. E. Hockenbury. Copyright © 2013 by Worth Publishers. Used with permission.

CULTURE AND HUMAN BEHAVIOR

The Stress of Adapting to a New Culture

differences affecting cultural stress

Refugees, immigrants, and even international students are often unprepared for the dramatically different values, language, food, customs, and climate that await them in their new land. The process of changing one's values and customs as a result of contact with another culture is referred to as *acculturation.* **Acculturative stress** is the stress that results from the pressure of adapting to a new culture (Sam & Berry, 2010).

acceptance of new culture reduces stress also speaking new language, education, & social support

Many factors can influence the degree of acculturative stress that a person experiences. For example, when the new society accepts ethnic and cultural diversity, acculturative stress is reduced (Mana & others, 2009). The transition is also eased when the person has some familiarity with the new language and customs, advanced education, and social support from friends, family members, and cultural associations (Schwartz & others, 2010). Acculturative stress is also lower if the new culture is similar to the culture of origin.

how attitudes affect stress

Cross-cultural psychologist John Berry (2003, 2006) has found that a person's attitudes are important in determining how much acculturative stress is experienced (Sam & Berry, 2010). When people encounter a new cultural environment, they are faced with two questions: (1) Should I seek positive relations with the dominant society? (2) Is my original cultural identity of value to me, and should I try to maintain it?

4 patterns of acculturation

The answers produce one of four possible patterns of acculturation: integration, assimilation, separation, or marginalization (see the diagram). Each pattern represents a different way of coping with the stress of adapting to a new culture (Berry, 1994, 2003).

1* *Integrated* individuals continue to value their original cultural customs but also seek to become part of the dominant society. They embrace a *bicultural* identity (Hunyh & others, 2011). Biculturalism is associated with higher self-esteem and lower levels of depression, anxiety, and stress, suggesting that the bicultural identity may be the most adaptive acculturation pattern (Schwartz & others, 2010). The successfully integrated individual's level of acculturative stress will be low (Lee, 2010).

2* *Assimilated* individuals give up their old cultural identity and try to become part of the new society. They adopt the customs and social values of the new environment, and abandon their original cultural traditions.

possible rejection by both cultures

Assimilation usually involves a moderate level of stress, partly because it involves a psychological loss—one's previous cultural identity. People who follow this pattern also face the possibility of being rejected either by members of the majority culture or by members of their original culture (Schwartz & others, 2010). The process of learning new behaviors and suppressing old behaviors can also be moderately stressful.

Joe Raedle/Getty Images

Acculturative Stress Acculturative stress can be reduced when immigrants learn the language and customs of their newly adopted home. Here, two friends, one from China, one from Cuba, help each other in an English class in Miami, Florida.

**separation may be self-imposed or discriminating*

3* Individuals who follow the pattern of *separation* maintain their cultural identity and avoid contact with the new culture. They may refuse to learn the new language, live in a neighborhood that is primarily populated by others of the same ethnic background, and socialize only with members of their own ethnic group.

higher stress with separation

In some cases, separation is not voluntary, but is due to the dominant society's unwillingness to accept the new immigrants. Thus, it can be the result of discrimination. Whether voluntary or involuntary, the level of acculturative stress associated with separation tends to be high.

4* Finally, the *marginalized* person lacks cultural and psychological contact with *both* his traditional cultural group and the culture of his new society. By taking the path of marginalization, he lost the important features of his traditional culture but has not replaced them with a new cultural identity.

**marginalized = higher level of stress*

Although rare, the path of marginalization is associated with the greatest degree of acculturative stress. Marginalized individuals are stuck in an unresolved conflict between their traditional culture and the new society, and may feel as if they don't really belong anywhere. Fortunately, only a small percentage of immigrants fall into this category (Schwartz & others, 2010).

Question 1: Should I seek positive relations with the dominant society?

Question 2: Is my original cultural identity of value to me, and should I try to maintain it?		Yes	No
	Yes	Integration	Separation
	No	Assimilation	Marginalization

Patterns of Adapting to a New Culture According to cross-cultural psychologist John Berry, there are four basic patterns of adapting to a new culture (Sam & Berry, 2010). Which pattern is followed depends on how the person responds to the two key questions shown.

No matter what method you prefer, remember these important guidelines:

1. **Read before you mark.** Finish reading a section before you decide which are the most important ideas and concepts.
2. **Think before you mark.** When you read a text for the first time, everything can seem important. After you complete a section, reflect on it to identify the key ideas. Ask yourself: What are the most important ideas? What terms has the instructor emphasized in class? What will I see on the test? Knowing the likely answers to these questions can help you avoid marking too much material. On a practical note, if you find that you have made mistakes in how you have highlighted or that your textbooks were already highlighted by another student, use a different color highlighter.
3. **Take notes along with marking.** If you only make notes or underline in your textbook, you will have to read all the pages again. Rather than relying on marking alone, consider taking notes as you read. You can add your notes to the map, outline, list, or flash cards that you created while previewing the text. These methods are also more practical if you intend to review with a friend or study group. One more step in the note-taking process—putting your notes in your own words—will help you learn the material. When you rewrite your notes in your own words, you are not only predicting exam questions but also evaluating whether you can answer them.

A few words of caution about marking: For some students, highlighting or underlining is actually a form of procrastination and can lead to a false sense of security—just noting what's most important doesn't mean you've learned the material. Some students highlight or underline nearly everything they read, which does more harm than good. Remember, highlights and underlines are intended to pull your eye to key words and important facts. You won't be able to identify important concepts quickly if they're lost in a sea of color or lines. Ask yourself whether highlighting or underlining helps you take a more active role in your learning process. If not, you might want to try a different technique, such as making margin notes or annotations.

Reading with Concentration

Students often have trouble concentrating or understanding the content when they read textbooks. This is normal, and many factors contribute to this problem: the time of day, your energy level, your interest in the material, and your study location.

your turn Write and Reflect

Improving Your Powers of Concentration

The next time you are reading a textbook, monitor your ability to concentrate. Check your watch when you begin and check it again when your mind begins to wander. How many minutes did you concentrate on your reading? Write a journal entry listing some strategies to keep your mind from wandering.

Consider these suggestions and decide which would help you improve your reading ability:

- **Find a quiet place to study.** Choose a room or location away from traffic and distracting noises, such as the campus information commons. Avoid studying in your bed because your body is conditioned to go to sleep there.
- **Mute or turn off your electronic devices.** Store your cell phone in your book bag or some other place where you aren't tempted to check it. If you are reading on a device like a laptop or tablet, download what you need and disconnect from Wi-Fi so that you aren't tempted to e-mail, chat, or check social media sites.
- **Read in blocks of time, with short breaks in between.** Some students can read for 50 minutes, while others may find that a 50-minute reading period is too long. By reading in small blocks of time throughout the day instead of cramming in all your reading at the end of the day, you should be able to process material more easily.
- **Set goals for your study period.** A realistic goal might be "I will read twenty pages of my psychology text in the next 50 minutes." Reward yourself with a 10-minute break after each 50-minute study period.
- **Engage in physical activity during breaks.** If you have trouble concentrating or staying awake, take a quick walk around the library or down the hall. Stretch or take some deep breaths, and think positively about your study goals. Then go back to studying.
- **Actively engage with the material.** Write study questions in the margins, take notes, or recite key ideas. Reread confusing parts of the text, and make a note to ask your instructor for clarification on any material that remains unclear.
- **Focus on the important portions of the text.** Pay attention to the first and last sentences of paragraphs and to words in italics or bold type.
- **Understand the words.** Use the text's glossary or a dictionary to define unfamiliar terms.
- **Use organizers as you read.** Have the maps, outlines, lists, or flash cards you created during your preview available as you read, and add to them as you go. The next page shows an example of an organizer to use when you are reading; you can use it to organize a chapter you are currently reading in this or any other class.

Date:	Title:
Textbook:	Chapter:
What is the overall idea of the reading?	
What is the main idea of each major section of the reading?	Section 1: Section 2: Section 3:
What are the **supporting ideas** presented in the reading? Examples? Statistics? Any reference to research?	1. 4. 2. 5. 3.
What are the key terms and what do they mean?	
What are the conclusions from the reading?	
What are two or three things that I remember after reading?	1. 2. 3.

Reviewing

The final step in active textbook reading is reviewing. **Reviewing** involves looking through your assigned reading again. Many students expect to be able to read through their text material once and remember the ideas four, six, or even twelve weeks later when it's time for their exam. More realistically, you will need to include regular reviews in your study process. Your notes, study questions, margin notes and annotations, flash cards, visual maps, or outlines will prove very useful during the reviewing process. Your study goal should be to review the material from each chapter every week. Here are some strategies:

- Consider ways to use your senses to review.
- Recite aloud.
- Tick off each item on a list on your fingers.
- Post diagrams, maps, or outlines around your living space so that you will see them often and will likely be able to visualize them while taking the test.

Mark and Review

Marking the text and reviewing carefully are among the best approaches to getting more from your reading. These strategies seem to be good enough for George Clooney. Are they good enough for you?

Michael Buckner/Getty Images for American Foundation for Equal Rights

STRATEGIES FOR READING TEXTBOOKS

As you begin to read, be sure to learn more about the textbook and its author by reading the sections at the beginning of the book, such as the preface, foreword, introduction, and the author's biographical sketch. The **preface**, which is a brief overview near the beginning of a book, is usually written by the author(s) and will tell you why they wrote the book and what material the book covers. It will also explain the book's organizational structure and give insight into the author's viewpoint—all of which can help you see the relationships among the facts presented and comprehend the ideas discussed throughout the book. Reading the preface can come in handy if you are feeling a little lost at different points in the term. The preface often lays out the tools available in each chapter to guide you through the content, so if you find yourself struggling with the reading, be sure you go back and read this section.

The **foreword** is often an endorsement of the book written by someone other than the author. Some books have an additional **introduction** that describes the book's overall organization and its contents, often chapter by chapter. Some textbooks include study questions at the end of each chapter. Take time to read and respond to these questions, whether or not your instructor requires you to do so.

your turn Stay Motivated

Do ALL the Required Reading

Some first-year students, especially those who have trouble managing their time, believe that they can skip some of the required reading and still get good grades on tests and exams. The best students, however, will tell you that this isn't a smart strategy. Instructors assign readings because they believe they're important to your understanding, and concepts and details in the readings will be on the tests. Maintain your motivation to do well by reading all the materials assigned by your instructors.

All Textbooks Are Not Created Equal

Textbooks in different **disciplines**—areas of academic study—can differ in their organization and style of writing. Some may be easier to understand than others, but don't give up if the reading level is challenging.

Math and science texts are filled with graphs and figures that you will need to understand in order to grasp the content and the classroom lectures. They are also likely to have less text and more practice exercises than other textbooks. If you have trouble reading and understanding any of your textbooks, get help from your instructor or your college's learning center.

Textbooks cover a lot of material in a limited space, and they won't necessarily provide all the information you want to know about a topic. If you find yourself interested in a particular topic, go to the **primary sources**—the original research or documents on that subject. You'll find those sources referenced in almost all textbooks, either at the end of each chapter or at the back of the book.

You can also refer to other related sources that make the text more interesting and easier to understand. Your instructors might use the textbook only to supplement their lectures. Some instructors expect you to read the textbook carefully, while others are much more concerned that you understand broad concepts that come primarily from their lectures. Ask your instructors what the tests will cover and what types of questions will be used.

Finally, not all textbooks are written in the same way. Some are better designed and written than others. If your textbook seems disorganized or hard to understand, let your instructor know your opinion. Other students likely feel the same way. Your instructor might spend some class time explaining the text, and he or she can meet with you during office hours to help you with the material.

is**this**you?

The Challenge of Being "First"

Are you the first person in your family to go to college? If so, you are in good company. Many "first-generation" students attend colleges and universities today. Make sure that you understand the rules and regulations and the unique higher-education terminology at your institution. If you or your family members feel lost or confused, talk to your college success instructor and ask about what services are available for first-generation students. Also, remember that some of our nation's most successful individuals were the first in their families to attend and graduate from college.

Math Texts

While the previous suggestions about textbook reading apply across the board, mathematics textbooks present some special challenges because they usually have lots of symbols and few words. Each statement and every line in the solution of a problem needs to be considered and processed slowly. Typically, the author presents the material through definitions, theorems, and sample problems. As you read, pay special attention to definitions. Learning all the terms that relate to a new topic is the first step toward understanding.

Math texts usually include derivations of formulas and proofs of theorems. You must understand and be able to apply the formulas and theorems, but unless your course has a particularly theoretical emphasis, you are less likely to be responsible for all the proofs. So if you get lost in the proof of a theorem, go to the next item in the section. When you come to a sample problem, it's time to get busy. Pick up a pencil and paper, and work through the problem in the book. Then cover the solution and think through the problem on your own.

Of course, the exercises in each section are the most important part of any math textbook. A large portion of the time you devote to a math course will be spent completing these assigned exercises. It is absolutely necessary to work out these exercises before the next class, whether or not your instructor collects the work. Success in mathematics requires regular practice, and students who keep up with their math homework, either by working alone or in groups, perform better than students who don't, particularly when they include in their study groups other students who have more advanced math skills.

After you complete the assignment, skim through the other exercises in the problem set. Reading the unassigned problems will increase your comprehension. Finally, talk through the material to yourself, and be sure your focus is on understanding the problem and its solution, not on memorization. Memorizing something might help you remember how to work through one problem, but it does not help you learn the steps involved so that you can use them to solve other, similar problems.

your turn Work Together

Tackle Math as a Team

In a small group, discuss with classmates two or three of your challenges in learning from your math textbooks. Find students who are taking the same math course, share some strategies that you use to study the material for this course, and consider forming a study group.

Science Texts

Your approach to your science textbook will depend somewhat on whether you are studying a math-based science, such as physics, or a text-based science, such as biology. In either case, you need to become familiar with the overall format of the book. Review the table of contents and the **glossary** (a list of key words and their definitions), and check the material in the **appendixes** (supplemental materials at the end of the book). There you will find lists of physical constants, unit conversions, and various charts and tables. Many physics and chemistry books also include a mini-review of the math you will need in those science courses. (See Figure 5.)

Notice the organization of each chapter, and pay special attention to graphs, charts, and boxes. The amount of technical detail might seem overwhelming. Remember that textbook authors take great care to present material in a logical format, and they include tools to guide you through the material. Chapter-opening learning objectives and end-of-chapter summaries can be useful to study both before and after reading the chapter. You will usually find answers to selected problems in the back of the book. Use the answer key or the student solutions manual to make sure that you're solving problems and answering questions accurately.

FIGURE 5 › Reading Science Textbooks

This page from an allied-health-themed chemistry textbook includes abbreviations you'd need to know for dosages, practice exercises, and a formula for calculating medicine dosages. If you need help with any of your textbooks, ask your instructor or classmates. Source: Excerpt from page 23 of *Essentials of General, Organic, and Biochemistry*, 2nd ed., by Denise Guinn. Copyright © 2012 by W. H. Freeman. Used by permission.

PRACTICE EXERCISES

23 Using the conversions on page 12, convert the following units into calories:
a. 5.79 kcal **b.** 48.8 J

24 How many joules are there in 2.45 cal?

25 How many joules are there in 2,720 Calories, the amount of energy the average person consumes in a day?

Dosage Calculations

For some medicines prescribed for patients, the dosage must be adjusted according to the patient's weight. This is especially true when administering medicine to children. For example, a dosage of "8.0 mg of tetracycline per kilogram body weight daily" is a dosage based on the weight of the patient. A patient's weight is often given in pounds, yet many drug handbooks give the dosage per kilogram body weight of the patient. Therefore, to calculate the correct amount of medicine to give the patient, you must first convert the patient's weight from pounds into kilograms with an English-metric conversion, using Table 1-3.

It is important to recognize that the dosage is itself a conversion factor between the mass or volume of the medicine and the weight of the patient. Whenever you see the word *per*, it means *in every* and can be expressed as a ratio or fraction where *per* represents a division operation (divided by). For example, 60 miles *per* hour can be written as the ratio 60 mi/1 hr. Similarly, a dosage of 8.0 mg *per* kg body weight can be expressed as the fraction 8.0 mg/1 kg. Hence, dosage *is* a conversion factor:

$$\frac{8\text{ mg}}{1\text{ kg}} \quad \text{or} \quad \frac{1\text{ kg}}{8\text{ mg}}$$

Dimensional analysis is used to solve dosage calculations by multiplying the patient's weight by the appropriate English-metric conversion factor and then multiplying by the dosage conversion factor, as shown in the following worked exercise.

Some common abbreviations indicating the frequency with which a medication should be administered include *q.d.* and *b.i.d.*, derived from the Latin meaning administered "daily" and "twice daily," respectively. If the medicine is prescribed for two times daily or four times daily, divide your final answer by two or four to determine how much to give the patient at each administration.

WORKED EXERCISE Dosage Calculations

1-19 Tetracycline elixir, an antibiotic, is ordered at a dosage of 8.0 mg per kilogram of body weight q.d. for a child weighing 52 lb. How many milligrams of tetracycline elixir should be given to this child daily?

Solution

Step 1: Identify the conversions. Since the dosage is given based on a patient's weight in kilograms, an English-to-metric conversion must be performed. From Table 1-3 this is 1.000 kg = 2.205 lb. The dosage itself is already a conversion factor.

Step 2: Express each conversion as two possible conversion factors. The English-to-metric conversion factors for the patient's weight are

$$\frac{1\text{ kg}}{2.205\text{ lb}} \quad \text{or} \quad \frac{2.205\text{ lb}}{1\text{ kg}}$$

The dosage *is* a conversion factor between the mass of medicine in milligrams and the weight of the patient in kilograms:

$$\frac{8.0\text{ mg}}{1\text{ kg}} \quad \text{or} \quad \frac{1\text{ kg}}{8.0\text{ mg}}$$

As you begin an assigned section in a science text, skim the material quickly to gain a general idea of the topic and to familiarize yourself with any new vocabulary and technical symbols. Then look over the end-of-chapter problems so that you'll know what to look for in your detailed reading of the chapter. State a specific goal: "I'm going to learn about recent developments in plate tectonics," or "I'm going to distinguish between mitosis and meiosis," or "Tonight I'm going to focus on the topics in this chapter that were stressed in class."

Should you underline and highlight, or should you outline the material in your science textbooks? You might decide to underline or highlight for a subject such as anatomy, which involves a lot of memorization. In most sciences, however, it is best to outline the text chapters.

Social Sciences and Humanities Texts

Many of the suggestions that apply to science textbooks also apply to reading in the **social sciences** (academic disciplines that examine human aspects of the world, such as sociology, psychology, anthropology, economics, political science, and history). Social science textbooks are filled with special terms that are specific to a particular field of study. (See Figure 6.) These texts also describe research and theory building and contain references to many primary sources. Your social science texts might also describe differences in opinions or perspectives. Social scientists do not all agree on any one issue, and you might be introduced to a number of ongoing debates about particular topics. In fact, your reading can become more interesting if you seek out differing opinions on an issue. You might have to go beyond your course textbook, but your library is a good source of various viewpoints about ongoing controversies.

Textbooks in the **humanities** (branches of knowledge that investigate human beings, their culture, and their self-expression, such as philosophy, religion, literature, music, and art) provide facts, examples, opinions, and original material such as stories or essays. You will often be asked to react to your reading by identifying central themes or characters.

your turn Make Good Choices

Buy Your Course Materials

Textbooks are expensive, and it may be tempting to think that you can borrow one from another student, find the text in the library, or even do well in the course without having access to the textbook. No one will force you to purchase your textbooks—it's really up to you. To succeed in college, however, it's critically important that you choose to buy them and do all the assigned reading. Read the Tech Tip in this chapter for information on the benefits of e-books and for help in evaluating whether these are a good option for you.

FIGURE 6 › Social Science Textbook Page

Strategies for reading and note taking should change depending on what kind of textbook you are reading. When reading a social science textbook, such as the economics book shown here, you can see how a section is broken into subsections. Headings help guide you through the content. A table is included with examples that illustrate what is being discussed and help you understand the material.

Determinants of Elasticity

Price elasticity of demand measures how sensitive sales are to price changes. But what determines elasticity itself? The four basic determinants of a product's elasticity of demand are (1) the availability of substitute products, (2) the percentage of income or household budget spent on the product, (3) the difference between luxuries and necessities, and (4) the time period being examined.

Substitutability The more close substitutes, or possible alternatives, a product has, the easier it is for consumers to switch to a competing product and the more elastic the demand. For many people, beef and chicken are substitutes, as are competing brands of cola, such as Coke and Pepsi. All have relatively elastic demands. Conversely, if a product has few close substitutes, such as insulin for diabetics or tobacco for heavy smokers, its elasticity of demand tends to be lower.

Proportion of Income Spent on a Product A second determinant of elasticity is the proportion (percentage) of household income spent on a product. In general, the smaller the percent of household income spent on a product, the lower the elasticity of demand. For example, you probably spend little of your income on salt, or on cinnamon or other spices. As a result, a hefty increase in the price of salt, say 25%, would not affect your salt consumption because the impact on your budget would be tiny. But if a product represents a significant part of household spending, elasticity of demand tends to be greater, or more elastic. A 10% increase in your rent upon renewing your lease, for example, would put a large dent in your budget, significantly reducing your purchasing power for many other products. Such a rent increase would likely lead you to look around earnestly for a less expensive apartment.

Luxuries Versus Necessities The third determinant of elasticity is whether the good is considered a luxury or a necessity. Luxuries tend to have demands that are more elastic than those of necessities. Necessities such as food, electricity, and health care are more important to everyday living, and quantity demanded does not change significantly when prices rise. Luxuries such as trips to Hawaii, yachts, and designer watches, on the other hand, can be given up when prices rise.

Time Period The fourth determinant of elasticity is the time period under consideration. When consumers have some time to adjust their consumption patterns, the elasticity of demand becomes more elastic. When they have little time to adjust, the elasticity of demand tends to be more inelastic. Thus, as we saw earlier, when gasoline prices rise suddenly, most consumers cannot immediately change their transportation patterns, therefore gasoline sales do not drop significantly. However, as gas prices continue to remain high, we see shifts in consumer behavior, to which automakers respond by producing smaller, more fuel-efficient cars.

Table 1 provides a sampling of estimates of elasticities for specific products. As we might expect, medical prescriptions and taxi service have relatively inelastic price elasticities of demand, while foreign travel and restaurant meals have relatively elastic demands.

Selected Estimates of Price Elasticities of Demand — TABLE 1

Inelastic		Roughly Unitary Elastic		Elastic	
Salt	0.1	Movies	0.9	Shrimp	1.3
Gasoline (short run)	0.2	Shoes	0.9	Furniture	1.5
Cigarettes	0.2	Tires	1.0	Commuter rail service (long run)	1.6
Medical care	0.3	Private education	1.1	Restaurant meals	2.3
Medical prescriptions	0.3	Automobiles	1.2	Air travel	2.4
Pesticides	0.4			Fresh vegetables	2.5
Taxi service	0.6			Foreign travel	4.0

Source: Compiled from numerous studies reporting estimates for price elasticity of demand.

techtip

EMBRACE THE E-BOOK

In college we have textbooks, workbooks, and notebooks. While textbook publishers continue to make traditional books available, the same content is increasingly available in digital formats. In most courses today, students are required to access some course material digitally. For students who are used to buying or renting printed books from the college bookstore, this can be confusing.

© W2 Photography/Corbis

The Problem

You have heard about electronic books that are alternatives to traditional textbooks, but you aren't sure what device to buy to read e-books. You really want to know the advantages and disadvantages that an e-book has when compared to a traditional book.

The Fix

Explore different platforms that deliver e-book content, and discover how reading with a digital reader differs from (and can even be better than) reading traditional books.

How to Do It

Go to the library. Many libraries have tablets of different kinds. Ask a librarian to download a book in a variety of formats for you, so you can try different tablets out before choosing one to buy.

Try the different media available. E-books give you access to the pages of the text, as well as video, audio, and Web content.

PROS OF E-BOOKS

- Digital reading devices are eminently portable and can hold thousands of books.
- E-books save trees, can be bought without shipping costs, and have a low carbon footprint.
- E-readers let you buy books online from anywhere with Web access, and you can start reading within minutes.
- You can type notes in an e-book as well as highlight passages and copy and paste sections.
- You can print out pages simply by hooking the device up to your printer.
- You can access many e-books for free from the public library; you can even use the British Library's Online Gallery to peruse some of the world's oldest and rarest books.
- Some e-books come with bonus audio, video, or animation features.
- Many digital reading devices accept audio books and can read to you aloud.
- The backlit screen means that you can read in bed with the light off, without disturbing anyone.
- You can adjust the size of the text.
- Some e-readers have a built-in dictionary. Others link to reference Web sites like Google or Wikipedia when a Wi-Fi or 3G connection is available.
- E-books are searchable and even sharable.

CONS OF E-BOOKS

- Digital reading devices are expensive, can break if you drop them, and are more likely to be stolen than books.
- Looking at a screen can cause some eye fatigue.
- It's harder to flip through pages of an e-book than a printed book.
- If you have limited or temporary access to e-books for your courses, your access will expire after the academic term. But you can keep the print textbooks you buy and build your own library.

GOOD TO KNOW

Some electronic readers are no-frills, basic models designed to replicate the experience of reading a paper book. Others offer Web browsers, video, music, and thousands of free and for-purchase apps. Because most are Web-enabled, you can use them for other things like listening to music or audio books, checking e-mail, creating presentations, and writing papers. This increased functionality might be distracting but can also make you more productive.

EXTRA STYLE POINTS: Price your textbooks in both the print and digital formats. Factoring in the cost of the e-reader, which format is cheaper?

Supplementary Material

Whether or not your instructor requires you to read material in addition to the textbook, you will learn more about a topic if you go to some of the primary and supplementary sources that are referenced in each chapter of your text. These sources can be journal articles, research papers, or original essays, and they can be found online or in your library. Reading the original source material will give you more detail than most textbooks do.

Many of these sources were originally written for other instructors or researchers, so they often refer to concepts that are familiar to other scholars, but not necessarily to first-year college students. If you are reading a journal article that describes a theory or research study, one technique for easier understanding is to read the article backwards—from the end to the beginning. Read the article's conclusion and discussion sections first, and then go back to see how the author performed the experiment or formed the ideas. In almost all scholarly journals, articles are introduced by an **abstract**, which is a paragraph-length summary of the article's methods and major findings. Reading the abstract is a quick way to get the main points of a research article before you start reading it. As you're reading research articles, always ask yourself: So what? Was the research important to what we know about the topic, or, in your opinion, was it unnecessary?

IMPROVING YOUR READING

With effort, you *can* improve your reading. Remember to be flexible and to adjust *how* you read depending on *what* you are reading. Here are a few suggestions:

- Evaluate the importance and difficulty of the assigned readings, and adjust your reading style and the time you set aside to do the reading. How you read your math textbook is different than how you read your psychology textbook. When reading your math textbook, you should have a notebook to record your solutions to the problems. When you read your psychology textbook, you should highlight the important ideas or make margin notes.
- Connect one important idea to another by asking yourself: Why am I reading this? Where does this fit in? Writing summaries and preparing notes and outlines can help you connect ideas across chapters.
- When the textbook material is exactly the same as the lecture material, you can save time by concentrating mainly on one or the other.

It takes a planned approach to read and understand textbook materials and other assigned readings and to remember what you have read.

Monitoring Your Reading

You can monitor your comprehension while reading textbooks by asking yourself: Do I understand this? If not, stop and reread the material. Look up words that are not clear. Try to clarify the main points and how they relate to one another.

Another way to check that you understand what you are reading is to try to recite the material aloud, either to yourself or to your study partner. Using a study group to monitor your comprehension gives you immediate feedback and is highly motivating. After you have read with concentration from the first section of the chapter, proceed to each subsequent section until you have finished the chapter.

After you have completed each section and before you move on to the next section, ask again: What are the key ideas? What will I see on the test? At the end of each section, try to guess what information the author will present in the next section.

Developing Your Vocabulary

Textbooks are full of new words and terms. A **vocabulary** is a set of words in a particular language or field of knowledge. As you become familiar with the vocabulary of an academic field, reading the texts related to that field becomes easier.

If words are such a basic and essential component of our knowledge, what is the best way to learn them? The following are some basic vocabulary-building strategies:

- **Notice and write down unfamiliar terms while you preview a text.** Consider making a flash card for each term or making a list of terms.
- **Think about the context when you come across challenging words.** See whether you can guess the meaning of an unfamiliar term by using the words around it.
- **Consider a word's parts.** If context by itself is not enough to help you guess the meaning of an unfamiliar word, try analyzing the term to discover its root (or base part) and any prefixes (parts that come before the root) or suffixes (parts that follow the root). For example, *transport* has the root *port,* which means "carry," and the prefix *trans,* which means "across." Together the word means "carry across" or "carry from one place to another." Knowing the meaning of prefixes and suffixes can be very helpful. For example, *anti* means "against," and *pro* means "for."
- **Use the glossary of the text or a dictionary.** Textbook publishers carefully compile glossaries to help students learn the vocabulary of a given discipline. If the text has no glossary, have a dictionary on hand. If a given word has more than one definition, search for the meaning that fits your text. The online Merriam-Webster's Dictionary (**merriam-webster.com**) is especially helpful for college students.
- **Use new words in your writing and speaking.** If you use a new word a few times, you'll soon know it. In addition, any flash cards you have created will come in handy for reviewing the definitions of new words at exam time.

your turn Write and Reflect

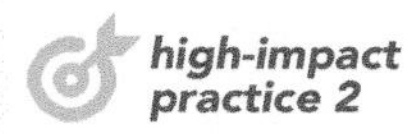

Building Your Vocabulary

Choose a chapter in this or another textbook. As you read it, list the words that are new to you or that you don't understand. Using a dictionary, write out the definition of each word, and then write a short paragraph using the word in an appropriate context. Set a goal to add at least one new word a week to your personal vocabulary.

What to Do When You Fall Behind on Your Reading

From time to time, life might get in the way of doing your assigned readings on time. You may get sick or have to take care of a sick family member, you may have to work extra hours, or you may have a personal problem that prevents you from concentrating on your courses for a short time. Unfortunately, some students procrastinate and think they can catch up. That is a myth. The less you read and do your assignments, the harder you will have to work to make up for lost time.

A Marathon, Not a Sprint

If you fall behind in your reading, you're not alone—many students do. Remember that your studies are more like a marathon than a sprint; you should take time to catch up, but do so at a steady pace. Do your assigned readings, study with others, get help, and do not give up!

If you try to stay on schedule with your assigned readings but fall behind, do not panic. Here are some suggestions for getting back on track:

- **Add one or two hours a day to your study time to go back and read the material that you missed.** In particular, take advantage of every spare moment to read; for example, read during your lunch hour at work, while you are waiting for public transportation, or in the waiting room at the doctor's office.
- **Join a study group.** If everyone in the group reads a section of the assigned chapter and shares and discusses his or her notes, summaries, or outlines with the group, you can cover the content more quickly.
- **Ask for help.** Visit your college learning center to work with a tutor who can help you with difficult concepts in the textbook.
- **Talk to your instructor.** Ask for extra time to make up your assignments if you have fallen behind for a valid reason such as sickness or dealing with a personal problem. Most instructors are willing to make a one-time exception to help students catch up.
- **Do not give up.** You may have to work harder for a short period of time, but you will soon get caught up.

If English Is Not Your First Language

The English language is one of the most difficult languages to learn. Words are often spelled differently from the way they sound, and the language is full of **idioms**—phrases that cannot be understood from the individual meanings of the words. For example, if your instructor tells you to "hit the books," she does not mean for you to physically pound your texts with your fist, but rather to study hard.

If you are learning English and are having trouble reading your texts, don't give up. Reading slowly and reading the material more than once can help you improve your comprehension. Make sure that you have two good dictionaries—one in English and one that links English with your primary language—and look up every key word you don't know. Be sure to practice thinking, writing, and speaking in English, and take advantage of your college's services. Your campus might have English as a second language (ESL) tutoring and workshops. Ask your adviser or your first-year seminar instructor to help you find out where those services are offered on your campus.

checklist for success

Reading to Learn

- **Be sure to practice the four steps of active reading: previewing, marking, reading with concentration, and reviewing.** If you practice these steps, you will understand and retain more of what you read.
- **Take your course textbooks seriously.** They contain essential information you'll be expected to learn and understand. Never try to "get by" without the text.
- **Remember that not all textbooks are the same.** They vary by subject area and style of writing. Some may be easier to comprehend than others, but don't give up if the reading level is challenging.
- **Learn and practice the different techniques suggested in this chapter for reading and understanding texts on different subjects.** Which texts are easiest for you to understand? Which are the hardest? Why?
- **In addition to the textbook, be sure to read all supplemental assigned reading material.** Also, try to find additional materials to take your reading beyond what is required. The more you read, the more you will understand, and the better your performance will be.
- **As you read, be sure to take notes on the material.** Indicate in your notes what specific ideas you need help in understanding.
- **Get help with difficult material before too much time elapses.** College courses use sequential material that builds on previous material. You will need to master the material as you go along.
- **Discuss difficult readings in study groups.** Explain to one another what you do and don't understand.
- **Find out what kind of assistance your campus offers to increase reading comprehension and speed.** Check out your learning and counseling centers for free workshops. Even faculty and staff sometimes take advantage of these services. Most everyone wants to improve reading speed and comprehension.
- **Use reading to build your vocabulary.** Learning new words is a critical learning skill and outcome of college. The more words you know, the more you'll understand, and your grades will show it.

build your experience

REFLECT ON CHOICES

In this chapter you have learned that reading textbooks is an essential part of being a successful student. The choice of how to approach your reading is up to you. Reflect on the strategies that have been suggested, list those that you already use, and make a separate list of those you want to try in the future.

APPLY WHAT YOU HAVE LEARNED

Now that you have read and discussed this chapter, consider how you can apply what you have learned to your academic life and your personal life. The following prompts will help you reflect on the chapter material and its relevance to you both now and in the future.

1. Choose a reading assignment for one of your upcoming classes. After previewing the material, begin reading until you reach a major heading or until you have read at least a page or two. Now stop and write down what you remember from the material. Go back and review what you read. Were you able to remember all the main ideas?

2. It is easy to say that there is not enough time in the day to get everything done, especially when you're faced with a long reading assignment. Your future depends on how well you do in college, however. Challenge yourself not to use that excuse. How can you modify your daily activities to make time for reading?

USE YOUR RESOURCES

> **Learning Assistance Center**
Find out about your campus's learning assistance center and any reading assistance that is available there. Most centers are staffed by full-time professionals and student tutors. Both the best students and struggling students use learning centers.

> **Peer Leaders**
Your peer leader is a great source of information on campus resources and the availability of tutoring. Ask him or her for suggestions about where you can go for help with your reading and comprehension.

> **Fellow Students**
Your best help can come from a fellow student. Look for the best students, those who appear to be the most serious and conscientious. Hire a tutor if you can, or join a study group. You are much more likely to be successful.

> **College or University Online Resources**
Dartmouth College offers "Active Reading: Comprehension and Rate" at **dartmouth.edu/~acskills/success/reading.html**. Mount Saint Vincent University in Canada offers "Reading Textbooks Effectively" at **msvu.ca/en/home/studentservices/academicadvisingsupport/studyskills/readingtextbookseffectively.aspx**, and Niagara University's Office for Academic Support offers "21 Tips for Better Textbook Reading" at **niagara.edu/oas-21-tips**.

LaunchPad

LaunchPad for *Your College Experience* is a great resource. Go online to master concepts using the LearningCurve study tool and much more. macmillanhighered.com/gardner12e

wavebreakmedia/Shutterstock

7 GETTING THE MOST FROM CLASS

YOU WILL EXPLORE

Benefits to your learning that result from being engaged in class

Ways to prepare before class

Why you should participate in class by listening critically and speaking up

Methods for assessing and improving your note-taking skills and how to use your notes to be engaged in learning

High-impact practices 2 (writing) and 3 (collaboration)

Dillon Watts, 19

History major
Sacramento State University

Monkey Business Images/Shutterstock. Licensed material is being used for illustrative purposes only, person depicted in the Licensed Material is a model.

“Taking notes should never be a substitute for paying attention and understanding the deeper elements of lectures and verbal discourse.”

Dillon Watts grew up in Sacramento, California. After graduating from high school, he attended Sacramento City College for one year and then transferred to Sacramento State University. In reflecting on his experience in college classes so far, he says, "Most of the time the questions you have are questions that will help the whole class. Everyone in the class benefits from an instructor's answer." He points out, however, that no one appreciates a student asking questions just for the participation points or to show off. "I always try to be direct and simple when asking questions so that the class can get direct and simple answers," Dillon says.

This same no-nonsense attitude is also present in the way he prepares for class. He explains, "I just make sure to be there on time, every time, and to stay until the class is over. I make an effort to pay attention, and I'm careful to write down key points of the lecture. I also do all the assigned reading, and I find it pretty easy to maintain good grades.

"In a class with lots of information, I take notes really well. Sometimes it makes it harder to actually pay attention to concepts, but it certainly pays off for tests and such. In less formal classes such as speech or ethics, which are very idea-heavy, I tend to not take notes that much or even at all. Taking notes should never be a substitute for paying attention and understanding the deeper elements of lectures and verbal discourse," he says.

Dillon plans to get a master's degree at Stanford, Berkeley, or another California school. In ten years he hopes to be a journalist or a philosophy or history instructor. He also hopes to put his class-participation skills to good use. "It is my dream to take part in debates and public speeches," he says. His advice to other first-year students: "Do your best. Try to get as much as you can out of your classes and to do your best, whether or not you feel like it. It always pays off in the end."

To access the LearningCurve study tool, video activities, and more, go to LaunchPad for *Your College Experience*. macmillanhighered.com/gardner12e

Dillon's advice is sound when you consider that in order to earn high grades in any college class you take, you'll need to master certain skills such as listening, taking notes, and being engaged in learning. Engagement in learning means that you take an active role in your classes by attending, listening critically, asking questions, contributing to discussions, and providing answers. These active-learning behaviors will enhance your ability to understand abstract ideas, find new possibilities, organize those ideas, and recall the material once the class is over, resulting in strong performance on exams, as many exam questions are based on material covered in class lectures and discussions.

This chapter shows you several note-taking methods. Choose the one that works best for you. Because writing down everything the instructor

assess your strengths

Students who are engaged in college life, both in and out of class, practice many of the behaviors that are reviewed in this chapter. What about you? Were you engaged in classes and activities in high school? Which were your favorites and why? Most students find that engagement makes them more enthusiastic and actually increases their learning. As you begin to read this chapter, consider your strengths in the area of engagement.

set goals

What are your most important objectives in learning the material in this chapter? Do you have a good method of note taking? Do you devote time and energy to academic work by attending class and studying out of class? Use this chapter to help you develop strategies and goals that relate to engagement in learning. Do all the assigned reading and warm up for each class session so you can see how being prepared for class makes a difference. Consider scheduling visits with your instructors during their office hours to show them your notes from recent classes and ensure that you are writing down the most important points.

says is probably not possible and because you might need some help to determine which are the most important ideas presented, ask questions in class and become comfortable reviewing your notes with your instructor, either after class or during office hours. You might consider making an audio recording of the lecture and discussion, if you have the instructor's permission. Reviewing your notes with a tutor, someone from your campus learning center, a friend from class, or in a study group can also help you clarify your understanding of a lecture's most important points.

BECOME ENGAGED IN LEARNING

Engaged students are those who are fully involved with the college experience and spend the time and energy necessary to learn, both in and out of class. Engaged learners who have good listening and note-taking skills get the most out of college.

You can learn by listening to a lecture, and you can better understand that lecture by considering what the information presented means to you. Practice the techniques of **active learning** by talking with others, asking questions in class, studying in groups, and seeking out information beyond the lecture material and required reading. Explore other information sources in the library or on the Internet. Think about how the material relates to your own life or experience. For instance, what you learn in a psychology class might help you recognize patterns of behavior in your own family, or the material presented in a sociology class may shed light on the group dynamics in a team or group to which you belong. When you are actively engaged in learning, you will not

Stay Engaged

Students of all kinds benefit from active learning strategies, whether in arts and sciences courses or professional training situations, like the one in which these military cadets are engaged.

Yana Paskova/For *The Washington Post* via Getty Images

only learn the material in your notes and textbooks, but you will also build valuable skills that you can apply to college, work, and your personal life, such as:

- **Working with others.** Learning to work with others is one of the most important skills you can develop for success in college and your career.
- **Improving your thinking, listening, writing, and speaking skills.** These are the primary skills that define a college-educated person.
- **Functioning independently and teaching yourself.** Your first year of college will help you become an **independent learner.** Independent learners are self-motivated and do not always wait for an instructor to point them in the right direction.
- **Managing your time.** Time management sounds easy, but it is a challenge for almost all students, regardless of their academic abilities.
- **Gaining sensitivity to cultural differences.** The world we live in requires all of us to develop our own knowledge about, and respect for, cultures that are different from our own.

Engagement in learning requires your full and active participation in the learning process. Your instructors will set the stage and provide valuable information, but it's up to you to do the rest. For instance, if you disagree with what your instructor says, politely share your opinion. Most instructors will listen. They might still disagree with you, but they might also appreciate your efforts to think independently.

Not all instructors teach in a way that includes active learning. Ask your friends to recommend instructors who encourage students to participate in class, work in groups, explore materials independently, and otherwise engage fully in learning.

PREPARE FOR CLASS

Have you ever noticed how easy it is to learn the words of a song? It's easier to remember song lyrics than other kinds of information because songs follow a tune, have a beat, and often relate to things in our personal lives. It is easier to remember new information if you can connect it to what you already know. In your first-year classes, you'll listen to and read material that might seem hard to understand. Beginning on the first day of class, you will be more likely to remember what you hear and read if you try to link it to something you have already learned or experienced.

Preparing for class is a very important first step toward success. Here are some strategies that will help you begin listening, learning, and remembering before each class session:

1. **Do the assigned reading.** Doing the assigned reading before class will help you understand new terms, listen better, and pick out the most important information when taking notes in class. Some instructors assign readings during class; others expect you to follow the **syllabus** (course outline) to keep up with the assigned readings. As you read, take good notes (more on note taking later in this chapter). In books you own, **annotate** (add explanatory notes in the margins), highlight, or underline key points. In books you do not own, such as library books, make a photocopy of the pages and then annotate or highlight the photocopies.
2. **Pay careful attention to your course syllabus.** The syllabus you receive at the start of each course will include the course requirements, your instructor's expectations, and how the course will be graded. Instructors expect students to understand and follow the syllabus with few or no reminders. You might find that this is a key difference between college and high school.
3. **Make use of additional materials provided by the instructors.** Many instructors post lecture outlines or notes in the course management system (CMS) before class. Download and print these materials for easy use during class. CMS materials often provide hints about the topics that the instructor considers most important; they can also create an organizational structure for taking notes.
4. **Warm up for class.** Review chapter introductions and summaries that refer to related sections in your text, and quickly review your notes from the previous class period. This prepares you to pay attention, understand, and remember.
5. **Get organized.** Decide how you want to take notes. If you handwrite your notes, using three-ring binders can help you organize them, as you can punch holes in syllabi and other course handouts and keep them with your class notes. You might want to buy notebook paper with a large left-hand margin, so that you can annotate your lecture notes (more on this later in the chapter). You can also download and print blank notebook paper from several free Web sites.

   If you take notes on a laptop or tablet, keep your files organized in separate folders for each of your classes, and make sure that the file name of each document includes the date and topic of the class. See the Tech Tip in this chapter for more information on using electronic devices to take effective notes.

PARTICIPATE IN CLASS

Learning is not like watching sports; it's like playing a sport. To play a sport—and not just watch it—you have to participate. Participation is the heart of **active learning**. To really learn, you must listen carefully, talk about what you are learning, write about it, connect it to past experiences, and make what you learn part of yourself. When you participate in class, whether to answer a question or to ask a question of your own, you are more likely to remember the information discussed than if you listen passively to someone else.

Listen Critically and with an Open Mind

Listening in class is different from listening to a TV show, listening to a friend, or even listening during a meeting. In such everyday activities, you might not be required to remember or use the information you hear. Knowing how to listen in class can help you get more out of what you hear, understand better what you have heard, and save time. Here are some suggestions:

1. **Be ready for the message.** Prepare yourself to hear, to listen, and to receive the message. If you have done the assigned reading, you will already know details from the text, so you can focus your notes on key concepts from the lecture. You will also notice information that the text does not cover, and you will be prepared to pay closer attention when the instructor presents new material.
2. **Listen to the main concepts and central ideas, not just to facts and figures.** Although facts are important, they will be easier to remember and will make more sense when you can place them within concepts, themes, and ideas.
3. **Listen for new ideas.** Even if you are an expert on a topic, you can still learn something new. Do not assume that college instructors will present the same information you learned in a similar course in high school. Even if you listen to the same lecture multiple times, if you pay attention, you will be able to pick out and learn new information each time. As an engaged student, make a note of questions in your mind as you listen, but save the judgments for later.
4. **Repeat mentally.** Words can go in one ear and out the other unless you make an effort to remember them. Think about what you hear, and say it silently in your own words. If you cannot translate the information into your own words, ask the instructor for more explanation.
5. **Decide whether what you have heard is unimportant, somewhat important, or very important.** While most of what your instructors say and do in class is important, occasionally they may make comments or tell stories that are only somewhat related to the class material, or may not be related at all. If an instructor's comment is really unrelated to the focus of the class, you don't need to write it down. If it's very important, make it a major point in your notes by highlighting or underlining it, or use it as a major topic in your

outline if that's the method you use for taking notes. If it's somewhat important, try to relate it to a very important topic by writing it down as a part of that topic.

6. **Keep an open mind.** Every class holds the promise of letting you discover new ideas and uncover different opinions. Some instructors might intentionally present information that challenges your ideas and values. College is supposed to teach you to think in new ways and train you to provide support for your own beliefs. Instructors want you to think for yourself; they don't necessarily expect you to agree with everything they or your classmates say. However, if you want people to respect your values and ideas, you must show respect for theirs by listening to what they say with an open mind.
7. **Ask questions.** Early in the term, determine whether your instructor wants you to ask questions during the lecture. Some instructors prefer that students ask their questions after the lecture, during separate discussion sections, labs, or office hours. If your instructor answers questions when students ask them, speak up if you did not hear or understand what was said. Ask for explanations immediately, if possible; other students are likely to have the same questions. If you can't hear another student's question or response, ask him or her to repeat the question.
8. **Sort, organize, and categorize.** When you listen, try to match what you are hearing with what you already know. Take an active role in deciding how best to remember what you are learning. If you find yourself daydreaming during a lecture, quickly refocus your thoughts on the topic and actively take notes. After class or during your instructor's next office hours, ask him or her to help you fill in any gaps in your notes.

is this you?

Balancing Sports and Study

Are you a student athlete? If so, you might find that it's tough to balance the demands of team practice and games with being a good student. To keep up with your studies, you'll need to go to every class and take advantage of all the academic help available to you through the athletic department and other campus resources. Whatever your athletic goal might be—whether it is to play on a professional team or just enjoy your sport as a college student—keep your eyes on the prize: a college degree.

Speak Up

Naturally, you will be more likely to participate in a class when the instructor emphasizes class discussion, calls on students by name, shows signs of approval and interest, and avoids criticizing students for an incorrect answer. Often, answers you and other students offer may not be quite correct, but they can lead to new perspectives on a topic.

Whether you are in a large or a small class, you might be nervous about asking a question, fearing you will make a fool of yourself. However, it is likely that other students have the same question but are too nervous to ask. If so, they may thank you silently or even aloud! Many instructors set time aside to answer questions in class, so to take full advantage of these opportunities, try using the techniques listed on the next page.

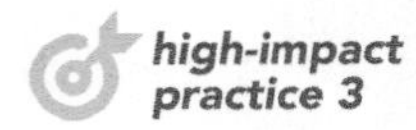

your turn Work Together

Do You Ask Questions in Class?

Think about the number of times during the past week you have raised your hand in class to ask a question. How many times has it been? Do you ask questions frequently, or is this something you avoid? Make a list of the reasons you either do or don't ask questions in class. Would asking more questions help you earn better grades? Be prepared to share your reflections with a small group. Did you hear anything from your peers that encourages you to participate more in class?

1. **Take a seat as close to the front as possible and keep your eyes on the instructor.** Sitting close to the front can help you concentrate better and avoid distractions from other students. It will also make it easier to maintain eye contact with your instructors.
2. **Focus on the lecture and class discussions.** Avoid distractions. Sit away from friends who can distract you, do not engage in side conversations, and turn off all electronic devices that you are not using for class.
3. **Raise your hand when you don't understand something.** If you don't understand something, you have a right to ask for an explanation. Never worry that you're asking a stupid question. Don't let embarrassment or shyness stop you. The instructor might answer you immediately, ask you to wait until later in the class, or throw your question to the rest of the class. In each case, you benefit in several ways. The instructor will get to know you, other students will get to know you, and you will learn from both the instructor and your classmates. But don't overdo it, or you'll risk disrupting class. Office hours provide the perfect opportunity for following up on class lectures.
4. **Speak up in class.** Ask a question or volunteer to answer a question or make a comment. This becomes easier every time you do it, and you will be more likely to remember what happens in class if you are an active participant.
5. **When the instructor calls on you to answer a question, don't bluff.** If you know the answer, give it. If you're not certain, begin with, "I think . . . , but I'm not sure I have it all correct." If you don't know, just say so.
6. **If you have recently read a book or article that is relevant to the class topic, bring it in.** Use it either to ask questions about the topic or to provide information that was not covered in class.

Hands Up!

Participating in class not only helps you learn but also shows your instructor that you're interested and engaged. You may be anxious the first time you raise your hand, but you may quickly find that participating in class raises your interest and enjoyment.

Jonathan Stark

TAKE EFFECTIVE NOTES

What are effective notes? They are notes that cover all the important points of the lecture or reading material without being too detailed or too limited. Most important, effective notes prepare you to do well on quizzes and exams. They also help you understand and remember concepts and facts. Becoming an effective note-taker takes time and practice, but this skill will help you improve your learning and your grades in the first year of college and beyond.

your turn Make Good Choices

Going Back in Time

Think back to high school. Did you choose to save any of your high school notes? Do you remember the note-taking method you used? If you have an old notebook, look at the way you took notes in high school and think about whether this method works for you now. Is it time to choose a better method of taking notes? Consider this question as you learn about different note-taking formats.

Note-Taking Formats

You can make class time more productive by using your listening skills to take effective notes, but first you have to decide on one of the following four commonly used formats for note taking: the Cornell, outline, paragraph, and list formats. Any format can work as long as you use it consistently.

Serious Business

The importance of developing good note-taking skills cannot be overstated. Carefully read about different note-taking formats presented on the next several pages, study the examples carefully, and try out each one. Find the format that works best for you. Use it to its fullest, and you're on your way to college success.

wavebreakmedia/Shutterstock

FIGURE 1 › Note Taking in the Cornell Format

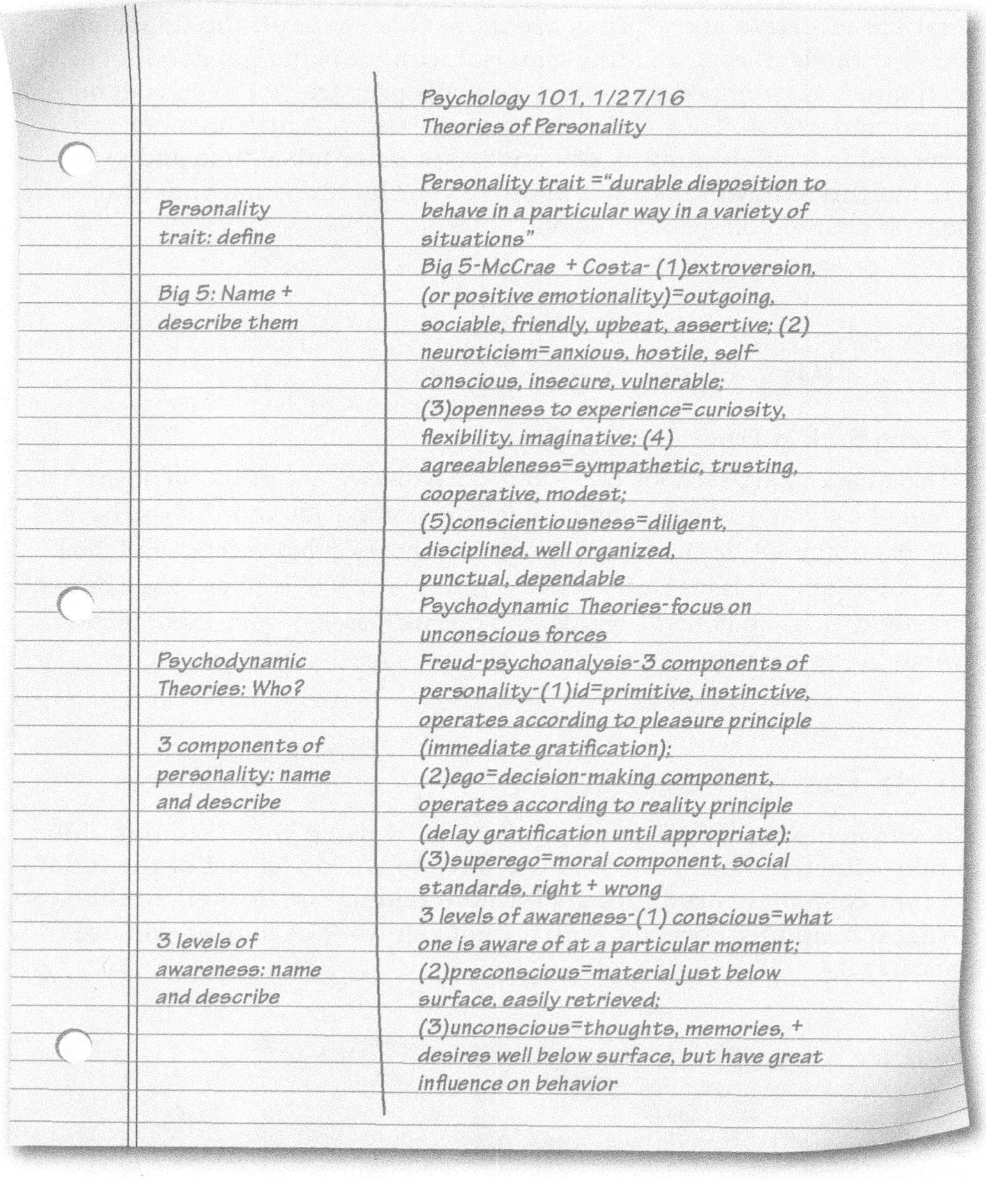

	Psychology 101, 1/27/16 Theories of Personality
Personality trait: define	Personality trait ="durable disposition to behave in a particular way in a variety of situations"
Big 5: Name + describe them	Big 5-McCrae + Costa- (1)extroversion, (or positive emotionality)=outgoing, sociable, friendly, upbeat, assertive; (2) neuroticism=anxious, hostile, self-conscious, insecure, vulnerable; (3)openness to experience=curiosity, flexibility, imaginative; (4) agreeableness=sympathetic, trusting, cooperative, modest; (5)conscientiousness=diligent, disciplined, well organized, punctual, dependable
Psychodynamic Theories: Who?	Psychodynamic Theories-focus on unconscious forces Freud-psychoanalysis-3 components of personality-(1)id=primitive, instinctive, operates according to pleasure principle (immediate gratification);
3 components of personality: name and describe	(2)ego=decision-making component, operates according to reality principle (delay gratification until appropriate); (3)superego=moral component, social standards, right + wrong
3 levels of awareness: name and describe	3 levels of awareness-(1) conscious=what one is aware of at a particular moment; (2)preconscious=material just below surface, easily retrieved; (3)unconscious=thoughts, memories, + desires well below surface, but have great influence on behavior

Cornell Format. Using the **Cornell format**, one of the best-known methods for organizing notes, you create a "recall" column on each page of your notebook or your document by drawing a vertical line about 2 to 3 inches from the left border (see Figure 1). As you take notes during class—whether writing down or typing ideas, making lists, or using an outline or paragraph format—write only in the wider column on the right; leave the left-hand recall column blank. You will use the recall column to write down or type the main ideas and important details for tests and exams as you go through your notes, which you should do as soon as possible after class, preferably within an hour or two. Many students have found the recall column to be an important part of note taking, one that becomes an effective study tool for tests and exams.

FIGURE 2 › Note Taking in the Outline Format

Psychology 101, 1/27/16: Theories of Personality

I. Personality trait = "durable disposition to behave in a particular way in a variety of situations"
II. Big 5-McCrae + Costa
  A. Extroversion (or positive emotionality)=outgoing, sociable, friendly, upbeat, assertive
  B. Neuroticism=anxious, hostile, self-conscious, insecure, vulnerable
  C. Openness to experience=curiosity, flexibility, imaginative
  D. Agreeableness=sympathetic, trusting, cooperative, modest
  E. Conscientiousness=diligent, disciplined, well organized, punctual, dependable
III. Psychodynamic Theories-focus on unconscious forces--Freud—psychoanalysis
  A. 3 components of personality
    1. Id=primitive, instinctive, operates according to pleasure principle (immediate gratification)
    2. Ego=decision-making component, operates according to reality principle (delay gratification until appropriate)
    3. Superego=moral component, social standards, right + wrong
  B. 3 levels of awareness
    1. Conscious=what one is aware of at a particular moment
    2. Preconscious=material just below surface, easily retrieved
    3. Unconscious=thoughts, memories, + desires well below surface, but have great influence on behavior

Outline Format. Some students find that an **outline** is the best way for them to organize their notes. In a formal outline, Roman numerals (I, II, III, etc.) mark the main ideas. Other ideas relating to each main idea are marked by uppercase letters (A, B, C, etc.). Arabic numerals (1, 2, 3, etc.) and lowercase letters (a, b, c, etc.) mark related ideas in descending order of importance or detail. Using the outline format allows you to add details, definitions, examples, applications, and explanations (see Figure 2).

FIGURE 3 › Note Taking in the Paragraph Format

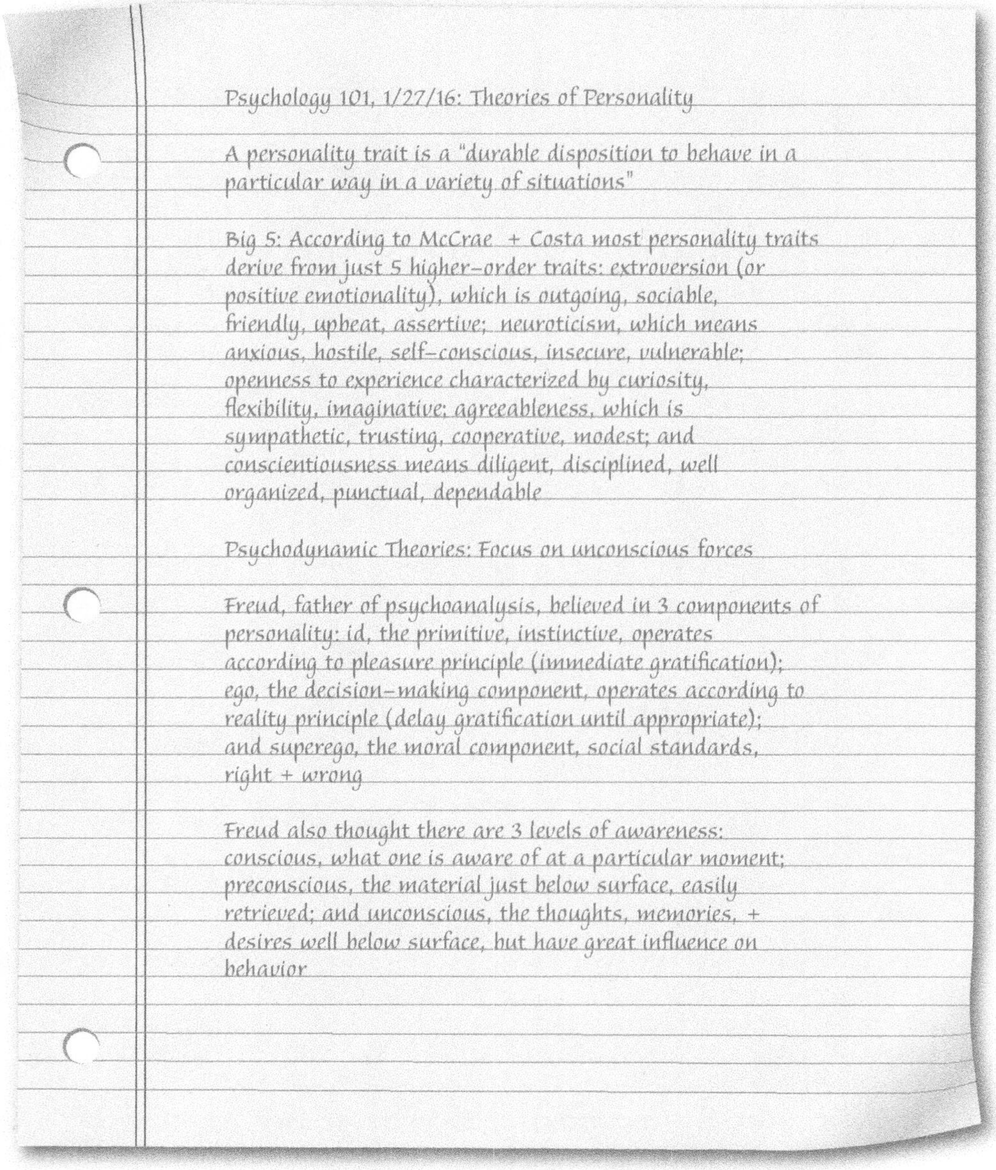

Psychology 101, 1/27/16: Theories of Personality

A personality trait is a "durable disposition to behave in a particular way in a variety of situations"

Big 5: According to McCrae + Costa most personality traits derive from just 5 higher-order traits: extroversion (or positive emotionality), which is outgoing, sociable, friendly, upbeat, assertive; neuroticism, which means anxious, hostile, self-conscious, insecure, vulnerable; openness to experience characterized by curiosity, flexibility, imaginative; agreeableness, which is sympathetic, trusting, cooperative, modest; and conscientiousness means diligent, disciplined, well organized, punctual, dependable

Psychodynamic Theories: Focus on unconscious forces

Freud, father of psychoanalysis, believed in 3 components of personality: id, the primitive, instinctive, operates according to pleasure principle (immediate gratification); ego, the decision-making component, operates according to reality principle (delay gratification until appropriate); and superego, the moral component, social standards, right + wrong

Freud also thought there are 3 levels of awareness: conscious, what one is aware of at a particular moment; preconscious, the material just below surface, easily retrieved; and unconscious, the thoughts, memories, + desires well below surface, but have great influence on behavior

Paragraph Format. When you take notes while you read, you might decide to write **summary paragraphs**—two or three sentences that sum up a larger section of material (see Figure 3). This method might not work well for class notes because it's difficult to summarize a topic until your instructor has covered it completely. By the end of the lecture, you might have forgotten critical information.

FIGURE 4 › Note Taking in the List Format

Psychology 101, 1/27/16: Theories of Personality

- A personality trait is a "durable disposition to behave in a particular way in a variety of situations"
- Big 5: According to McCrae + Costa most personality traits derive from just 5 higher-order traits
    - extroversion, (or positive emotionality)=outgoing, sociable, friendly, upbeat, assertive
    - neuroticism=anxious, hostile, self-conscious, insecure, vulnerable
    - openness to experience=curiosity, flexibility, imaginative
    - agreeableness=sympathetic, trusting, cooperative, modest
    - conscientiousness=diligent, disciplined, well organized, punctual, dependable
- Psychodynamic Theories: Focus on unconscious forces
- Freud, father of psychoanalysis, believed in 3 components of personality
    - id=primitive, instinctive, operates according to pleasure principle (immediate gratification)
    - ego=decision-making component, operates according to reality principle (delay gratification until appropriate)
    - superego=moral component, social standards, right + wrong
- Freud also thought there are 3 levels of awareness
    - conscious=what one is aware of at a particular moment
    - preconscious=material just below surface, easily retrieved
    - unconscious=thoughts, memories, + desires well below surface, but have great influence on behavior

List Format. The list format can be effective in taking notes on terms and definitions, facts, or sequences, such as the body's digestive system (see Figure 4). It is easy to use lists in combination with the Cornell format, with key terms on the left and their definitions and explanations on the right.

Note-Taking Techniques

Whatever note-taking format you choose, follow these important steps:

1. **Identify the main ideas.** The first principle of effective note taking is to identify and write down the most important ideas around which the lecture is built. Although supporting details are important as well, focus your note taking on the main ideas. These ideas can be buried in details, statistics, examples, or problems, but you will need to identify and record them for further study. Some instructors announce the purpose of a lecture or offer an outline of main ideas, followed by details. Other instructors develop PowerPoint presentations. If your instructor makes such materials available on a

Web site prior to class, you can print them out and take notes on the outline or next to the PowerPoint slides during the lecture. Some instructors change their tone of voice or repeat themselves for each key idea. Some ask questions or provide an opportunity for discussion. If an instructor says something more than once, chances are it is important. Ask yourself, "What does my instructor want me to know at the end of today's class?"

2. **Don't try to write down everything.** Some first-year students try to do just that. They stop being thinkers and become just note-takers. As you take notes, leave spaces so that you can fill in additional details that you might have missed during class but remember or read about later. Take the time to review and complete your notes as soon as you can after class. Once you have decided on a format for taking notes, you might also want to develop your own system of abbreviations. For example, you might write "inst" instead of "institution" or "eval" instead of "evaluation." Just make sure you will be able to understand your abbreviations when it's time to review.
3. **Don't be thrown by a disorganized lecturer.** When a lecture is disorganized, it's your job to try to organize the material presented into general and specific points. When information is missing, you will need to indicate in your notes where the gaps are. After the lecture, review the reading material, ask your classmates to fill in these gaps, or ask your instructor for help. Some instructors have regular office hours for student appointments, while others are willing to spend time after class answering students' questions. However, it is amazing how few students use these opportunities for one-on-one instruction. The questions you ask might help your instructor realize which parts of the lecture need more attention or repetition.
4. **Keep your notes and supplementary materials for each course separate.** Whether you use folders, binders, or some combination, label your materials with the course number and name. Before class, label and date the paper you will use to take notes; after class, organize your notes chronologically. In your folder or binder, create separate tabbed sections for homework, lab assignments, graded and returned tests, and other materials. If you take notes electronically, you should create separate files and folders for each class, with specific names and dates. You can create a folder for each course and add subfolders for notes, assignments, and projects within each folder.
5. **Download notes, outlines, diagrams, charts, and graphs from the CMS site and bring them to class.** You might be able to save yourself a lot of time during class if you do not have to copy graphs and diagrams while the instructor is talking. Instead, you can focus on the ideas being presented while adding labels and notes to the printouts.
6. **If handouts are distributed in class, label them and place them near your notes.** Buy a portable three-hole punch, and use it to add handouts to your binder or folder as you review your notes each day.

your turn Write and Reflect

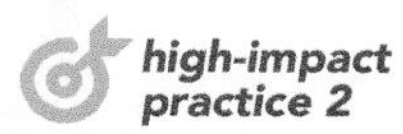

What Note-Taking Method Works Best for You?

Over the next week, try a variety of note-taking methods, such as the Cornell format, the outline format, and a random format where you write down what you think is important in no particular order. Then compare your notes and decide which format you like best—which is easiest for you and which helps you the most when you study and prepare for tests. Write a short essay describing your experience using these methods.

Taking Notes in Nonlecture Courses. Always be ready to change your note-taking methods based on the situation. Group discussion is a popular way to teach in college because it engages students in active participation. On your campus, you might also have courses with **Supplemental Instruction (SI)** opportunities, which allow students to discuss the information covered in class lectures and discussions outside of class.

How do you keep a record of what's happening in such classes? Let's assume that you are taking notes on a problem-solving group assignment. You would begin your notes by writing down the problem that the group is being asked to solve. As the group discussion continues, you would list the solutions that are offered. These would be your main ideas. The important details might include the pros and cons of each viewpoint or suggested solution. The important thing to remember when taking notes in nonlecture courses is that you need to record the information presented by your classmates as well as the information presented by your instructor, and you need to consider all reasonable ideas, even those that differ from your own.

When a course has separate lecture and discussion sessions, you will need to understand how the discussion sessions relate to and supplement the lectures. If the material covered in the discussion session differs from what was covered in the lecture, you might need to ask for help in organizing your notes. When similar topics are covered, you can combine your lecture and discussion notes so that you have full coverage of each topic.

How you organize the notes you take in a class discussion session depends on the purpose or form of the discussion. It usually makes sense to begin with a list of the issues or topics under discussion. Another approach is to list the questions raised for discussion. If the discussion explores reasons for and against a particular argument, divide your notes into columns or sections for each set of reasons. When different views are presented in discussion, record all the ideas. Your instructor might ask you to compare your own opinions to those of other students and explain why and how you formed those opinions.

Taking Notes in Science and Mathematics Courses. Many mathematics and science courses build on one another from term to term and from year to year. When you take notes in these courses, you will likely need to go back to them in the future. For example, when taking organic

techtip

TAKE BETTER NOTES IN BETTER WAYS

Studies have shown that people remember only half of what they hear, which is a major reason to take notes during lectures. Solid note taking will help you distill key concepts and make it easier to study for tests. Note taking also engages the brain in a process known as rehearsal. Writing things down is important for you to start the process of creating your own way of understanding the materials.

© Erik Isakson/Tetra Images

The Problem

You don't take good notes because you aren't sure what is important. You have access to technology, but aren't sure how to use it to take notes.

The Fix

Along with making use of the note-taking formats presented in this chapter, use your smart phone, tablet, or laptop to save information and create tools that will help you study.

How to Do It

1. Microsoft Word is great for most classes. To highlight main ideas, you can bold or underline text, change the size and color, highlight whole sections, and insert text boxes or charts. You can make bullet points or outlines and insert comments. As you review your notes, you can cut and paste to make things more coherent. You can also create a folder for each class so you can find everything you need easily.
2. Microsoft Excel is especially good for any class that involves calculations or financial statements. You can embed messages in the cells of a spreadsheet to explain calculations. (The notes will appear whenever you hover your cursor over that cell.)
3. Microsoft PowerPoint can be invaluable for visual learners. Instead of creating one giant, potentially confusing Word file, you can make a slideshow with a new slide for each key point. Some instructors also post the slides that they plan to use in class before class begins. You can write notes on printouts of the slides, or download them and add your notes in PowerPoint.

Some Cool Apps for Note Taking and Reviewing:

- Pocket (iOS and Android) allows you to store and review written content from your phone.
- Evernote (iOS and Android) lets you take a picture of handwritten or printed notes—or anything else you want to recall later—then you can file content and search it by keyword later.
- CamScanner (iOS and Android) allows you to photograph, scan, and store notes.
- Scan Edit (iOS) lets you scan any document and convert it into a PDF, saving time and money.
- Tiny Tap (iOS) lets you create multiple-choice quizzes that you can take as practice and share with other students.
- StudyBlue (iOS, Android, and Web Apps) allows you to make amazing-looking flash cards.

EXTRA STYLE POINTS: No matter what program or app you use, some rules always apply:

- Write down main points using phrases or key terms instead of long sentences.
- Date your notes; keep them in order and in one place; save files using filenames with the course number, name, and date of the class; and back up everything.
- Keep a pen and paper handy for sketching graphs and diagrams.
- If you find it hard to keep up, keep practicing your listening and typing skills. Consider a typing class, program, or app to learn how to type properly.
- If you prefer a spiral notebook and a ballpoint pen, that's OK; these formats are tried and true.
- Practice teaching others what you learned in class. You can also learn note-taking strategies from your peers.

chemistry, you might need to review the notes you took in earlier chemistry courses. This can be particularly important if some time has passed since you completed your last related course, such as after a summer or winter break.

Taking notes in math and science courses can be different from taking notes in other classes. The following tips can help:

- Write down any equations, formulas, diagrams, charts, graphs, and definitions that the instructor puts on the board or screen.
- Write the instructor's words as precisely as possible. Technical terms often have exact meanings that cannot be changed.
- Use standard symbols, abbreviations, and scientific notation.
- Write down all worked problems and examples step by step. The steps are often necessary in answering exam questions. Actively engage in solving the problem yourself as it is being solved during class. Be sure that you can follow the logic and understand the sequence of steps. If you have questions you cannot ask during the lecture, write them down in your notes so that you can ask them in a discussion session, in the lab, or during the instructor's office hours.
- Consider taking your notes in pencil or erasable pen. You might need to make changes if you are copying long equations while trying to pay attention to the instructor. You want to keep your notes as neat as possible. Later, you can use colored ink to add other details.
- Listen carefully to other students' questions and the instructor's answers. Take notes on the discussion and during question-and-answer periods.
- Use asterisks, exclamation points, question marks, or symbols of your own to highlight both important points in your notes and questions that you need to come back to when you review.
- Refer to the textbook after class; the text might contain better diagrams and other visual representations than you can draw while taking notes in class. If they are not provided in handouts or on the instructor's Web site, you might even want to scan or photocopy diagrams from the text and include them with your notes in your binder.
- Keep your binders for math and science courses until you graduate (or even longer if you are planning to go to graduate or professional school). They will serve as good review materials for later classes in math and science. In some cases, these notes can also be helpful in the workplace.

Using Technology to Take Notes. While some students use laptops, tablets, or other mobile devices for note taking, others prefer taking notes by hand so that they can easily circle important items or copy equations or diagrams while they are being presented. If you handwrite your notes, entering them on a computer after class for review purposes might be helpful, especially if you are a kinesthetic learner who prefers to learn through experience and practice. After class, you can also cut and paste diagrams and other visuals into your notes and print a copy, since a printout might be neater and easier to read than notes you wrote by hand.

Some students—especially aural learners, who prefer to hear information—find it is advantageous to record lectures. But if you record, don't become passive; listen actively. Students with specific types of learning disabilities might be urged to record lectures or use the services of note-takers, who type on a laptop while the student views the notes on a separate screen.

Review Your Notes

Unless we take steps to remember it, we forget much of the information we receive within the first twenty-four hours; in fact, the decline of memory over time is known as the **forgetting curve**. So if you do not review your notes almost immediately after class, it can be difficult to remember the material later. In two weeks, you will have forgotten up to 70 percent of it! Forgetting can be a serious problem when you are expected to learn and remember many different facts, figures, concepts, and relationships for a number of classes.

Immediate reviewing will help your overall understanding as well as your ability to remember important details during exams. Use the following three strategies:

1. **Write down the main ideas.** For five or ten minutes, quickly review your notes and select key words or phrases. Fill in the details you still remember but missed writing down during class. You might also want to ask your instructor or a classmate to quickly look at your notes to see if you have covered the major ideas.
2. **Repeat your ideas out loud.** Repeat a brief version of what you learned from the class either to yourself or to someone else. For many, the best way to learn something is to teach it to others. You will understand something better and remember it longer if you try to explain it in your own words. This helps you discover your own reactions and find the gaps in your understanding of the material. Asking and answering questions in class can also provide you with the feedback you need to make sure that your understanding is accurate.
3. **Review your notes from the previous class just before the next class session.** As you sit in class the next time it meets, waiting for the instructor to begin, use the time to quickly review your notes from the previous class session. This will prepare you for the lecture that is about to begin and help you to ask questions about material from the earlier lecture that was not clear to you.

What if you have three classes in a row and no time to study between them? Repeat the information as soon as possible after class. Review the most recent class first. Never delay doing this; if you do, it will take you longer to review, select main ideas, and repeat the ideas. With practice, you can complete the review of your main ideas from your notes quickly, perhaps between classes, during lunch, or while waiting for or riding the bus.

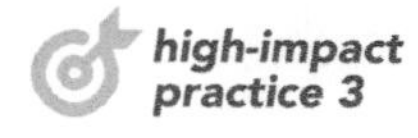

Compare Notes

Comparing notes with other students in a study group, SI session, or learning community has a number of benefits: You will probably take better notes when you know that someone else will see them, you can tell whether

Many Heads Are Better Than One
Educational researchers have discovered that learning is enhanced by group study. Give it a try.
Clerkenwell/Getty Images

your notes are as clear and organized as those of other students, and you can use your comparisons to see whether you agree on what the most important points are.

Take turns testing each other on what you have learned. This will help you predict exam questions and find out if you can answer them. In addition to sharing specific information from the class, you can also share tips on how you take and organize your notes. You might get new ideas that will help your overall learning.

Be aware, however, that merely copying another student's notes, no matter how good those notes are, does not benefit you as much as comparing notes. If you had to be absent from a class because of illness or a family emergency, it's fine to look at another student's notes to see what you missed, but just rewriting those notes might not help you learn the material. Instead, summarize the other student's notes in your own words to enhance your understanding of the important points.

Class Notes and Homework

Once you have reviewed your notes, you can use them to complete homework assignments. Follow these steps:

1. **Do a warm-up for your homework.** Before doing the assignment, look through your notes again. Use a separate sheet of paper to rework examples, problems, or exercises. If there is related assigned material in the textbook, review it. Go back to the examples. Try to respond to the questions or complete the problems without looking at the answers or solutions. Keep in mind that it can help to go back through your course notes, reorganize them, highlight the important items, and create new notes that let you connect with the material.

2. **Do any assigned problems, and answer any assigned questions.** When you start doing your homework, read each question or problem and ask: What am I supposed to find or find out? What is most important? What is not that important? Read each problem several times, and state it in your own words. Solve the problem without referring to your notes or the text, as though you were taking a test. In this way, you will test your knowledge and know whether you are prepared for exams.
3. **Don't give up too soon.** Start your homework with the hardest subject first while you are most energetic. When you face a problem or question that you cannot easily solve or answer, move on only after you have tried long enough. After you have completed the whole assignment, come back to any problems or questions that you could not solve or answer. Try once more, and then take a break. You might need to think about a particularly difficult problem for several hours or even days. Inspiration might come when you are waiting at a stoplight or just before you fall asleep.
4. **Complete your work.** When you finish an assignment, talk to yourself about what you learned from it. Think about how the problems and questions were different from one another, which strategies were successful, and what form the answers took. Be sure to review any material you have not mastered. Ask for help from the instructor, a classmate, a study group, the campus learning center, or a tutor to learn how to answer questions that stumped you.

your turn Stay Motivated

Use What You Have Learned

Now that you've read these suggestions about taking notes and studying for class, which ideas are you motivated to implement in your own note taking? Come to class ready to explain which ideas appeal to you most and why.

checklist for success

Getting the Most from Class

- **Practice the behaviors of engagement.** These behaviors include listening attentively, taking notes, and contributing to class discussion. Engagement also means participating in out-of-class activities without being "required" to do so.
- **Seek out professors who practice "active" teaching.** Ask other students, your seminar instructor, and your adviser to suggest the most engaging professors.
- **Prepare for class before class; it is one of the simplest and most important things you can do.** Read your notes from the previous class and do the assigned readings.
- **Go to class.** A huge part of success is simply showing up. You have no chance of becoming engaged in learning if you're not there.
- **Identify the different types of note taking covered in this chapter and decide which one(s) might work best for you.** Compare your notes with those of another good student to make sure that you are covering the most important points.
- **As you review your notes before each class, make a list of any questions you have and ask both fellow students and your instructor for help.** Don't wait until just before the exam to try to find answers to your questions.

build your experience

REFLECT ON CHOICES

high-impact practice 2

This chapter offers several options for effective note taking. Before you make a choice to try a new note-taking format, think back on those we suggested: Cornell, outline, paragraph, and list. Which one is most similar to the method you currently use, and which is most different? Reread the material, and do a brief written comparison of the recommended formats. Which do you think is most complex, which would be the easiest to use, and, given your learning style, which format would help you best understand and remember the material?

APPLY WHAT YOU HAVE LEARNED

Now that you have read and discussed this chapter, consider how you can apply what you have learned to your academic life and your personal life. The following prompts will help you reflect on the chapter material and how you can use it both now and in the future.

1. What is your least engaging class—the one in which the instructor does not encourage you to engage in active learning? Think of some ways you could make this class more engaging, such as asking questions or doing extra reading on the class material. Make a list of your ideas and share it with your college success instructor. He or she might have other ideas to suggest to you.
2. This chapter makes the point that it is easier to learn and remember new material when you can connect it to something you already know or have experienced. Which of your first-year classes connects most directly to something you learned in the past or something that happened to you? Write a brief paper in which you describe these connections.

USE YOUR RESOURCES

- **Learning Assistance Center**
  Almost every campus has a learning assistance center, and this chapter's topic is one of their specialties. More and more, the best students—and good students who want to be better students—use learning centers as much as students who are having academic difficulties. Services at learning centers are offered by both full-time professionals and highly skilled student tutors.
- **Fellow College Students**
  Often, the best help we can get comes from those who are closest to us: fellow students. Keep an eye out in your classes, residence hall, co-curricular groups, and other places for the most serious, purposeful, and directed students. They are the ones to seek out. Find a tutor. Join a study group. Students who do these things are the ones most likely to stay in college and be successful. It does not diminish you in any way to seek assistance from your peers.
- **Computer Center**
  If you need help using Word, Excel, PowerPoint, or electronic note-taking systems, visit the computer center on your campus.
- **Math Center**
  Your college may have a special center that provides help for math courses. If you are having difficulty figuring out what kind of notes to take in math classes, visit this center to ask for assistance.
- **Disabled Student Services**
  Your institution's office of disabled student services can help arrange for a note-taker if you cannot take notes because of a documented disability.
- **Toastmasters International**
  This organization offers public speaking tips at **toastmasters.org**. When you feel more confident about speaking in public, you will participate more in class. Find additional guidelines for speaking in class at **school-for-champions.com/grades/speaking.htm**.

LaunchPad for *Your College Experience* is a great resource. Go online to master concepts using the LearningCurve study tool and much more. **macmillanhighered.com/gardner12e**

Ammentorp Photography/Shutterstock

8 STUDYING

YOU WILL EXPLORE

Ways to concentrate and study more effectively

How memory works and myths about memory

Skills to improve your memory

High-impact practices 2 (writing) and 3 (collaboration)

Joe Miranda, 19

Engineering major
Spokane Falls Community College

> **"Two of the biggest challenges of making the transition from high school to college were learning time management and study skills."**

Early in high school, Joe Miranda did well enough in his classes to be able to play basketball and football. He hoped to be a college athlete, but then a knee injury derailed those plans. In his senior year of high school in Spokane, Washington, one of Joe's teachers recommended that he look into engineering as a profession. Joe had always been interested in math and science, but he hadn't done much planning for college. He researched different careers and types of engineering and found that environmental engineering excited him. Then he researched programs close to home.

Joe plans to complete his associate's degree in pre-engineering at Spokane Falls Community College (SFCC) and then transfer to Washington State University. SFCC has a six-quarter pre-engineering program intended to prepare students for transfer to a four-year engineering college in their junior year. When he was in high school, Joe didn't take the college-prep courses he needed to enter the engineering program at SFCC right away. As a result, he is taking lower-level college courses that will allow him to ramp up to higher-level courses like calculus and advanced chemistry, which he'll need in order to transfer. Joe knows all his time and effort will be worth it. "I found a great tutor at the learning center on campus who is helping me keep up the good grades I am getting," he says.

Joe is good at math and science, but that doesn't mean his transition to college was easy. "In high school," he says, "my studying habits were slim to none. I was the type of high school student who was able to pass a test just from listening and from what I remembered from class."

At SFCC, Joe had to change some of his study habits when he found that he wasn't able to remember everything the instructors required him to learn. "Two of the biggest challenges in making the transition from high school to college were learning time management and study skills," Joe says. He notes that, compared with high school, his college classes go twice as fast and instructors expect students to do a lot more work on their own. One of the first steps Joe took to adjust his study habits was to stop setting aside huge blocks of unstructured study time. "I learned that studying for more than four hours straight is not the best for me. I need to study for an hour, take a half hour break, and then study another hour. I realized that after an hour, I had trouble remembering things." By taking breaks to eat, exercise, or watch TV, Joe knows that he's giving his brain time to process information.

His one piece of advice to other first-year students? "The first year is going to be the hardest because it's so different," he says. "Just push through it. You'll find that it all starts making sense."

To access the LearningCurve study tool, video activities, and more, go to LaunchPad for *Your College Experience*. **macmillanhighered.com/gardner12e**

You might have learned to study effectively while you were in high school, or like Joe, you might find that your high school study habits no longer work now that you're in college. You will need to discover ways of structuring your study time that work best for you. Joe quickly learned that a four-hour study session was too long for him. But however you structure your study sessions, you will

assess your strengths

What study skills have you learned and practiced, and how do you need to improve? As you read this chapter, consider the strengths you have in studying and remembering course material.

set goals

What are your most important objectives in learning the material in this chapter? Do you need to improve your ability to concentrate, your study skills, and your memory? Consider how you might improve the environment in which you study.

need to allocate regular times each week to review course material, do assigned reading, and keep up with your homework. Occasionally, you will also want to do additional (unassigned) reading and investigate particular topics that interest you, as these are strategies that will help you retain knowledge.

Studying, comprehending, and remembering are essential to getting the most from your college experience. Although many students think that the only reason to study is to do well on exams, a far more important reason is to learn and understand course information. If you study to increase your understanding, you are more likely to remember and apply what you learn, not only to tests, but also to future courses and to life beyond college.

This chapter considers two related topics: concentration and memory. It begins with the role of concentration in studying—if you cannot concentrate, you'll find it next to impossible to remember anything. Next, the chapter offers a number of tools to help you make the best use of your study time. It concludes with a thorough discussion of what memory is, how it works, and how you can improve your memory.

is this you?

Making *A's* without Studying

Were you a straight-A student in high school who spent almost no time studying? In the first few weeks of college, maybe you went to class and listened, and you read through the assigned material on time. But you never took notes, reviewed your reading, or spent extra time preparing for tests and exams. You believed that your brainpower would carry you through college, just like it did in high school. But your first round of college exams gave you a horrible shock: You got a C in your easiest course, three D's, and an F. You quickly realized that something had to change. Clearly in college you can't coast effortlessly like you did in high school. This chapter will help you develop systematic strategies for studying that will help you pull up your grades before the end of the term.

STUDYING IN COLLEGE: MAKING CHOICES AND CONCENTRATING

Learning new material takes a lot of effort on your part. You must concentrate on what you hear and read. This might sound simple, but considering all the responsibilities that college students must balance, the opportunity to concentrate and really focus on what you're learning and studying can be hard to come by. Understanding how to maximize your ability to concentrate through what you do and where you do it is a good place to start.

Making a few changes in your behavior and in your environment will allow you to concentrate better and remember more. With concentration, you'll probably need fewer hours to study because you will use your time more efficiently. What are you willing to do to make this happen? Working through the following exercise, you'll begin to navigate some tough choices.

Tough Choices	Your Answer: Yes or No?
Are you willing to do assigned reading before you come to class?	
Are you willing to find a place away from home, either on campus or elsewhere, for quiet study?	
Are you willing to turn off your cell phone while you read?	
Are you willing to turn off distracting music or TV while you are studying?	
Are you willing to sit in a spot in class where you can see and hear better?	
Are you willing to go over your notes after class to revise or rewrite them?	
Are you willing to form study groups or work with partners?	
Are you willing to reduce stress through exercise, sleep, or meditation?	
Are you willing to take a few minutes on the weekend to organize the week ahead?	
Are you willing to study for tests four or five days in advance?	

Attending a college or university is a major responsibility, one you shouldn't take lightly. It is a lot of work, but it also offers you a lot of opportunities. For most people, a college degree is a pathway to a better, more fulfilling life. As a college learner, you may need to make different choices about how you manage your time and your study environment. Depending on your past study habits, some of these choices may not be easy. You may find that you have to invest more time in reading and reviewing, and that you have to study in groups with other students. Behaviors such as these can have a direct, positive impact on your ability to remember and learn the information you will need in the months and years ahead.

With these realities in mind, what did you learn about yourself from answering the questions in the exercise on the previous page? Think especially about the questions to which you answered "no." Which of these are you willing or unwilling to change right now? Remember: Changing behaviors that disrupt your ability to get the most out of college, both in and out of the classroom, will save you a lot of headaches in the future.

your turn Write and Reflect

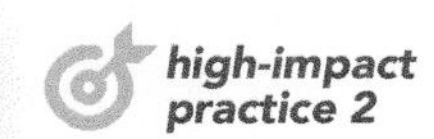

Are You Able to Concentrate?

The next time that you read a textbook, monitor your ability to concentrate. Check your watch when you begin, and check it again when your mind begins to wander. How many minutes did you concentrate on your reading? List some strategies to keep your mind from wandering. Write a journal entry containing ideas you have heard that you think will work well for you.

HOW MEMORY WORKS

Learning experts describe two different processes involved in memory (see Table 1). The first is **short-term memory**, which is defined as how many items you are able to understand and remember at one time. After less than 30 seconds—and sometimes much faster—you will forget the information stored in your short-term memory unless you take action either to keep that information in short-term memory or to move it to long-term memory.

Although short-term memory is significantly limited, it has a number of uses. It serves as an immediate holding tank for information, some of which you might not need for long. It helps you maintain a reasonable attention span so that you can keep track of topics mentioned in conversation, and it also enables you to stay on task with the goals you are pursuing at any given moment. But even these simple functions of short-term memory fail on occasion. If you are interrupted in any way, by a ringing phone or someone asking a question, you might find that your attention suffers and that you have to start over to reconstruct the contents of your short-term memory.

The second memory process is also important for college success. **Long-term memory**, the capacity to retain and recall information over the long term, from hours to years, can be divided into three categories:

- *Procedural memory* deals with knowing how to do something, such as solving a mathematical problem or driving a car. You use your procedural memory when you ride a bicycle, even if you haven't ridden one in years; when you cook a meal that you know how to prepare without using a recipe; or when you send a text message.
- *Semantic memory* involves facts and meanings without regard to where and when you learned those things. Your semantic memory is used when you remember word meanings or important dates, such as your mother's birthday.
- *Episodic memory* deals with particular events, their time, and their place. You use episodic memory when you remember events in your life—a vacation, your first day of school, or the moment your child was born. Some people can recall not only the event, but also the very time and place the event happened. For others, although the event stands out, the time and place are harder to remember.

TABLE 1

Short-Term Memory	Long-Term Memory
Stores information for about 30 seconds. Can handle from five to nine chunks of information at one time. Information is either forgotten or moved to long-term memory.	Can be described in three ways: Procedural—remembering how to do something Semantic—remembering facts and meanings Episodic—remembering events, including their time and place

Connecting Memory to Deep Learning

Multitasking has become a fact of life for many of us, but research summarized on the Web site of the American Psychological Association[1] shows that trying to do several tasks at once can make it harder to remember the most important things. It is hard to focus on anything for long if your life is full of daily distractions and competing responsibilities—school, work, commuting, and family responsibilities—or if you're not getting the sleep you need. Have you ever had the experience of walking into a room with a specific task in mind and immediately forgetting what that task was? You were probably interrupted, either by your own thoughts or by someone or something else. Or have you ever felt the panic that comes when your mind goes blank during a test, even though you studied hard and knew the material? If you spent all night studying, lack of sleep may have raised your stress level, causing you to forget what you worked hard to learn. Such experiences happen to most people at one time or another.

[1] www.apa.org/research/action/multitask.aspx.

To do well in college and in life, it's important that you improve your ability to remember what you read, hear, and experience. Concentration is a key element of learning and is so deeply connected to memory that you can't really have one without the other.

The benefits of having a good memory are obvious. In college, your memory will help you retain information and earn excellent grades on tests. After college, the ability to remember important details—names, dates, and appointments—will save you energy and time, and will prevent a lot of embarrassment.

Most memory strategies tend to focus on helping you remember bits and pieces of knowledge: names, dates, numbers, vocabulary words, formulas, and so on. However, if you know the date when the Civil War began and the name of the fort where the first shots were fired but you don't know why the Civil War was fought or how it affected history, you're missing the point of a college education. College is a time to develop **deep learning**, which involves understanding the why and how behind the details. So while remembering specific facts is necessary, to do well in college and in your career, you will need to understand major themes and ideas. You will also need to improve your ability to think deeply about what you're learning.

your turn Stay Motivated

The Fun of Improving Your Memory

What might motivate you to improve your memory? Do your friends complain that you keep forgetting the times you had planned to meet? Have you forgotten the due date for a paper, or have you forgotten your mother's birthday? If you want to develop a better memory, try some fun strategies for memory improvement. For example, many memory games are available that you can play for a few minutes every day; some of them can be accessed online or on your mobile device. Check out these free apps: Brain Workout for Android or Music Game for iPhone.

Myths about Memory

To understand how to improve your memory, let's first look at what we know about how memory works. Although scientists keep learning new things about how our brains function, author Kenneth Higbee[2] suggests some myths about memory, some of which you might have heard, and

[2]Kenneth L. Higbee, *Your Memory: How It Works and How to Improve It*, 2nd rev. ed. (New York: Marlowe, 2001).

techtip

USE THE CLOUD

Most of us have created files on computers. We usually store them on the computer's internal hard drive or on a removable drive, such as a thumb or flash drive. But colleges are moving away from allowing students to store data on their student accounts, so moving from computer to computer when you are working can present a problem. Also, if you don't have the latest word processing or presentation software on your own computer, it might be difficult to use files for your classes that were created in these software programs.

Cloud computing allows you to use the Internet as a storage device. Some sites even have pared-down versions of word processing, spreadsheet, and presentation software that you can use for free.

Another great advantage of cloud computing is the ability to share your files or folders with others. You can create a personal digital library and decide who gets to check out what file. It also tracks the changes that you and others have made to a file and keeps you from having multiple different versions if you are sharing the file with a group.

Pixsooz/Shutterstock

The Problem

You store your class files on a drive or laptop that you don't always have with you. How can you access your files anytime you need?

The Fix

Save your files to the cloud and have access to them from any Internet-connected device.

How to Do It

Sign up for a free account from a cloud storage site. These sites allow you to save files to an online location. You'll have your own private, password-protected storage space. Cloud storage is great for collaboration because you can choose to share all or some of your files with your classmates and friends. Here are four sites with free storage.

1. ***Dropbox*** (dropbox.com) is probably the best known cloud storage site. Users get 2 GB of free storage. You can upgrade to up to 500 GB for a monthly fee, or earn more storage space by referring others to the site. Dropbox has both a Web interface that you can access from any computer and a downloadable client that you can save to your computer. (A client is a piece of hardware or software that accesses a service made available by a server.) This client makes Dropbox look like any other folder on your computer, but when you add files to it, Dropbox actually adds them to your online folder. Dropbox is available as a stand-alone app on iPhone, iPad, and Android devices, and it works with other document-editing apps for mobile devices.
2. ***Google Drive*** (drive.google.com) allows users to store and share documents up to 5 GB. A great feature of Google Drive is that you can edit documents in real time with others. If you're writing a group paper, all your coauthors can view and edit the same document simultaneously. There is even a chat window so you can talk to each other while editing. Like Dropbox, Google Drive is available as a stand-alone app, and it integrates well with iPhone, iPad, and Android apps. If you have a Gmail account, you already have an account for Google Drive.
3. ***MediaFire*** (mediafire.com) lets you work collaboratively and access your files using stand-alone apps on iPhone, iPad, and Android devices. Its key feature is 50 GB of free storage space.
4. ***Microsoft OneDrive*** uses the Microsoft Office Suite and allows you to create, store, and share files. It comes with 15 GB of free space, but you can expand that space for a fee. It also has a free, stand-alone app for smart phones or tablets. If you have a Hotmail account, you can access OneDrive.

some you might even believe. Here are five of these memory myths and what experts say about them:

1. **Myth:** Some people have bad memories.
   Reality: Although the memory ability you are born with is different from that of others, nearly everyone can improve his or her ability to remember and recall. Improving your concentration will benefit your ability to remember!
2. **Myth:** Some people have photographic memories.
   Reality: Some individuals have truly exceptional memories, but these abilities result more often from learned strategies, interest, and practice than from the natural ability to remember.
3. **Myth:** Memory benefits from long hours of practice.
   Reality: Experts believe that practice often improves memory, but they argue that the way you practice is more important than how long you practice.
4. **Myth:** Remembering too much can clutter your mind.
   Reality: For all practical purposes, the storage capacity of your memory is unlimited. In fact, the more you learn about a particular topic, the easier it is to learn even more. How you organize the information is more important than the quantity of the information.
5. **Myth:** People use only 10 percent of their brain power.
   Reality: No one knows exactly how much of our brain's resources we actually tap. However, most researchers believe that we all have far more mental ability than we actually use.

IMPROVING YOUR MEMORY

Just as you can use strategies to improve your ability to concentrate, you can also improve your ability to store information in your brain for future use. Psychologists and learning specialists have developed a number of strategies you can use when studying. Some of these strategies might be new to you, but others will be familiar.

Have you ever had to memorize a speech or lines from a play? How you remember the lines might depend on your learning style. If you're an aural learner, you might decide to record your lines, along with those of other characters, and listen to them on tape. If you're a visual learner, you might remember best by visualizing where your lines appear in the script. If you learn best by reading, you might simply read the script over and over. If you're a kinesthetic learner, you might need to walk or move as you read the script.

Although knowing specific words will help, remembering concepts and ideas can be much more important. To store such ideas in your mind, ask yourself these questions as you review your notes and textbook material:

1. What is the basic idea in what I'm reading?
2. Why does the idea make sense? Is it logical?

3. How does this idea connect to other ideas in the material or to experiences in my life?
4. What are some possible arguments against the idea?

To prepare for an exam that will cover large amounts of material, you need to reduce your notes and text pages into manageable study units. Review your materials with these questions in mind: Is this one of the key ideas in the chapter or unit? Will I see this on the test? Five study tools in particular can help you remember what you have learned: review sheets, mind maps, flash cards, summaries, and mnemonics.

Review Sheets

Use your notes to develop **review sheets**—lists of key terms and ideas that you need to remember. If you're using the Cornell format to take notes, you'll make these lists in the recall column. Also be sure to use your lecture notes to test yourself or others on the information presented in class.

Mind Maps

A **mind map** (see Figure 1 on the next page) is essentially a visual review sheet that shows the relationships between ideas; its visual patterns provide you with clues to jog your memory. Because they are visual, mind maps help many students—particularly English language learners—remember information more easily.

An Elephant (Almost) Never Forgets

Although elephants apparently do have pretty good memories, they're like the rest of us in that they occasionally forget. Work to develop your memory by using the specific strategies in this chapter. One of the most important strategies you can use is considering the big-picture context behind bits and pieces of information.

"Is this the memory seminar?"

FIGURE 1 › Sample Mind Map

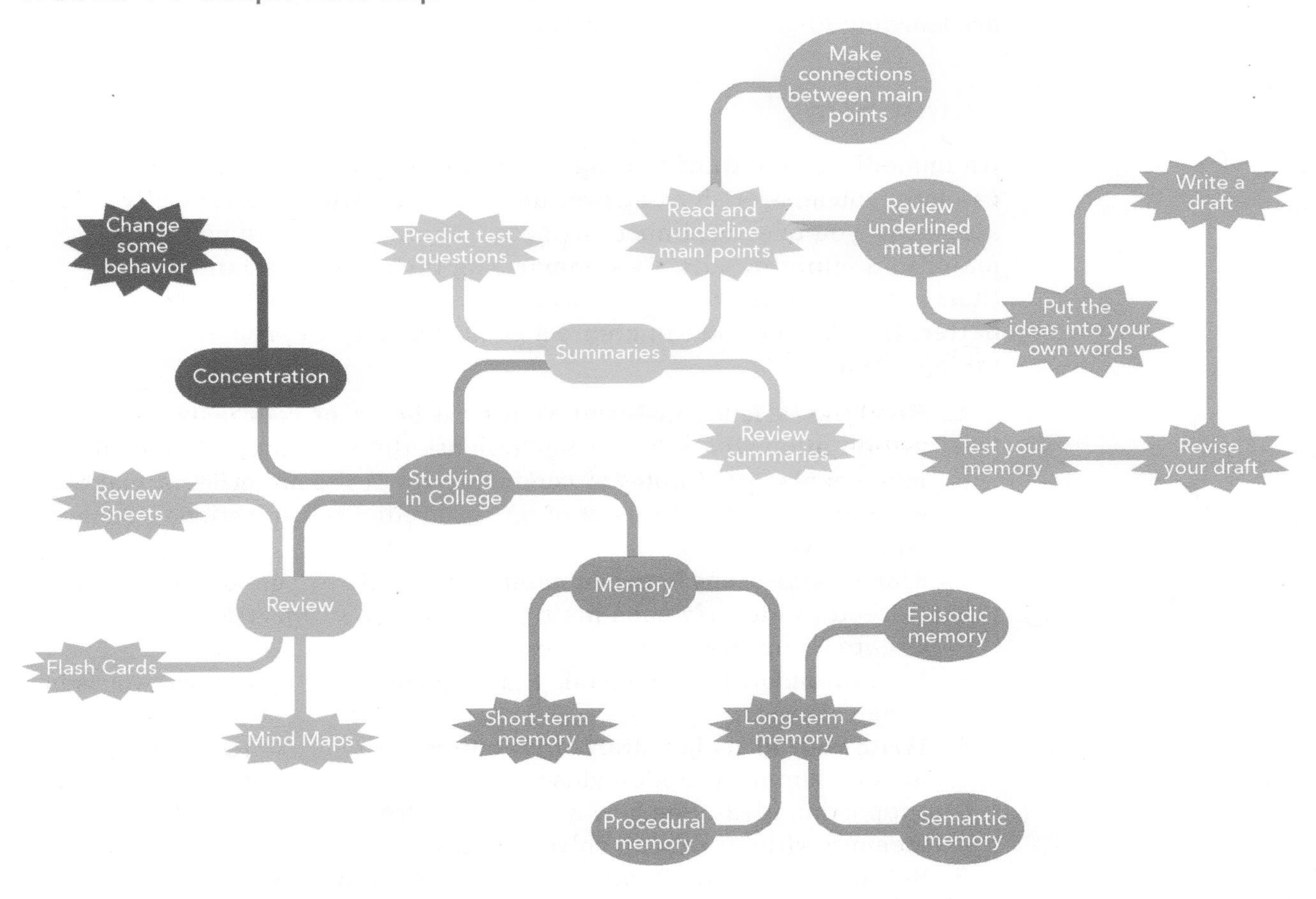

To create a mind map, start with a main idea and place it in the center. Then add major categories that branch out from the center. To these branches, add pieces of related information to form clusters. You can use different shapes and/or colors to show the relationships among the various pieces of information. You can find many apps for creating mind maps on your computer or mobile device. Figure 1 shows a mind map of this chapter, created by using an app called Total Recall. Other mind-map apps include MindMeister and SimpleMind.

Flash Cards

Just as you can create flash cards during the process of active reading, you can also use them as a tool for improving your memory. Flash cards—with a question, term, or piece of information on one side and the answer, definition, or explanation on the other—can serve as memory aids. One of the advantages of flash cards is that you can keep them in your backpack or jacket, or on your mobile device. Then you can look at them anywhere, even when you don't have enough time to take out your notebook to study.

Flash cards can help you make good use of time that might otherwise be wasted, such as time spent on the bus or waiting for a friend. Flash cards are excellent tools for improving your vocabulary, especially if you are learning English as a second language.

Summaries

An immediate benefit of writing summaries of class topics is that they can help you answer short-answer and essay questions successfully. They also allow you to see connections between ideas and help you identify major and minor details. By summarizing the main ideas and putting them into your own words, you will be able to remember information better. Here's how you can create a good summary in preparation for taking a test:

1. **Read the assigned material, your class notes, or your instructor's presentation slides.** Underline or mark the main ideas as you go, make explanatory notes or comments about the material, or make an outline on a separate sheet of paper. Predict test questions based on your active reading.
2. **Make connections between main points and key supporting details.** Reread to identify each main point and its supporting evidence. Create an outline in the process.
3. **Review underlined material.** Put those ideas into your own words in a logical order.
4. **Write your ideas in a draft.** In the first sentence, state the purpose of your summary. Follow this statement with each main point and its supporting ideas. See how much of the draft you can develop from memory without relying on your notes.
5. **Review your draft.** Read it over, adding missing details or other information.
6. **Test your memory.** Put your draft away, and try to repeat the contents of the summary out loud to yourself or to a study partner who can let you know whether you have forgotten anything.
7. **Schedule time to review your summary and double-check your memory shortly before the test.** You might want to do this with a partner, but some students prefer to review alone. Some instructors might be willing to help you with this process and give you feedback on your summaries.

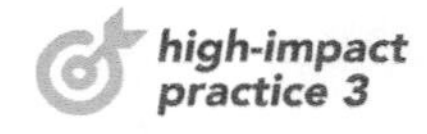

your turn Work Together

Using Learning Styles to Study and Remember

With your instructor's help, identify other students in your class who share your learning style. Get together to brainstorm strategies for remembering material for exams using your learning style, and keep track of the most helpful ideas.

Mnemonics

Mnemonics (pronounced "ne-MON-iks") are different methods or tricks to help you remember information. Mnemonics tend to fall into four basic categories:

1. **Acronyms.** Acronyms, which are new words created from the first letters of several words, can be helpful in remembering. The names of the Great Lakes can be more easily recalled by remembering the word *HOMES* for **H**uron, **O**ntario, **M**ichigan, **E**rie, and **S**uperior.
2. **Acrostics.** An acrostic is a verse in which certain letters of each word or line form a message. Many piano students were taught the notes on the treble clef lines (E, G, B, D, F) by remembering the acrostic "**E**very **G**ood **B**oy **D**eserves **F**udge." Many students are taught the following to remember the planets of our solar system: **M**y **V**ery **E**xcellent **M**other **J**ust **S**erved **U**s **N**achos (**M**ercury, **V**enus, **E**arth, **M**ars, **J**upiter, **S**aturn, **U**ranus, **N**eptune).
3. **Rhymes or songs.** Do you remember learning "Thirty days hath September, April, June, and November. All the rest have thirty-one, excepting February alone. It has twenty-eight days' time, but in leap years twenty-nine"? If so, you were using a mnemonic rhyming technique to remember the number of days in each month.
4. **Visualization.** You can use visualization to connect a word or concept with a visual image. The more ridiculous the image, the more likely you are to remember the word or concept. For example, if you want to remember the name of George Washington, you may think of a person you know by the name of George. You should then picture that person washing a ton of dishes. Now every time you think of the first president of the United States, you see George washing a ton of dishes.[3]

your turn Make Good Choices

Choose Review Methods That Work for You

This chapter has offered several strategies for reviewing material before you take a test or exam, including review sheets, mind maps, flash cards, summaries, and mnemonics. Some of these strategies might work better for certain subject areas. For instance, mnemonics and flash cards will help when you have to remember definitions or other specific bits of information. Review sheets, mind maps, and summaries work more effectively when you need to understand broad concepts. When you begin studying for your next test, let the type of test and the material it will cover help you choose the best study method.

[3]Example from Jim Somchai, "Memory and Visualization," EzineArticles.com, ezinearticles.com/?Memory-and-Visualization&id=569553.

Mnemonics are a sort of mental filing system that provide a way of organizing material. They probably aren't needed if what you are studying is logical and organized, but they can be really useful when material doesn't have a pattern of its own. Although using mnemonics can be helpful in remembering information, it takes time to think up rhymes, associations, or visual images that have limited use when you need to analyze or explain the material in depth.

STUDYING TO UNDERSTAND AND REMEMBER

Studying will help you accomplish two goals: understanding and remembering. While memory is a necessary tool for learning, what's most important is that you study to develop a deep understanding of course information. When you really comprehend what you are learning, you will be able to place names, dates, and specific facts in context. You will also be able to exercise your critical-thinking abilities.

Here are some methods that might be useful when you're trying to remember detailed information:

- **Pay attention and avoid distractions.** This suggestion is the most basic, but the most important. If you're sitting in class thinking about everything except what the professor is saying, or if you're reading and you find that your mind is wandering, you're wasting your time. Force yourself to focus. Review your responses to the questions posed in the exercise you completed earlier in this chapter about what you're willing to do to improve your concentration.
- **Be confident that you can improve your memory.** Recall successes from the past when you learned things that you didn't think you could or would remember. Choose memory improvement strategies that best fit your preferred learning styles: aural, visual, read/write, or kinesthetic. Identify the courses where you can make the best use of each memory strategy.
- **Overlearn the material.** Once you think you understand the material you're studying, go over it again to make sure that you'll remember it for a long time. Test yourself, or ask someone else to test you. Repeat what you're trying to remember out loud and in your own words.
- **Explain the material to another person.**
- **Make studying a part of your daily routine.** Don't allow days to go by when you don't open a book or work on course assignments. Make studying a daily habit!
- **Check the Internet.** If you're having trouble remembering what you have learned, Google a key word and try to find interesting details that will engage you in learning more about the subject. Many first-year courses cover such a large amount of material that you might miss some interesting details unless you look for them yourself. As your interest increases, so will your memory about the topic. Make sure to check multiple online sources.

- **Go beyond memorizing words and focus on understanding and then remembering the big concepts and ideas.** Keep asking yourself questions like: What is the main point here? Is there a big idea? Whenever you begin a course, review the syllabus, talk with someone who has already taken the course, and take a brief look at all the reading assignments. Having the big picture will help you understand and remember the details of what you're learning. For example, the big picture for a first-year college success class is to give students the knowledge and strategies to be successful in college.
- **Look for connections between your life and what's going on in the content of your courses.** College courses might seem unrelated to you and your goals, but if you look more carefully, you'll find many connections between course material and your daily life. Seeing those connections will make your courses more interesting and will help you remember what you're learning. For example, if you're taking a sociology class and studying marriage and the family, think about how your own family experiences relate to those described in your readings or in the lectures.
- **Get organized.** If your desk or your computer is organized, you won't waste time trying to remember where you put a particular document or what name you gave to a file. And as you rewrite your notes, putting them in an order that makes sense to you (for example, by topic or by date) will help you learn and remember them.

your turn Work Together

high-impact practice 3

Is It Worth the Time and Effort to Get Organized?

With a small group of your classmates, share how organized you are in your living space and on your computer. Is your living space more or less organized than your laptop, desktop, or iPad? Do group members think that being organized is important? How does being disorganized affect time management? Work with your peer leader to come up with strategies to be more organized. Keep track of the initial time you spend getting organized, and the time you save over a two- or three-week period by being more organized.

- **Reduce the stress in your life.** Many college students experience stress because they have to juggle college, work, and family life. Stress-reducing habits, such as eating well and getting enough exercise and sleep, are especially important for college students. Remember, too, that your college probably has a counseling center or health center where you can seek help in dealing with whatever might be causing stress in your daily life.

- **Collaborate.** In your first year of college, join a group of students who study together. Your instructors or the college learning center can help you organize study groups. Study groups can meet throughout the term or can get together only to review for midterm or final exams.
- **Get a tutor.** Tutoring is not just for students who are failing. Often the best students ask for help to make sure that they understand course material. Most tutors are students, and at most community colleges, tutoring services are free.

Work Together

One way to enhance your memory is to study with others. Each of you can check specific facts and details and share the strategies you use to remember them. You can also motivate and support one another.
Digital Vision/Getty Images

As you learned in this chapter, memory and concentration play very important roles in achieving success in college because they help you understand, remember, and deeply learn the material so that you can apply that learning to your career and life.

checklist for success

Studying

- **Make studying a part of your daily routine.** Don't allow days to go by when you don't crack a book or keep up with course assignments.
- **Manage your study time wisely.** Create a schedule that will allow you to prepare for exams and complete course assignments on time. Be aware of "crunch times" when you might have several exams or papers due at once. Create some flexibility in your schedule to allow for unexpected distractions.
- **Collaborate.** One of the most effective ways to study is in a group with other students.
- **Be confident that you can improve your memory.** Remind yourself occasionally of things you have learned in the past that you didn't think you could or would remember.
- **Choose the memory improvement strategies that best fit your preferred learning style(s): aural, visual, read/write, or kinesthetic.** Identify the courses where you can make the best use of each memory strategy.
- **Go beyond simply trying to memorize words, and focus on trying to understand and remember the big concepts and ideas.** Keep asking yourself: What is the main point here? Is there a big idea? Am I getting it?
- **Be alert for external distractions.** Choose a place to study where you can concentrate, and allow yourself uninterrupted time to focus on the material you are studying.
- **Get a tutor.** Tutoring is not just for students who are failing. Often the best students seek assistance to ensure that they fully understand course material. Most tutors are students, and most campus tutoring services are free.

build your experience

REFLECT ON CHOICES

high-impact practice 2

Reflect on what you have learned about college success in this chapter and how you will apply the chapter information or strategies in college and in your career. Without opening your book, write a brief paper summarizing what you learned in this chapter. Then go back to the chapter subheadings to see what you remembered and what you might have forgotten. Which of the strategies presented in this chapter were already familiar to you, and which new ones will you choose to adopt?

APPLY WHAT YOU HAVE LEARNED

Now that you have read and discussed this chapter, consider how you can apply what you have learned to your academic life and your personal life. The following prompts will help you reflect on the chapter material and its relevance to you both now and in the future.

1. Give mnemonics a try. Choose a set of class notes that you need to study for an upcoming quiz or exam. As you study, pick one concept and create your own acronym, acrostic, rhyme, song, or visualization to help you remember.

2. The way that students study in high school is often very different from the way they need to study in college. It can be difficult to adapt to new ways of doing things. Write a one-page paper describing how you studied in high school and how you can improve on those habits to do well in college.

USE YOUR RESOURCES

› **Learning Assistance Center**
Here, staff can help you develop effective memory strategies. Pay a visit and ask about specific workshops or one-on-one assistance with memory.

› **Peers and Your Peer Leader**
Ask fellow students and your peer leader to share their own tips for improving memory.

› **Your Instructor**
Ask your instructor if there is someone on your campus who is an expert on memory strategies. If so, make an appointment to meet that person.

› **The Library**
Your college or university library will have many books on the topic of memory. Some were written by researchers for the research community, but others were written for people like you. Download or check out a book on memory to see what you can learn. Here are some good options: Tony Buzan, *Use Your Perfect Memory*, 3rd ed., (New York: Penguin Books, 1991); Kenneth L. Higbee, *Your Memory: How It Works and How to Improve It*, 2nd ed., (New York: Marlowe, 2001); Harry Lorayne, *Super Memory, Super Student: How to Raise Your Grades in 30 Days* (Boston: Little, Brown, 1990). Ask your college librarian to help you identify some helpful online resources as well, such as this site that offers memorization techniques, maintained by the Alamo Community College District: **alamo.edu/memory**.

LaunchPad

LaunchPad for *Your College Experience* is a great resource. Go online to master concepts using the LearningCurve study tool and much more. macmillanhighered.com/gardner12e

Chris Ryan/Getty Images

9 TEST TAKING

YOU WILL EXPLORE

Ways to prepare for exams physically, emotionally, and academically

Tips for test taking

Strategies for taking different types of tests and handling various question types

How to overcome test anxiety

What cheating is, how to avoid it, and how to maintain academic honesty

High-impact practices 2 (writing) and 3 (collaboration)

Nicole Bradley, 24

Nursing major
University of Washington

"The first step to improving my test-taking abilities was changing my attitude about my 'academic self.'"

Nicole Bradley grew up all over the country, moving with her parents as part of a military family. "My parents were young and adventurous and willing to move wherever the military sent them," she says. At age sixteen, she landed in Bothell, Washington, near Seattle, and was able to finish high school. Soon after her graduation, Nicole gave birth to a son and found herself working to support herself and her child. For a while, college was the furthest thing from her mind, but eventually she realized that she wanted more for her son—and for herself. "Ultimately, being a single mother is what motivates me, not only to provide a better life for both of us, but also to set an example that was not always set for me," she explains.

Part of going to college and raising a family involves finding that ever-elusive work-life balance in areas such as preparing for tests. Nicole always thought that she just wasn't good at taking tests or learning, so she usually finished in the middle of the pack on tests and exams. "The first step to improving my test-taking abilities," she says, "was changing my attitude about my 'academic self.'" Once Nicole worked to improve her attitude, she began looking at the test-preparation strategies that worked best for her. One thing she figured out was that note taking was integral to a good performance on tests. "I found that I remember things best by relating them to things that I already know," she says. Now she knows to take careful notes during class, underline key terms, and make additional marginal notes so that when she gets home, she can create associations to help with memory. She also knows that her brain works best when the rest of her body is well cared for and has plenty of rest, good food, exercise, and often meditation and relaxation. "It works better than cram studying, and I get a lot more out of my courses and do better on my exams," she explains.

As with many things in life, Nicole realizes that with test taking, you sometimes have to get it wrong before you get it right. Her advice to other first-year students? "Go back over the questions you got wrong on a test and try to figure out what you got wrong and why."

To access the LearningCurve study tool, video activities, and more, go to LaunchPad for *Your College Experience*. macmillanhighered.com/gardner12e

Tests and exams are the primary ways that instructors will evaluate your learning. In general, tests are shorter than exams and will count less toward your overall course grade. A course might have only a final exam, or it might have a midterm and a final. These exams generally take two or more hours to complete and comprise a major component of your final grade in a course.

You can prepare for tests and exams in many ways. Sometimes you'll have to recall names, dates, and other specific bits of information. Many instructors, especially in courses such as literature and history, will also expect you to have a good overall understanding of the subject matter. Even in math and science courses, your instructors want you not only to remember the correct theory, formula, or equation, but also to understand

assess your strengths

Tests and exams are an unavoidable component of college life. Good students will practice strategies to improve their exam scores. As you read this chapter, think of specific examples of your strengths in preparing for and taking different kinds of exams.

set goals

What are your most important objectives for learning the material in this chapter? Do you need to improve your abilities as a test taker, or do you need to deal with test anxiety that prevents you from doing your best? Consider what you might do to improve in these areas, such as leaving plenty of time to study in advance of exams.

and apply what you have learned. Knowing your preferred learning style, managing your time and energy, and using study and memory strategies will help you prepare for any kind of test or exam you face. This chapter provides you with several strategies to prepare for and take tests and exams successfully, describes types of tests and test questions you may encounter, and includes tips for managing test anxiety and maintaining academic honesty.

GETTING READY . . .

Believe it or not, you actually began preparing for tests on the first day of the term. Your lecture notes, assigned readings, and homework are all part of that preparation. As you get closer to the test day, you should know how much additional time you will need for review, what material the test will cover, and what format the test will take. It is very important to double-check the exam dates on the syllabus for each of your classes, as in Figure 1 on the next page, and to incorporate these dates into your overall plans for time management—for example, in your daily and weekly to-do lists.

Prepare for Test Taking

Tests are usually a major portion of your grade in college, so proper preparation for them is essential. Of course you need to understand the material, but there are many ways you can prepare for exams in addition to your regular study routines.

Find Out about the Test. Ask your instructor about the test format, how long the test will last, and how it will be graded. Find out the types of questions and the content that will be covered. Talk with your instructor to clarify any misunderstandings you might have about your reading or lecture notes. If you have a part-time instructor who does not have office hours, try to talk to him or her before or after class. Some instructors might let you view copies of old exams so that you can see the types of questions they use. Never miss the last class before an exam; your instructor might take part or all of that class session to summarize and review valuable information.

FIGURE 1 > Exam Schedule from Sample Course Syllabus

History 111, US History to 1865
Fall 2016

Examinations

Note: In this course, most of your exams will be on Fridays, except for the Wednesday before Thanksgiving and the final. This is to give you a full week to study for the exam and permit me to grade them over the weekend and return the exams to you on Monday. I believe in using a variety of types of measurements. In addition to those scheduled below, I reserve the right to give you unannounced quizzes on daily reading assignments. Also, current events are fair game on any exam! Midterm and final exams will be cumulative (on all material since beginning of the course). Other exams cover all classroom material and all readings covered since the prior exam. The schedule is as follows:

Friday, 9/9: Objective type

Friday, 9/23: Essay type

Friday, 10/14: Midterm: essay and objective

Friday, 11/4: Objective

Wednesday, 11/16: Essay

Tuesday, 12/20: Final exam: essay and objective

Design an Exam Plan. Use information about the test as you design an exam-preparation plan. Create a schedule that will give you time to review for the exam without waiting until the night before. Develop a to-do list of the major steps you need to take to be ready, and schedule review dates. Be sure that your schedule is flexible enough to allow for unexpected distractions or emergencies. If you are able to schedule your study sessions over several days, your mind will continue to process the information between study sessions, which will help you during the test. Be sure you have read and learned all the material one week before the exam. That way, you can use the week before the exam to review. In that final week, set aside several one-hour blocks for review, and make specific notes on what you plan to do during each hour. Also, let your friends and family know when you have important exams coming up and how that will affect your time with them.

Use Online Quizzing. Many textbooks have related Web sites that offer a number of study tools such as flash cards, videos, or online quizzing. Ask your instructors about these sites, and also check the preface of your textbooks for information on accessing these sites. You might also use Google to find them.

Join a Study Group. Joining a study group is one of the best ways to prepare for exams. Group members can share different views of the most important topics to review, quiz one another on facts and concepts, and gain support from other serious students. Some instructors will provide time in class for the formation of study groups, or you might choose to approach classmates on your own. You can always ask your instructor, academic adviser, or the college's tutoring or learning center professionals to help you find other interested students and decide on guidelines for the group. Study groups can meet throughout the term, or they can just review for midterms or final exams. Group members should prepare questions or discussion points before the group meets. If your study group decides to meet just before exams, allow enough time to share notes and ideas.

high-impact practice 3

Talk to Other Students. Other students, especially those who have previously taken a course you are currently taking from the same instructor, may be able to give you a good idea of what to expect on tests and exams. If your college is small, you shouldn't have any trouble finding students who have taken the same courses you are taking now. If you're at a large college, your instructor may be able to suggest a former student who could serve as a tutor. But keep in mind that your instructor might decide to take a different approach in your class than he or she did in past classes.

Get a Tutor. Most colleges and universities offer free tutoring services. Ask your academic adviser, counselor, or college learning center staff members about arranging for tutoring. Keep in mind that some of the best

Strength in Numbers
Study groups can meet anytime, but studying and reviewing with others in your class can be most helpful just before and just after a test or exam.

students seek out tutoring, not just students who are struggling. Most students who receive tutoring are successful in their courses. Many learning centers employ student tutors who have done well in the same courses you are taking. These students might have some good advice on how to prepare for tests given by particular instructors. If you earn good grades in a specific course, you could eventually become a tutor and be paid for your services. Serving as a tutor also deepens your own learning and helps you become more successful in your major.

Prepare for Math and Science Exams

Math and science exams often require additional—and sometimes different—preparation techniques. Here are some suggestions for doing well on these exams:

- Do your homework regularly even if it is not graded, and do all the assigned problems. As you do your homework, write out your work as carefully and clearly as you will be expected to on your tests. This practice will allow you to use your homework as a review for the test. Figure 2 shows a page from a textbook with practice problems.
- Attend each class, always be on time, and stay for the entire class. Many instructors use the first few minutes of class to review homework, and others may end the class by telling you what will be on the test.
- Build a review guide throughout the term. As you begin your homework each day, write out a problem from each homework section in a notebook that you use solely to review material for that course. Then when you need to review for your exam, you can come back to this notebook to make sure you have a representative problem from each section you've studied.
- Throughout the term, keep a list of definitions or important formulas and put them on flash cards. Review several of them as part of every study session. Another technique is to post the formulas and definitions in your living space—on the bathroom wall, around your computer work area, or on the door of the microwave. Seeing this information frequently will help you keep it in your mind.

If these strategies don't seem to help you, ask a tutor to give you a few practice exams so you can review your responses together.

Prepare Physically

Keeping your body healthy is another key part of preparing yourself for quizzes, tests, and exams. The following strategies will help you prepare physically:

- **Maintain your regular sleep routine.** To do well on exams, you will need to be alert so that you can think clearly, and you are more likely to be alert when you are well rested. Last-minute, late-night cramming does not allow you to get sufficient sleep, so it isn't an effective study strategy. Most students need seven to eight hours of sleep the night before the exam.

FIGURE 2 › Solving Practice Problems

Completing plenty of practice problems, like the ones shown here, is a great way to study for math and science classes. So try your hand at all the problems provided in your textbook—even those that your instructor hasn't assigned—and check out Web sites offering such problems. Source: Excerpt from page 315, COMAP, *For All Practical Purposes: Mathematical Literacy in Today's World*, 9th ed. Copyright © 2013 by W. H. Freeman. Used by permission.

(c) What is the probability that 5 cards drawn at random from a 52-card deck will yield a royal flush?

■ **30.** Biblical permutations: The King James Version of the Old Testament has its 39 books canonized in a different order than the Hebrew Bible does. What mathematical expression would yield the number of possible orders of these 39 books? Is this number larger than you expected?

8.4 Continuous Probability Models

31. Generate two random real numbers between 0 and 1 and take their sum. The sum can take any value between 0 and 2. The density curve is the shaded triangle shown in Figure 8.13.

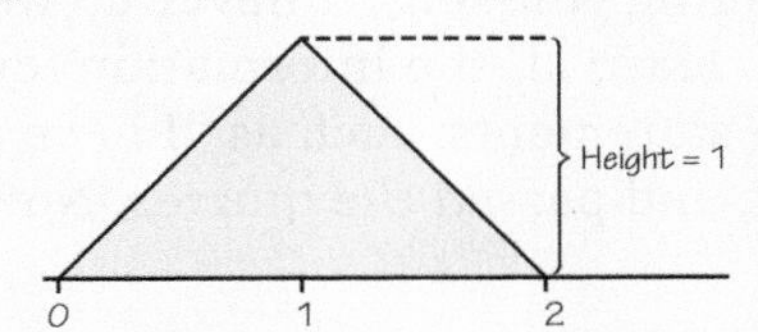

Figure 8.13 The density curve for the sum of two random numbers, for Exercise 31.

(a) Verify by geometry that the area under this curve is 1.
(b) What is the probability that the sum is less than 1? (Sketch the density curve, shade the area that represents the probability, and then find that area. Do this for part (c) as well.)
(c) What is the probability that the sum is less than 0.5?

32. Suppose two data values are each rounded to the nearest whole number. Make a density curve for the sum of the two roundoff errors (assuming each error has a continuous uniform distribution).

33. On the TV show *The Price Is Right*, the "Range Game" involves a contestant being told that the suggested retail price of a prize lies between two numbers that are $600 apart. The contestant has one chance to position a red window with a span of $150 that will contain the price. On one episode, the price of a piano is between $8900 and $9500. If we assume a uniform continuous distribution (i.e., that all prices within the $600 interval are equally likely), what is the probability that the contestant will be successful?

8.5 The Mean and Standard Deviation of a Probability Model

34. You have a campus errand that will take only 15 minutes. The only parking space anywhere nearby is a faculty-only space, which is checked by campus police about once every hour. If you're caught, the fine is $25.

(a) Give the probability model for the money that you may or may not have to pay.
(b) What's the expected value of the money that you will pay for your unauthorized parking?

35. Exercise 15 gives a probability model for the grade of a randomly chosen student in Statistics 101 at North Carolina State University, using the 4-point scale. What is the mean grade in this course? What is the standard deviation of the grades?

36. In Exercise 14, you gave a probability model for the intelligence of a character in a role-playing game. What is the mean intelligence for these characters?

37. Exercise 16 gives probability models for the number of rooms in owner-occupied and rented housing units. Find the mean number of rooms for each type of housing. Make probability histograms for the two models and mark the mean on each histogram. You see that the means describe an important difference between the two models: Owner-occupied units tend to have more rooms.

38. Typographical and spelling errors can be either "nonword errors" or "word errors." A nonword error is not a real word, as when "the" is typed as "teh." A word error is a real word, but not the right word, as when "lose" is typed as "loose." When undergraduates write a 250-word essay (without spell-checking), the number of nonword errors has this probability model:

Errors	0	1	2	3	4
Probability	0.1	0.2	0.3	0.3	0.1

The number of word errors has this model:

Errors	0	1	2	3
Probability	0.4	0.3	0.2	0.1

(a) What is the mean number of nonword errors in an essay?
(b) What is the mean number of word errors in an essay?
(c) How does the difference between the means describe the difference between the two models?

39. Find (and explain how you found) the mean for:

(a) the continuous probability model in Exercise 31.
(b) the probability model in Exercise 32.

■ **40.** The idea of insurance is that we all face risks that are unlikely but carry a high cost. Think of a fire destroying your home. Insurance spreads the risk: We all pay a small amount, and the insurance policy pays a large amount to those few of us whose homes burn down. An insurance

- **Follow your regular exercise program.** Exercise is a positive way to relieve stress and to give yourself a much-needed break from long hours of studying.
- **Eat right.** Eat a light breakfast before a morning exam, and avoid greasy or acidic foods that might upset your stomach. Limit the amount of caffeinated beverages you drink on exam day because caffeine can make you jittery. Choose fruits, vegetables, and other foods that are high in energy-rich complex carbohydrates. Avoid eating sweets before an exam; the immediate energy boost they create can be quickly followed by a loss of energy and alertness. Ask the instructor whether you may bring a bottle of water with you to the exam.

Prepare Emotionally

Just as physical preparation is important, so is preparing your attitude and your emotions. You'll benefit by paying attention to the following ideas:

- **Know the material.** If you have given yourself enough time to review, you will enter the classroom confident that you are in control. Study by testing yourself or quizzing others in a study group so that you will be sure you really know the information.
- **Practice relaxing.** Some students experience test anxiety, which can lead to upset stomachs, sweaty palms, racing hearts, and other unpleasant physical symptoms. The section on test anxiety later in this chapter includes an anxiety quiz; if that quiz reveals that test anxiety is a problem for you, consult your counseling center about relaxation techniques. Some campus learning centers also provide workshops on reducing test anxiety.
- **Use positive self-talk.** Instead of telling yourself, "I never do well on math tests" or "I'll never be able to learn all the information for my history essay exam," make positive statements, such as "I have always attended class, done my homework, and passed the quizzes. Now I'm ready to do well on the test!"

your turn Stay Motivated

Avoid Becoming Discouraged

Are you sometimes down on yourself when you've performed poorly on a test or exam? Does your disappointment negatively affect your motivation to do well in a particular course or in college? Remember that a positive attitude, plus a clear plan for improvement, will both help you stay motivated to do your best and make you more resilient. Believe in your ability to overcome the temporary stumbling blocks that are part of everyone's college experience.

TIPS FOR TEST TAKING

Throughout your college career, you will take tests in many different formats, in many subject areas, and with many different types of questions. It may surprise you to find that your first-year tests are likely to be more challenging than those in later years because, as a new student, you are still developing your college test-taking skills. The following test-taking tips apply to any test situation.

1. **Write your name on the test.** Usually you will have to write your name on a test booklet or answer sheet. Some instructors, however, may require you to fill in your student ID number.
2. **Look over the whole test and stay calm.** Carefully read all the directions before beginning the test so that you understand what to do.

Ask the instructor or exam monitor for clarification if you don't understand something. Be confident. Don't panic. Answer one question at a time.

3. **Make the best use of your time.** Quickly review the entire test and decide how much time you will spend on each section. Be aware of the point values of different sections of the test. If some questions are worth more points than others, you need to spend more of your time answering them.
4. **Jot down idea starters before the test.** Check with your instructor ahead of time to be sure that it is OK to write some last-minute notes on the test or on scrap paper. If so, then before you even look at the test questions, turn the test paper over and take a moment to write down the formulas, definitions, or major ideas you have been studying. This will help you go into the test with confidence and knowledge, and your notes will provide quick access to the information you may need throughout the test.
5. **Answer the easy questions first.** Expect that you won't completely understand some questions. Make a note to come back to them later. If different sections have different types of questions (such as multiple-choice, short-answer, and essay questions), first finish the types of questions that are easiest for you to answer. Be sure to leave enough time for any essays.
6. **If you feel yourself starting to panic or go blank, stop whatever you are doing.** Take a deep breath, and remind yourself that you will be OK and you do know the material and can do well on this test. If necessary, go to another section of the test and come back later to the item that triggered your anxiety.
7. **Try to answer each question, even if you can only provide a partial answer.** You may not be able to answer all the questions fully; provide as much information as you can remember. Particularly for math and science test questions, you may get some credit for writing down equations and descriptions of how to solve the problems even if you cannot fully work them out or if you run out of time before you finish them.
8. **If you finish early, don't leave immediately.** Stay and check your work for errors. Reread the directions one last time.

TYPES OF TESTS

While you are in college, you will take many different types of tests. Some may be used in specific subjects such as English or math; others can be used in any class you might take. This section discusses the different test types and presents helpful tips for succeeding on each one.

Problem-Solving Tests

In science, mathematics, engineering, and statistics courses, some tests will require you to solve problems and show all the steps that led to the solution. Even if you know a shortcut, it is important to document how you got from step A to step B. For these tests, you must also be careful to avoid errors in your scientific notation. A misplaced sign, parenthesis, or bracket can make all the difference.

If you are allowed to use a calculator during the exam, it is important to check that your input is accurate. The calculator does what you tell it to, and if you miss a zero or a negative sign, the calculator will not give you the correct answer to the problem.

Read all directions carefully. Whenever possible, after you complete the problem, work it in reverse to check your solution. Also check to make sure that your solution makes sense. You can't have negative bushels of apples, for example, or a fraction of a person, or a correlation less than negative 1 or greater than 1.

Machine-Scored Tests

For some tests, you may have to enter your answers on a Scantron form. The instructor will feed those forms into a machine that scans the answers and prints out your score. When taking any test, especially a machine-scored test, carefully follow the directions. In addition to your name, be sure to provide all other necessary information on the answer sheet. Each time you fill in an answer, make sure that the number on the answer sheet corresponds to the number of the item on the test.

Although scoring machines have become more sophisticated over time, they might still misread stray marks or incomplete bubbles on your answer sheet. When a machine-scored test is returned to you, check your answer sheet against the scoring key, if one is provided, to make sure that you receive credit for all the questions you answered correctly.

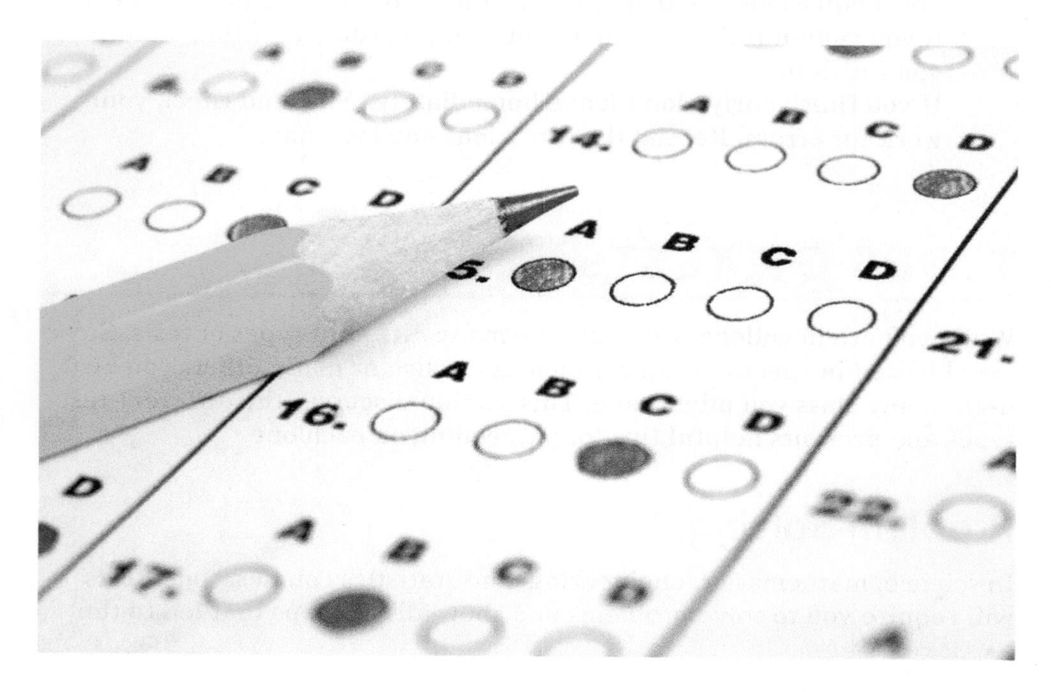

Example of a Scantron Answer Sheet

Each time you fill in a Scantron answer sheet, make sure that the number on the answer sheet corresponds to the number of the item on the test, and make sure that all bubbles are filled in completely.

Vixit/Shutterstock

Computerized Tests

Computerized tests are often taken in a computer lab or testing center and are usually *not* administered online. (Read this chapter's Tech Tip about *online* tests.) Computerized tests and test questions can be significantly different from one another depending on the kind of test, the academic subject, and whether the test was written by the instructor, a textbook company, or another source. Be sure to take advantage of any practice test opportunities to get a better sense of what these tests and test questions will be like. Often they are timed, as is the case with most computerized placement tests. The more experience you have with computerized tests, the more comfortable you will be taking them, which is true with the other test types.

Some multiple-choice computerized tests allow you to scroll through all the questions, while others only allow you to see one question at a time. Some computerized tests might not allow you to return to questions you've already completed to double-check your answers.

For computerized tests in math and other subjects that require you to solve problems, be sure to check each answer before you submit it. Also, know in advance whether you are allowed to use additional materials, such as a calculator or scratch paper, for working the problems.

Laboratory Tests

In many science courses, you will have laboratory tests that require you to move from one lab station to the next to solve problems, identify parts of models or specimens, or explain chemical reactions. To prepare for lab tests, always attend your labs, take good notes, and study your lab notebook carefully before the test.

You might also have lab tests in foreign language courses that can include both oral and written sections. Work with a partner or study group to prepare for oral exams. Have group members ask one another questions that require the use of key vocabulary words.

Open-Book and Open-Notes Tests

Although you may like the idea of being able to refer to your book or notes during an exam, open-book and open-note tests are usually harder than other tests, not easier. You won't really have time to read whole passages during an open-book exam. Study as completely as you would for any other test, and do not be fooled into thinking that you don't need to know the material. The best way to prepare for an open-book test is to study as you would for any other test. But as you prepare, you can develop a list of topics and the page numbers where they are covered in your text or in your lecture notes. Type a three-column grid (or use an Excel spreadsheet) with your list of topics in alphabetical order in the first column and corresponding pages from your textbook and lecture notebook in the second and third columns so that you can refer to them quickly when necessary.

During the test, keep an eye on the time. Don't waste time looking up information in your text or notes if you are sure of your answers. Instead, wait until you have finished the test, and then, if you have extra time, go back and look up answers and make any necessary changes.

techtip

CONQUER ONLINE TESTS

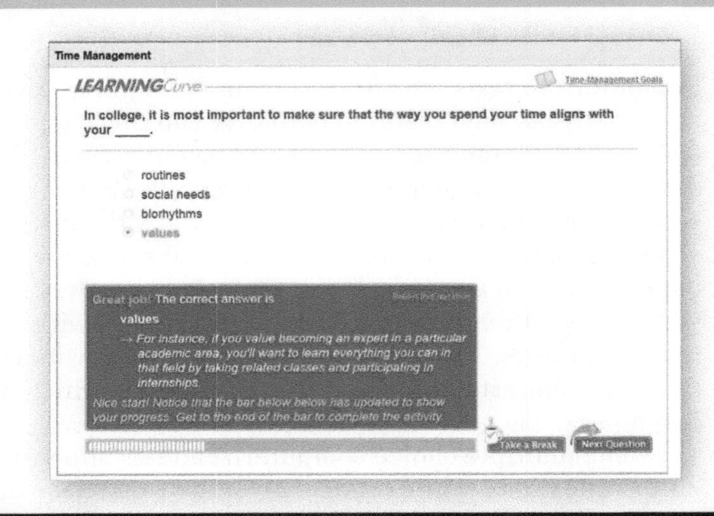

The Problem

You don't know how to take an online test—a test that is administered online.

The Fix

Learn to avoid rookie errors that can trip you up.

How to Do It

1. ***Study with other people.*** Whether an online test is part of a self-paced online course or a face-to-face course, start a study group, either in person or online, as far in advance of the exam as possible.
2. ***Get organized.*** An online, open-book quiz or test can take longer than a normal test if you're not sure where to locate the information you need. When you prepare, study like you would for a normal, in-class, timed test; your notes and books should be for occasional reference only. Don't think you can learn everything you need to know on the day of the test.
3. ***Resist the temptation to surf the Web for answers.*** The answer you pick might not be what your instructor is looking for. It's much better to check your notes to see what you were taught in class.
4. ***Work together.*** If your instructor allows collaboration on tests, open up an instant message window with a fellow student. Take the test together, and take it early.
5. ***Stay focused.*** When you're taking an online test, it's easy to fall prey to real-life diversions like Facebook, iTunes, or a sudden urge to rearrange your closet. Whatever you do, take the test seriously. Go somewhere quiet where you can concentrate—not Starbucks. A quiet, remote spot in the library is ideal.
6. ***Budget your time.*** Keep an eye on the clock so that you'll be sure to finish the entire test. Tackle the easy questions first. Once you get the easy questions out of the way, you can revisit the harder ones.
7. ***Practice using the test interface.*** Ask your instructor if you can practice with a "zero-points" quiz so you can familiarize yourself with the testing site and the question setup. You don't want to be nervous about how the site works while you are answering questions on a test that will affect your grade. The sample online question shown above is from LearningCurve, an online self-assessment system that is designed to work with your textbook.
8. ***Ask about special rules.*** Online tests can be set up differently than regular tests. Find out in advance if there's a penalty for wrong answers, if you can retake the test, and if you can go back and change an answer.
9. ***Plan for an intermittent connection.*** There's always the risk of losing your Internet connection in the middle of the test. To be on the safe side, type your answers and essays into a Word document. Then leave time at the end of the test session to cut and paste them into the test itself.
10. ***Use all the time allotted.*** If you finish early, take a few minutes to check your answers and spelling carefully. (That's good advice for traditional tests, too.)

EXTRA STYLE POINTS: Use study guides or a study session from each class to create your own online practice test. If you use Google Drive, you can create a file called a "form," which allows you to create a test, quiz, or survey that you can use with your study group. Everyone in the group can use it at times that are convenient for them, rather than only when the group can get together.

Take-Home Tests

Some instructors may allow you to take tests outside class and refer to your textbook, notes, and other resources. Take-home tests are usually more difficult than in-class tests. Read the directions and questions as soon as you receive the test to help you estimate how much time you will need to complete it. Remember that your instructor will expect your essay answers to look more like out-of-class papers—proofread and edited—than like the essays you would write during an in-class test.

It is probably no surprise that issues of academic honesty can arise for take-home tests. If you usually work with a study group or in a learning community for the course, check with the instructor in advance to determine if any type of group work is allowed on the test.

TYPES OF QUESTIONS

Your instructors choose not only what types of exams they give you, but also what types of questions to include on the test so you can demonstrate what you are learning in the course. You may take an exam that has one type of question or multiple types of questions. This section includes strategies to help you answer different types of questions successfully.

Essay Questions

Essay questions require students to write a few paragraphs in response to each question. Many college instructors have a strong preference for essay questions for a simple reason: They require deeper thinking than other types of questions. Generally, advanced courses are more likely to include essay exams. To be successful on essay exams, follow these guidelines:

1. **Budget your exam time.** Quickly go over the entire exam, and note the questions that are the easiest for you to answer. Estimate the approximate amount of time you should spend on each essay question based on its point value. Remember, writing long answers to questions that have low point values can be a mistake because it takes up precious time you might need to answer questions that count more toward your total grade. Be sure you know whether you must answer all the questions or if you should choose which questions to answer. Wear a watch so that you can monitor your time, and don't forget to leave a few minutes to review and proofread your essay.
2. **Actively read the whole question.** Many well-prepared students write good answers to questions that were not asked, or write good answers to only part of the question. When that happens, they may lose points or even fail the exam.
3. **Develop a brief outline of your answer before you begin to write.** Make sure that your outline responds to all parts of the question. Use your first paragraph to introduce the main points; use the other paragraphs to describe each point in more depth. If you begin to lose

your concentration, you will be glad to have the outline to help you regain your focus. If you find that you are running out of time and cannot complete an essay question, provide an outline of key ideas at the very least. Instructors usually assign points on the basis of your coverage of the main topics from the material. That means you will usually earn more points by responding briefly to all parts of the question than by addressing just one part of the question in detail. You might receive some credit for your outline even if you cannot finish the essay.

4. **Write concise, organized answers.** Some students answer essay questions by quickly writing down everything they know on the topic. Long answers are not necessarily good answers. Answers that are too general, unfocused, or disorganized may not earn high scores.
5. **Know the key task words in essay questions.** Being familiar with key task words that appear in an essay question will help you frame your answer more specifically. Table 1 lists common key task words. If your instructor allows you to do so, consider circling or underlining key words in the question so that you are sure of how to organize your answer.

TABLE 1 › Key Task Words in Essay Questions

Analyze	Break the whole topic into parts to explain it better; show how the parts work together to produce the overall pattern.
Compare	Identify similarities in ideas, events, or objects. Don't just describe the elements; state how they are alike.
Contrast	Identify the differences between ideas, events, or objects. Don't just describe the ideas; state how they are different.
Criticize/Critique	Judge something; give your opinion. Criticism can be positive, negative, or mixed. A critique should generally include your own judgments (supported by evidence) and those of experts who agree with you.
Define	Give the meaning of a word or expression.
Describe	Give more information about a topic.
Discuss	Give broad statements backed up by detailed information. Discussion often includes identifying the important questions related to an issue and trying to answer these questions.
Evaluate	Discuss the strengths and weaknesses of an idea or a position. When you evaluate, you stress the idea of how well something meets a certain standard.
Explain	Clarify a statement. Explanations generally focus on why or how something has come about.
Justify	Argue in support of a decision or conclusion by showing evidence or reasons that support the argument. Try to support your argument with both logical and concrete examples.
Narrate	Relate a series of events in the order they occurred, as you do when you tell a story.
Outline	Present a series of main points in order. Some instructors want a formal outline with numbers and letters.
Summarize	Give information in brief form, without examples and details. A summary is short but covers all the important points.

Multiple-Choice Questions

Multiple-choice questions provide a number of possible answers, often between three and five. The answer choices are usually numbered (1, 2, 3, 4, . . .) or lettered (a, b, c, d, . . .), and the test taker is supposed to select the correct or the best one. Preparing for multiple-choice tests requires you to actively review all of the material that has been covered for a specific period, such as a week or a month. Reviewing flash cards, summary sheets, mind maps, or the recall column in your lecture notes is a good way to review large amounts of material efficiently.

Look for particular cues and quirks that multiple-choice questions include. Take extra care when choosing the answer to questions that contain words such as *not, except, all,* and *but.* Also read each answer choice carefully; be suspicious of choices that use words such as *always, never,* and *only.* These choices are often (but not always) incorrect. Often the correct answer is the option that is the most comprehensive.

In some multiple-choice questions, the first part of the question is an incomplete sentence called the stem, and the answer choices complete the sentence. In these questions, any answer choices that do not fit the grammar of the stem correctly are usually wrong. For example, in Figure 3, "Margaret Mead was an" is the stem. Which of the four answer options does not grammatically fit the stem, and can therefore be ruled out?

FIGURE 3 › Example of a Multiple-Choice Question

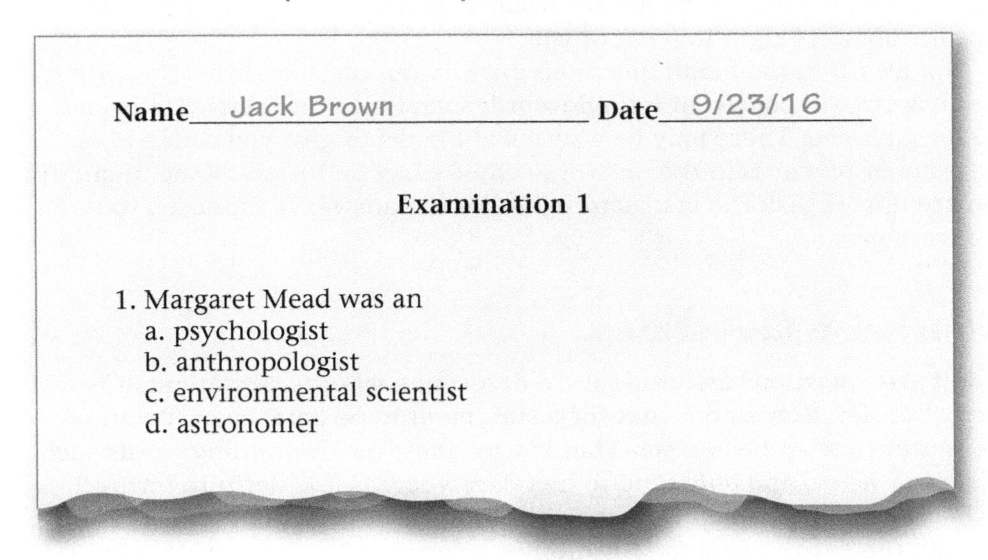

Name Jack Brown Date 9/23/16

Examination 1

1. Margaret Mead was an
   a. psychologist
   b. anthropologist
   c. environmental scientist
   d. astronomer

To avoid becoming confused by answer choices that sound alike, predict your own answer to the question before reading the options. Then choose the answer that best matches your prediction.

If you are totally confused by a question, place a check mark in the margin and come back to it later. Sometimes a question later in the exam may provide a clue to the answer of the question you are unsure about. If you have absolutely no idea, look for an answer that at least has some pieces of information. If there is no penalty for guessing, fill in an answer for every question, even if it is just a guess. If there is a penalty for guessing, don't just choose an answer at random; leaving the answer blank might be a wiser choice. Finally, always go back, if you have time at the end, and double-check that you chose the right answer for the right question, especially if you are using a Scantron form.

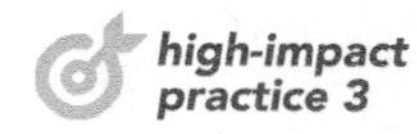

your turn Work Together

Is One Type of Exam Better than Another?

Many college instructors do not give essay exams in first-year courses, and instead use multiple-choice questions. With a small group of other students, discuss the kind of learning that multiple-choice exams measure, and the kind of learning they miss. Which type of exam do students in the group prefer? Share your reactions and ideas with the whole class.

Fill-in-the-Blank Questions

Fill-in-the-blank questions consist of a phrase, sentence, or paragraph with a blank space indicating where the student should provide the missing word or words. In many ways, preparing to answer fill-in-the-blank questions is similar to getting ready to answer multiple-choice items, but fill-in-the-blank questions can be harder because you do not have a choice of possible answers right in front of you.

Not all fill-in-the-blank questions are written the same way. Sometimes the answers will consist of a single word; sometimes the instructor is looking for a phrase. There may be a series of blanks to give you a clue about the number of words in the answer, or there may be just one long blank. If you are unsure, ask the instructor whether the answer is supposed to be one word or more.

True/False Questions

True/False questions ask students to determine whether a statement is correct or not. Remember that for a statement to be true, every detail of the sentence must be correct. That is why questions containing words such as *always, never,* and *only* tend to be false, whereas less definite terms such as *often* and *frequently* suggest the statement might be true. Read through the entire exam to see whether information in one question will help you answer another. Do not begin to second-guess what you know or doubt your answers just because a sequence of questions appears to be all true or all false.

Matching Questions

Matching questions are set up with terms in one column and descriptions or definitions in the other, and you must match the proper term with its definition. Before matching any items, review all of the terms and descriptions. Then match the terms you are sure of. As you do so, cross out both the term and its description, and use the process of elimination to help you answer the remaining items. To prepare for matching questions, try using flash cards and lists that you create from the recall column in your notes.

OVERCOMING TEST ANXIETY

Ace the Test—Any Type of Test

No matter what type of test you are taking, read each question carefully so that you have the best chance of selecting the right answer. And remember, when you take a machine-scored test, one of the simplest and most important steps you can take is to make sure you match the questions with your answer sheet numbers.

Test anxiety takes many different forms. Part of dealing with test anxiety is understanding why it happens and identifying its symptoms. Whatever the reason for test anxiety, you should know that it is common among college students.

Test anxiety has many causes. It can be the result of the pressure that students put on themselves to succeed. Some stress connected with taking exams is natural and can motivate you to perform better. However, when students put too much pressure on themselves or set unrealistic goals, the result can be stress that is no longer motivating. The expectations of parents, a spouse or partner, friends, and other people who are close to you can also create test anxiety.

Finally, some test anxiety is caused by lack of preparation. The awareness that you are not prepared, that you have fallen behind on assigned reading, homework, or other academic commitments, is usually the source of anxiety. Procrastination can also be a big problem because if you do poorly on the first test in a course, you will be under even more pressure to do well on other tests to pull up your course grade. This situation becomes even more difficult if the units of the course are cumulative—that is, if they build on one another, as in math and foreign languages—or if the final exam includes all the material that has been covered throughout the course.

Some test anxiety comes from a negative prior experience. Forgetting past failures can be a challenge; however, the past is not the present. If you carefully follow the strategies in this chapter, you are likely to do well on future tests. Remember that a little anxiety is OK, but if you find that anxiety is getting in the way of your performance on tests and exams, be sure to ask for help from your college counseling center.

Symptoms of Test Anxiety

Test anxiety can manifest itself in many ways. Some students feel it on the very first day of class. Other students begin showing symptoms of test anxiety when it's time to start studying for a test. Others do not get nervous until the night before the test or the morning of an exam day. And some students experience symptoms only while they are actually taking a test.

Symptoms of test anxiety can include:

- butterflies in the stomach
- queasiness
- nausea
- headaches
- an increased heart rate
- hyperventilation, which is unusually deep or rapid breathing as a result of anxiety
- shaking, sweating, or muscle cramps
- "going blank" during the exam and being unable to remember information

Test anxiety can undermine the success of any college student, no matter how intelligent, motivated, and prepared. That is why it is important to seek help from your college's counseling service or another professional if you think that you have severe test anxiety. If you are not sure where to go for help, ask your adviser or counselor, but seek help promptly! If your symptoms are so severe that you become physically ill (with headaches, hyperventilation, or vomiting), you should also consult your physician or campus health center.

Types of Test Anxiety

Students who experience test anxiety don't necessarily feel it in all testing situations. For example, you might do fine on classroom tests but feel anxious during standardized examinations such as a college placement test. One reason such standardized tests can create anxiety is that they can change your future. One way of dealing with this type of test anxiety is to ask yourself: What is the worst that can happen? Remember that no matter what the result, it is not the end of the world. How you do on standardized tests might limit some of your options, but going into these tests with a negative attitude will certainly not improve your chances for success.

Test anxiety can often be subject-specific. For example, some students have anxiety about taking math tests. It is important to understand the differences between anxiety that arises from the subject itself and general test anxiety. Perhaps subject-specific test anxiety relates to old beliefs about yourself, such as "I'm no good at math" or "I can't write well." Now is the time to try some positive self-talk and realize that by preparing well, you can be successful even in your hardest courses. If the problem continues, talk to a counselor to learn about strategies that can help you deal with such fears. Take the following test anxiety quiz to find out more about how you feel before taking tests.

Test Anxiety Quiz

Do you experience feelings of test anxiety? Read each of the following questions and consider your responses. If your answer to a question is "yes," place a check mark in the box. If your answer is "no," leave the box blank.

Mental

- ☐ Do you have trouble focusing and find that your mind easily wanders while studying the material or during the test itself?
- ☐ During the test, does every noise bother you—sounds from outside the classroom or sounds from other people?
- ☐ Do you often "blank out" when you see the test?
- ☐ Do you remember answers to questions only after the test is over?

Physical

- ☐ Do you get the feeling of butterflies, nausea, or pain in your stomach?
- ☐ Do you develop headaches before or during the test?
- ☐ Do you feel like your heart is racing, that you have trouble breathing, or that your pulse is irregular?
- ☐ Do you have difficulty sitting still, are you tense, or are you unable to get comfortable?

Emotional

- ☐ Are you more sensitive and more likely to lose patience with a roommate or friend before the test?
- ☐ Do you feel pressure to succeed, either from yourself or from your family or friends?
- ☐ Do you toss and turn the night before the test?
- ☐ Do you fear the worst—that you will fail the class or flunk out of college because of the test?

Personal Habits

- ☐ Do you often stay up late studying the night before a test?
- ☐ Do you have a personal history of failure in taking certain types of tests (essay, math, etc.)?
- ☐ Do you drink more than your usual amount of caffeine or forget to eat breakfast before a test?
- ☐ Do you avoid studying until right before a test, choosing to do other activities that are less important because you don't want to think about the test?

See the following for your Test Anxiety Reflection Score.

TEST ANXIETY REFLECTION SCORE

How many items did you check? Count your total, and then see what level of test anxiety you experience.

13–16 Severe: You may want to see if your college counseling center offers individual sessions to provide strategies for dealing with test anxiety. You have already paid for this service through your student fees, so if you have this level of anxiety, take advantage of help that is available for you.

9–12 Moderate: You may want to see if your counseling center offers a seminar on anxiety-prevention strategies. Such seminars are usually offered around midterms or just before final exams. Take the opportunity to do something valuable for yourself!

5–8 Mild: Be aware of what situations—whether it is certain types of classes or particular test formats—might cause anxiety and disrupt your academic success. If you discover a weakness, address it now before it is too late.

1–4 Slight: Almost everyone has some form of anxiety before tests, and it actually can be beneficial! In small doses, stress can improve your performance, so consider yourself lucky.

Strategies for Dealing with Test Anxiety

In addition to studying, eating right, and getting plenty of sleep, you can try a number of simple strategies to overcome the physical and emotional impact of test anxiety:

- **Breathe.** If at any point during a test you begin to feel nervous or you cannot think clearly, take a long, deep breath and slowly exhale to restore your breathing to a normal level.
- **Stretch.** Before you go into the test room, especially before a long final exam, stretch your muscles—legs, arms, shoulders, and neck—just as you would when preparing to exercise.
- **Sit in a relaxed position.** Pay attention to the way you are sitting. As you take the test, sit with your shoulders back and relaxed rather than hunched forward. Try not to clutch your pencil or pen tightly in your hand; take a break and stretch your fingers now and then.
- **Create positive mental messages.** Pay attention to the mental messages that you send yourself. If you are overly negative, turn those messages around. Give yourself encouraging, optimistic messages.
- **Keep your confidence high.** Do not allow others, including classmates, partners, children, parents, roommates, or friends, to reduce your confidence. If you belong to a study group, discuss strategies for relaxing and staying positive before and during tests.

Inhale . . . Exhale . . . Before a test or exam, it is a good idea to take a few minutes for some positive self-talk and a few deep breaths.

Getting the Test Back

Students react differently when they receive their test grades and papers. Some students dread seeing their test grades, but other students look forward to it. Either way, unless you look at your answers—the correct and incorrect ones—and the instructor's comments, you will have no way to evaluate your own knowledge and test-taking strengths. While checking over your graded test, you might also find that the instructor made a grading error that might have cost you a point or two. If that happens, you should let the instructor know.

Review your graded tests, because doing so will help you do better next time. You might find that your mistakes were the result of not following directions, being careless with words or numbers, or even thinking too hard about a multiple-choice question. Mistakes can help you learn, so refer to your textbook and notes to better understand the source and reason for each mistake. If you are a member of a study group, plan a test review with other group members; this allows you to learn from your mistakes and those of the others in the group.

If you have any questions about your grade, that is an excellent reason to visit your instructor during his or her office hours or before or after class; your concern will show the instructor that you want to succeed. When discussing the exam with your instructor, you might be able to negotiate a few points in your favor. Avoid making demands, though, and always be respectful.

your turn Write and Reflect

high-impact practice 2

What Advice Would You Give?

What do you do when an instructor returns an exam to you? Do you just look at the grade, or do you review the items you answered correctly and incorrectly? Write a one- or two-page paper in which you describe to new first-year students what steps they should take after receiving an exam back from an instructor—an exam on which they earned either a very good or very poor grade. Write persuasively, and then share your position verbally with a few other students in your class.

Above all, don't let a bad test grade get you down. One characteristic that differentiates successful students from unsuccessful ones is resilience—that is, whether they can bounce back from a disappointing grade or performance. Almost every college student has experienced disappointment—perhaps on a test or paper, the athletic field, or in music or dance. Don't run from a bad grade; learn from it. Review the mistakes you made, and talk with your instructor about what you misunderstood and how you can improve your performance on the next graded activity.

is this you?

Bouncing Back from a Bad Grade

You bombed a test, and now you are feeling hopeless and unsure about how to do better. First, know that a bad grade is not the end of the world. Almost every student performs poorly at some point in college. Don't let one D or F get you down. Use the opportunity to build your resilience—to become stronger and show your tough spirit. One way to bounce back from disappointment is to take control of the situation. Talk to the course instructor, work to understand what went wrong, and develop a strategy for improvement. That strategy might be finding a tutor, meeting on a regular basis with your instructor, or working with a learning center professional who can help you improve your skills in reading, studying, remembering, and preparing for tests. Your college success instructor can help you decide what first steps you need to take to improve your academic performance.

CHEATING

Imagine what our world would be like if researchers reported fake results that were then used to develop new machines or medical treatments, or to build bridges, airplanes, or subway systems. Fortunately, few researchers falsify their findings; most follow the rules of academic honesty. That honesty is a foundation of higher education, and activities that jeopardize it can damage everyone: your country, your community, your college or university, your classmates, and yourself.

What Is Cheating?

Different colleges define *cheating* in different ways. Some include the following activities in their definition of cheating: looking over a classmate's shoulder for an answer, using a calculator when it is not permitted, obtaining or discussing an exam or individual questions from an exam without permission, copying someone else's lab notes, purchasing term papers over the Internet, watching the video instead of reading the book, and copying computer files. Whatever your college's rules about cheating, it's essential that you follow them.

Many schools do not allow certain activities, in addition to lying or cheating. Here are some examples of prohibited behaviors:

- intentionally inventing information or results
- submitting the same piece of academic work, such as a research paper, for credit in more than one course
- giving your exam answers to another student to copy during an exam or before that exam is given to another class

- bribing anyone in exchange for any kind of academic advantage
- helping or trying to help another student commit a dishonest act

Why Students Cheat and the Consequences of Cheating

Students mainly cheat when they believe they cannot do well on their own. Some college students developed a habit of cheating in high school or even earlier, and do not trust their own ability to succeed in classes. Other students simply don't know the rules. For example, some students incorrectly think that buying a term paper isn't cheating. Some think that using a test file (a collection of actual tests from previous terms) is fair behavior.

Cultural and college differences may cause some students to cheat. In other countries and at some U.S. colleges, students are encouraged to review past exams as practice exercises. Some student government associations or student social organizations maintain test files for use by students. Some colleges permit sharing answers and information for homework and other assignments with friends. Make sure you know the policy at your college.

Pressure from others—family, peers, and instructors—might cause some students to consider cheating. And there is no doubt that we live in a competitive society, where winning can trump all other values. But in truth, grades are nothing if you cheat to earn them. Even if your grades help you get a job, it is what you have actually learned that will help you keep that job and be promoted. If you haven't learned what you need to know, you won't be ready to work in your chosen field.

Sometimes lack of preparation will cause students to cheat. Perhaps they tell themselves that they aren't really dishonest and that cheating just "one time" won't matter. But if you cheat one time, you're more likely to do it again.

Stop! Thief!

When students sit close to each other while taking a test, they may be tempted to let their eyes wander to someone else's answers. Don't let this happen to you. Cheating is the same as stealing. Also, don't offer to share your work or make it easy for other students to copy your work. Reduce temptation by covering your answer sheet.

Jonathan Stark

Cheating in college is not uncommon, and researchers have found that first-year students are more likely to cheat than other students are. Although you might see some students who seem to be getting away with cheating, such behaviors can have severe and life-changing results. In some cases, students who have cheated on exams have been suspended or expelled, and graduates have had their college degrees revoked.

Here are some steps you can take to reduce the likelihood of problems with academic honesty.

1. **Know the rules.** Learn the academic code for your college by going to its Web site or checking the student handbook.
2. **Set clear boundaries.** Refuse when others ask you to help them cheat. This might be hard to do, but you must say no. Leave your cell phone in your book bag; instructors are often suspicious when they see students looking at their cell phones during an exam.
3. **Improve time management.** Be well prepared for all quizzes, exams, projects, and papers.
4. **Seek help.** Find out where you can get help with study skills, time management, and test taking. If your skills are in good shape but the content of the course is too hard, consult your instructor, join a study group, or visit your campus learning center or tutorial service.
5. **Withdraw from the course.** Your college has a policy about dropping courses and a deadline to drop without penalty. You might decide to drop a course that's giving you trouble. Some students choose to withdraw from all classes and take time off before returning to school if they find themselves in over their heads or if a long illness, a family crisis, or something else has caused them to fall behind. But before withdrawing, you should ask about college policies in terms of financial aid and other scholarship programs. See your adviser or counselor before you decide to withdraw.
6. **Reexamine goals.** Stick to your own realistic goals instead of giving in to pressure from family members or friends to achieve impossibly high standards. You might also feel pressure to enter a particular career or profession that doesn't interest you. If that happens, sit down with counseling or career services professionals or your academic adviser and explore your options.

your turn Make Good Choices

Understand Academic Integrity

Sometimes students are confused about what constitutes dishonest behavior in their college classrooms. There are some actions that are on the line between cheating and being honest. Do you think it is acceptable to get answers from another student who took an exam you're about to take earlier in the term or in a prior term? What do you believe your instructors think? If you're not sure, ask your instructors how they view such behavior.

checklist for success

Test Taking

- **Learn as much as you can about the type of test you will be taking.** You will study differently for an essay exam than you will for a multiple-choice test.
- **Realize that you started preparing for test taking the very first day of the course.** Make the most of the first class sessions of the term—they are the most important ones *not* to miss. If you skip class, you are behind on your test preparation from day one.
- **Prepare yourself physically through proper sleep, diet, and exercise.** These behaviors are as important as studying the actual material. You may not control what is on the exams, but you can control your physical readiness to do your best.
- **Prepare yourself emotionally by being relaxed and confident.** Confidence comes from the knowledge that you have prepared well and know the material.
- **If you experience moderate to severe test anxiety, seek help from your counseling center.** Professionals can help you deal with this problem.
- **Develop a systematic plan of preparation for every test.** Be specific about when you are going to study, for how long, and what material you will cover.
- **Join a study group and participate conscientiously and regularly.** Students who join study groups perform better on tests. It's a habit you should practice.
- **Never cheat or plagiarize.** Experience the satisfaction that comes from learning and doing your own work and from knowing that you don't have to worry about getting caught or using material that may be incorrect.
- **Make sure that you understand what constitutes cheating and plagiarism on your campus so that you don't inadvertently do either.** If you are not clear about policies, ask your instructors or the professionals in your campus learning center or writing center.

your experience

ECT
N CHOICES

high-impact practice 2

Test taking is an inevitable part of college life. But you can choose how you are going to prepare for tests, deal with any test anxiety you might feel, and pay attention to your grades and instructor feedback. Reflect on your biggest problem in taking tests. Is it with certain types of tests or all of them? Is it related to certain subjects or any subject? Write a brief summary of strategies you have learned in this chapter to deal with this problem.

APPLY WHAT YOU HAVE LEARNED

Now that you have read and discussed this chapter, consider how you can apply what you have learned to your academic and personal life. The following prompts will help you reflect on the chapter material and its relevance to you both now and in the future.

1. Identify your next upcoming test or exam. What time of day is it scheduled, and what type of test will it be? What strategies have you read about in this chapter that will help you prepare for and take this test?
2. Is there one course you are taking this term that you find especially difficult? If you are anxious about taking tests in that class, adopt a positive self-message to help you stay focused. It could be a favorite quote or even something as simple as "I know I can do it!"

USE YOUR RESOURCES

- **Learning Center**
  Before you take your first tests, locate your campus's learning center. Almost every campus has one, and helping students study for tests is one of its specialties. The best students, good students who want to be the best students, and students with academic difficulties use learning centers and tutoring services. These services are offered by both full-time professionals and highly skilled student tutors, and they are usually free. If you are an online student, there may be a special learning center that focuses on helping you do your best in online courses.
- **Counseling Services**
  College and university counseling centers offer a wide array of services, including workshops and individual or group counseling for test anxiety. Sometimes these services are also offered by the campus health center. Ask your first-year seminar instructor where you can find counseling services on your campus. If you are an adult student, you may be very anxious about your first tests. Seek out services designed specifically for adults.
- **Fellow College Students and Peer Leaders**
  Often the best help we can get is the closest to us. Keep an eye out in your classes, residence hall, and extracurricular activities for the best students, those who appear to be the most serious, purposeful, and directed. Find a tutor. Join a study group. Talk with your peer leader. Students who do these things are much more likely to be successful than those who do not.
- **College and University Exam Preparation Resources**
  A wealth of helpful resources is available from many institutions. For instance, Florida Atlantic University's Center for Learning and Student Success (CLASS) offers a list of tips to help you prepare for exams: **fau.edu/CLASS/success/keys_to_success.php.** The State University of New York offers some excellent strategies for exam preparation: **blog.suny.edu/2013/12/scientifically-the-best-ways-to-prepare-for-final-exams.** And here is some exam preparation advice from the University of Leicester in England: **le.ac.uk/offices/ssds/healthy-living-for-students/preparation-for-exams.**

LaunchPad for *Your College Experience* is a great resource. Go online to master concepts using the LearningCurve study tool and much more. macmillanhighered.com/gardner12e

For Elinor and Emily
G.M.

For Princess Jo jo
L.S.

TRANSWORLD PUBLISHERS LTD
61-63 Uxbridge Road, London W5 5SA

TRANSWORLD PUBLISHERS (AUSTRALIA) PTY LTD
15-25 Helles Avenue, Moorebank, NSW 2170

TRANSWORLD PUBLISHERS (NZ) LTD
3 William Pickering Drive, Albany, Auckland

DOUBLEDAY CANADA LTD
105 Bond Street, Toronto, Ontario M5B IY3

Published 1997 by Doubleday
a division of Transworld Publishers Ltd

Designed by Ian Butterworth

A catalogue record for this book is available
from the British Library

ISBN 0 385 40783 1

Printed in Italy

THE DOUBLEDAY *book of*

PRINCESS STORIES

Geraldine McCaughrean
Illustrated by Lizzie Sanders

THE DOUBLEDAY *book of* PRINCESS STORIES

Geraldine McCaughrean

Illustrated by Lizzie Sanders

DOUBLEDAY

London · New York · Toronto · Sydney · Auckland

CONTENTS

The Gingerbread Boy

Beneath blue skies, a King once planted a forest. In the centre of the forest lay a blue lake, and in the centre of the lake, a green island. In the centre of the island grew a rose garden encircled by a high wall, and in the wall was a silver gate locked with a golden key. In the garden stood a palace, and inside the palace lived a little girl called Princess Mine.

Her mother, the Queen, was dead. But once a week, on Sundays, her father, the King, rowed over to the island. For he owned the golden key. He and Mine would laugh and talk, picnic among the roses or play hide-and-seek on the stairs. It was not a prison, you see. Princess Mine had done nothing wrong. It was just that her father was so lonely, and loved her so much, he wanted to keep her all to himself, keep all her love for himself.

'You are Mine,' he said. 'And what is mine, I do not share.'

In fact he passed a law decreeing that anyone crossing the lake and entering in at the silver gate must DIE!

Every day Mine walked along the empty corridors, sat in the empty halls and looked at the empty garden. And though the rooms were full of toys, she was very, very lonely.

When she had played with all her toys, she went to the library and read stories. But the children in the stories all had pets, or brothers and sisters, or neighbours or uncles or aunts.

Friends.

The lonely Princess envied them dreadfully — even those with wicked stepmothers, or witches living next door.

One day, when Mine had read all the storybooks in the library, she browsed through other kinds — about history, gardening, science. . . In the middle of reading a cookery book, she got up and ran to the empty palace kitchen, flung open the larder door and took out flour, milk, sugar, ginger and a few other things besides. Then she mixed some gingerbread dough, and rolled it out on the golden kitchen table.

First she shaped a dog, with two raisin eyes. Then she made a cat with a liquorice tail. Next she made a chicken with parsley for feathers, and last of all — best of all — a boy with cherries for cheeks. Mine dusted her gingerbread friends with icing sugar, sprinkled them with tears of loneliness. . . then ran and fetched a book of magic from the library. Finally she found what she was looking for:

'With my hands I made you.
With my heart I want you.
With a wish may you come to LIFE!'

Mine read out the spell, first in a whisper, then in a shout.

Woof! Woof! The dog came to life.

Miaow! The cat came to life.

Pck-pck-pck! The chicken came to life — though it did have green feathers.

Last of all — best of all — the boy came to life and climbed down from the table. He was a little shorter than Mine, but he could run almost as fast, and whistle, which she could not.

'I shall call you Ginger,' said the Princess.

'I shall call you Mine,' said the boy.

Princess Mine and Ginger ate picnics in the rose garden, and ran races and threw sticks for the gingerbread dog. They played hide-and-seek with the gingerbread cat, and fed the gingerbread chicken on raisins and cherries. They sprawled in the library reading books and playing chess. They did some cooking, too.

But every Sunday, Ginger and the animals hid themselves up in the palace loft, so that the King, on his weekly visit, would not find out about them.

Then, one Tuesday morning, very early, the King set out across the lake towards the green island. Under his arm was a bright, ribbony parcel for Princess Mine. Today was her birthday, and he wanted to surprise her.

The boat bumped the bank. In the lock the golden key turned. Up the stairs climbed footsteps so quiet that no-one woke. The floorboards made no squeak, the hinges no creak, as the bedroom door swung open.

'WHAT'S THIS!?'

There on the bed, piled as high as six eiderdowns, were rabbits and chicks, kittens and puppies, kids, hamsters, doves and mice. And underneath them all were Mine and Ginger, sleeping hand-in-hand.

'PREPARE TO DIE!' bawled the King.

With a great fluttering, scurrying scamper, the animals dashed out past the King, leaving Mine and Ginger blinking in the morning light.

'WHAT HAVE YOU TO SAY FOR YOURSELF, DAUGHTER?' demanded the King.

Mine shrugged. 'That I was lonely before, and that now I am not. That this palace of yours was once a prison to me; now it's full of friends. Everyone needs friends, Papa. Even you.' And she got out of bed and kissed him.

Well, all of a sudden the King saw how wrong he had been to leave her all alone and lonely. But it was too late. There was nothing he could do.

'I passed a law and the law cannot be broken,' he said, tears rolling down his cheeks. 'Even I cannot break it. All these friends of yours must die, because they crossed the lake, and entered in at the silver gate.'

'No, they didn't!' said Mine with a laugh.

'It's no good, child. Lying won't save them. How else could they be here?'

'Come with me and I'll show you,' said Princess Mine. She led the King downstairs to the palace kitchen. And there she took flour and sugar, butter, ginger and milk, and made some dough. She rolled it out — bigger then ever before — and cut out the figure of a lady. Then she fetched the magic book from the library and read out the spell. There stood a Queen — a little taller than the King, though not so fat. And she could whistle, which the King could not.

So Ginger and the animals did not have to die, because they had never crossed the lake, nor opened the silver gate.

But they did soon after. They all trooped outside, climbed into a rowing boat, and paddled across to the other bank. And there they joined the crowds flocking to see the wedding of the King to his gingerbread Queen.

You'll be glad to know that the two lived happily ever after. Because the King was not lonely any more.

Besides, the Queen could whistle, and she taught him how.

Golden Tree, Silver Tree and Copper

The western sea is silvery, but not so silvery as the fish who swim in it. Each year, trout swim up the long sea lochs past the high, grim walls of Scottish castles. And one such trout, once upon a time, swam always to the island of Eigg. There lived King Rowan and his wife, Silver Tree.

Once a year, the Queen asked a question of the sea trout, and her question was always the same:

'Fish who swims through all the sea
Whose is the fairest face you see?'

The trout always answered as she expected:

'On all the shores of ocean blue,
The fairest one by far is you',

which made the Queen happy, because she was vain.

Then King Rowan and Queen Silver Tree had a baby girl, and called her Golden Tree, that being the King's idea.

'Why? Is she more precious than me?' demanded the Queen.

'Not at all!' said the King. 'But see how golden her skin is compared with yours, pale as moonlight.' And he would not change his mind, no, he would not, which says something for the character of King Rowan, as his wife's temper was frightening.

Golden Tree had no such temper. She was as sweet and modest as the Queen was fierce and vain. To tell the truth, she was soon a lot more precious in the eyes of the King, the huntsmen, the gardeners and everyone on Eigg, who loved her dear as dear.

One year, when the trout were running, the tide brought in a Prince from the mainland in a boat with silver sails. 'I have heard tell of the beauty and sweetness of Princess Golden Tree,' he said to the King, 'and I have come to ask. . .' but then he saw Golden Tree and could not finish what he was going to say, because she was more beautiful than he had ever imagined.

'Daughter, daughter, do you like what you see of this Prince?' asked the King.

But Princess Golden Tree could not answer, because she had just seen Prince Pine, and she had never seen the like, neither awake nor in her dreams.

Meanwhile Queen Silver Tree was down at the lochside, calling out to the magic trout:

'Fish who swims through all the sea,
Whose is the fairest face you see?'

And the sea trout replied:

'As Spring gives way to Summer
And age gives way to youth,
The Princess Golden Tree has now
The fairest face, in truth',

which did not please the Queen. She picked up a pebble and threw it at the trout. Then she went raging back to the castle and flung herself down on her bed. Her skin turned paler than ever, and she vowed she would die without the proper medicine.

'And what is that, my dear?' said the King in great alarm.

'The heart of Golden Tree, roasted on a silver platter!'

Aghast, King Rowan thought quickly. 'Golden Tree is gone, my dear. A Prince came to ask for her, and I let her go — to the mainland where beauty is hardly noticed, as you know.'

'Fetch her back and kill her!' groaned Silver Tree. 'For her heart is all that can save me!'

So the King hurried down to the harbour, where Prince and Princess were still talking and not talking, gazing into each other's eyes. The King drew his dagger. . .

'Quick! Quick!' he said, cutting through the ship's mooring rope. 'Sail for the mainland! Your mother is so sick with jealousy of your beauty, Golden Tree, that I'm afeared you may die of it!'

Then, as the two sailed away, King Rowan went to the butcher's shop and bought a deer's heart and took it home for tea, saying it was the heart of Golden Tree.

A year later, when the trout were running, Queen Silver Tree went down to the sea loch again.

'Fish who swims through all the sea,
Whose is the fairest face you see?'

And the trout replied:

'In all my runs along the shores,
I never see the like of yours
Until I reach where Golden Tree
Sits with her baby on her knee.'

The Queen hurled a stone at the trout and stormed back to the castle. This time she did not take to her bed, but boarded a ship and, taking the helm, steered it across the ocean swell. Wind and rain in her face, she pointed ahead through mist and spray, shouting commands at the crew. No Viking raider ever ploughed more menacingly over the ocean swell. Above the castle of Princess Golden Tree, the gulls shrieked out a warning.

Prince Pine was away reaping heather, but Golden Tree saw the longship and knew the figure at the helm. So she locked every castle door and put her baby, little Copper Tree, safe in the cradle.

'Golden Tree, my dear!' called her mother at the door. 'You left so suddenly, I had no time to wish you well. Now I hear you have a baby! Let me in to see this granddaughter of mine!'

But Golden Tree pretended she could not open the door. 'Wait a little till my husband comes home!' she called through the lock. 'He has the keys to the door.'

'I will! But while we wait, won't you just put your little finger through the keyhole, so that I may kiss it?'

Golden Tree could see no harm in that, so she put her little finger through the keyhole and — ouch! — felt the stab of a rose thorn. The thorn was poisoned, and down she fell, as cold as death. And all that greeted Prince Pine on his return was the crying of his child and the sight of his wife on the floor.

He thought there was no living without her, and he found there was no parting from her loveliness. So, telling no-one, he made a coffin of glass for her and placed her in it, within a locked room, and kept the only key himself. In his sorrow, little Copper Tree was his only comfort, but though he loved her dearly as she grew, even she could not make him smile, not any more.

One day, when Prince Pine set off a-planting trees, Copper Tree found his keys and ran after him. But he was gone. Being an inquisitive little girl, she went about the castle matching each key to each lock, until she came to the door-that-must-stay-locked. Boldly she went inside.

And there, to her great amazement, she saw a lady encased in a coffin of glass and set about with fresh flowers (which the Prince brought every day from the hillside). It did not take her long to guess: this must be her mother!

Now the Prince had never noticed the thorn in Golden Tree's finger, but Copper Tree saw it at once. 'Poor lady,' she said. 'You have a nasty thorn in your finger. Let me pull it out, or you will have bad dreams...'

That night, Prince Pine came home and his little daughter greeted him. 'What, no smile for me, Daddy?'

'I fear I have not,' he replied. 'My face has forgotten how to smile.'

'Oh, but I could make it, if you'd just close your eyes!' she said.

Prince Pine closed his eyes with a terrible sigh. Copper Tree opened the door, and in came Golden Tree, as lovely as the day she had seemed to die. 'Open your eyes now, Daddy!'

The Prince opened his eyes — and never wanted to close them again, nor ever to stop smiling. For there were his two girls, Golden and Copper, laughing like rain on a sea loch.

Meanwhile the trout were running again, and Queen Silver Tree went down to the sea again.

'Fish who swims through all the sea,
Whose is the fairest face you see?'

asked Queen Silver Tree, way out on her western isle.

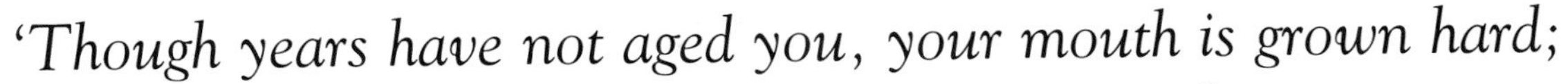

'Though years have not aged you, your mouth is grown hard;
And pride and cruelty your beauty have scarred.
Fairest by far across the sea
Is your daughter dear, kind Golden Tree;
And Copper Tree will fairer be —
So ask no more for flattery!'

At this, the Queen heaved a rock at the trout and ran back to the castle. She leapt aboard a boat and steered it herself across the ocean swell, to where the Prince's castle stood. The gulls screamed a warning.

The Prince was away mustering cattle, and Golden Tree was afraid when she looked out and saw the longboat coming, more dangerous than Vikings, blacker than thunderstorms.

'I'm afeared my mother has come to kill me a second time!' she said to Copper Tree. 'You must hide and I shall lock the door.'

But Copper Tree shook her head. 'No, Mother dear. We must go down and greet her. She is my grandmother, after all, and she may be changed, after all this time.'

So Golden Tree and Copper Tree went down to the shore to greet Queen Silver Tree. And sure enough she came ashore with a loving-cup in her hand.

'Drink to our meeting, daughter dear! Drink to our friendship, granddaughter dear!' and she held out the goblet — full to the brim with poison.

'We have a custom in these parts,' said Copper Tree, in her small, tinkling voice. 'A visitor must always drink first. So drink yourself, Grandmamma, and then we shall drink after.'

'Yes,' said Golden Tree. 'Drink.'

'Yes,' cried the gulls flying overhead. 'Drink.'

'Drink,' said the captain of the ship she had steered.

'Drink,' said the crew.

'Drink,' said the very stones of the beach.

'Drink,' said Prince Pine galloping down to the shore.

'Yes,' said King Rowan stepping down from the ship in person. 'Drink.'

So Queen Silver Tree drank, and fell dead just where she had meant her daughter and granddaughter to lie. They put her aboard the longship and set it out to sea, and the tides took it who-knows-where, out on the treeless ocean.

So Prince Pine and Golden Tree lived happily for ever, and Rowan was a true friend to them. But their best friend of all was Copper Tree, who learned from the sea trout to be wise. In fact, she learnt such wisdom that when the sea trout told her that she was the fairest in the world, she said, 'Get away with your flattering, you foolish fishy, or I'll cook you for supper!'

SPOILED

There was once a Princess whose parents loved her too much. They tried to make her happy every minute of every day, and so they brought her everything she asked for, and never told her, 'No'. There was a saying among the palace servants: 'What Winnie wants, Winnie must have.' And there seemed no end to what Winnie wanted.

On the day before her seventh birthday, her mother, the Queen, looked around the bedroom covered with toys and sighed. 'Whatever can we give you, darling Winnie? You seem to have everything already.'

Winnie took a deep breath: 'I want a gold-and-silver dress

and lots of pretty jewels and I want long golden ringlets. I want it always to be my birthday and I want to know everything, without ever going to school!'

Her father, the King, sighed. For the very first time, he shook his head and said, 'No. I'm sorry, Winnie. There's no money left in the exchequer, and your hair is the hair you were born with. And as for school. . .'

But Winnie was not listening. At the sound of that terrible word — NO — she had slammed out of the room, out of the palace and away into the wide world. 'If they won't give me what I want, I shall just have to get it for myself!'

She walked and walked until she came to a town and, in the centre of the town, a tall house. Parked outside was a glass coach with six white horses, and beside the coach stood an elderly lady.

Down the steps came the prettiest girl that Winnie had ever seen, wearing . . . a beautiful dress of gold and silver lace!

At once Winnie said, 'Oh! How I WANT that dress!'

The old lady looked from Winnie to the pretty girl and back again, then she sadly sighed and said, 'Go indoors, Cinderella. What Winnie wants, Winnie must have.'

So the girl cast her sad blue eyes in the direction of the skyline, where a distant castle twinkled with lights. 'Now I shall never go to the ball!' she sighed before turning back inside and taking off the dress. Winnie put it on. It fitted perfectly. And the skirts of gold and silver lace swished so sweetly as Winnie walked, that she could not hear Cinderella quietly sobbing on the step of the glass coach.

Outside the city, her path lay through a forest. All night Winnie walked until, at dawn, a tangle of rose briars blocked her way. Someone was hacking through them, for the briars shook to the sound. 'Are you going to take long?' called Winnie. 'I am in a fearful hurry.'

The most handsome Prince she had ever seen emerged and leaned forward on his sword to catch his breath. The sword hilt shone with every kind of precious gem. 'Good morning, maiden. It may take me many days to cut through these briars. You had better go another way.' Winnie did not hear him. She was too much intent on gazing at his sword.

'Oh, let me see! All those pretty jewels! How I do WANT them!'

The prince turned a little pale, and his smile faded. 'But the enchantment! The Sleeping—' Then, sighing, he bowed low and presented her with his sword. 'What Winnie wants, Winnie must have.' With only one more longing look at the turrets of a palace almost hidden behind the entanglement of briars, the prince mounted his horse and galloped away.

With the jewelled sword through her sash, Winnie danced off across the desert to where the sea pounded on a rocky shore. There, in the window of a high tower, sat Rapunzel, the happiest woman Winnie had ever seen. Her golden hair trickled down the wall, intertwining with passion flowers, and she whispered to Winnie, 'I hope one day you are as happy as I am, little girl.'

'I would be if I had hair like yours,' said Winnie, her voice sour with jealousy.

Rapunzel's smile melted away. 'But what when he comes?' she started to say. 'What when he cannot find the Golden Stair to climb?' Then Rapunzel sighed the saddest of sighs. 'What Winnie wants, Winnie must have.' And she dropped down from her window a pair of golden scissors. 'Take whatever you want.'

So Winnie climbed and snipped, climbed and snipped every last ringlet of hair. She fastened it to her own with tendrils of passion flowers and went on her way.

At the bottom of the world she came to a dreadful place where the Cog Wheel stands which turns the Earth. And there, straining with all his might to hold the wheel still, stood The Man Who Knows.

'Oo. It's so cold here,' said Winnie.

'Winnie wants it always to be her birthday,' said The Man Who Knows. 'So this side of the world must always be winter, so that her side may have the tenth of June for ever.'

Winnie was not listening. 'I came here because I want to know everything, without having to go to school.'

'Mmmm. Well, I will tell you just four things,' he said. 'Far away, in a big town, Cinderella is crying. Winnie wanted her dress. So now Cinderella cannot go to the ball.

Deep in the forest, Sleeping Beauty lies spellbound for ever. The prince who should have woken her has no sword to cut through the briars.

High in a tower, Rapunzel sits crying. Her prince came back for her, but had no golden plait to climb and so he rode away.'

'Stop! Stop!' cried Winnie. 'Is everyone in the world unhappy because of me?' She covered her eyes.

'No, no, my dear! Your mother and father are quite relieved you went away. Even now they are saying, "What a mercy, not to have to keep buying Winnie what she wants." '

'I didn't want to know that! I don't want it to be true! I don't want any of it to have happened!'

'Ah!' said The Man Who Knows. 'To make that so, I'd have to turn the world back to yesterday. I've never done that before.'

'Oh, turn it!' begged Winnie. 'Let me help! Oh, I do so WANT to undo today!'

'What Winnie wants, Winnie must have,' laughed the man. And, with a gigantic push, they rolled the world back one whole day.

It spun so fast that Winnie fell dizzily to the ground. When she opened her eyes, she was lying in her own bed. 'Mother, Mother! What day is it? I must know what day it is!'

'Why, it's the ninth of June, of course,' said her mother. 'The day before your birthday.'

'Oh, thank goodness!' said Winnie. 'I do so want. . .'

Her mother sighed. 'Yes, Winnie? And what do you want now?'

'To have a party!' cried Winnie. 'A party for you and for the servants and for everyone at school! To say thank you for all the lovely things I've got! That's all. Oh, let me, please!'

Her mother sighed, but it was a sigh of deep contentment. 'Then what Winnie wants, Winnie shall have.'

Princess High-and-Mighty

'All men are fools,' said Princess High-and-Mighty. 'The only man I would ever marry is the man I couldn't see or hear!' And so saying, she took herself off to a high tower with twelve windows, saying she would not — no, she would never — marry.

The King, her father, was appalled. His only child not marry? There would be no grandchildren to inherit the throne! Worse still, he would have to put up with her bad temper for the rest of his days. High-and-Mighty scared her father, not least by her habit of screwing up one eye and glaring at him with the other. When she did that, he knew she could see every grey hair of his beard, every breadcrumb left over from breakfast, every frayed thread in his coat. She had the eyesight of a hawk, and much the same nature.

The King racked his brains. 'So. You want a man you can neither see nor hear, do you?' he thought. 'Very well, young lady. I shall take you at your word.' And he issued a proclamation:

My daughter will marry the man who can reach her unseen and unheard.

Sucking his pen he added, as a footnote:
(Three tries permitted.)

To his surprise, men began to arrive by the dozen. Some were local, some came from abroad. They came because she was a Princess, of course, and very rich. They came because, if they married her, they would one day wear the crown of Polgarslovia. It would have been nice if they had wanted High-and-Mighty for herself, thought the King . . . but then who would?

They crept up to the tall tower on hands and knees. But before they were within one mile of it, a herald would come galloping with a letter from Princess High-and-Mighty. The letter simply said, *Seen you.*

They approached by night, falling into bogs, twisting their ankles in rabbit holes. But before they were within a mile of the tower, a beam of light would shine on them from one of the twelve windows and a voice would shout, *Heard you!*

They approached in hot-air balloons, but no sooner were they within range, than Princess High-and-Mighty fired an arrow from one of the twelve windows, and the balloons sank slowly to earth. They came in camouflage green, and disguised as sheep and cows. They came in covered wagons, and slung underneath their horses. But the Princess spotted each and every one, and her contempt for men grew, along with her determination never to marry.

Frank was a forester. He knew nothing about Princesses, and cared even less. All he cared about was animals. So when one day he saw a crow being mobbed by starlings, he swung his jacket to scare them away, then carried the bird about on his

shoulder until it was well again. Another time he found a vixen in a trap, and let her go. She followed him about after that, like a dog. Then once there was a fire in the forest, and he saw a toad cut off by a ring of flame, and actually braved the heat and smoke to rescue it.

'I think,' said the toad (much to Frank's surprise), 'that one good turn deserves another.'

'I agree,' said the crow on Frank's shoulder.

'We should help him find his fortune,' said the vixen.

'I never knew you could talk!' said Frank.

'You never asked,' said the vixen. 'In fact, that's your trouble. You never ask anything of life, and yet you deserve wealth and happiness more than any human I know. You should try for the hand of Princess High-and-Mighty. We would help you.'

Frank shook his head. 'No, thank you. The only girl I ever saw to my liking lives over yonder in a high tower with twelve windows. Don't know who she is, but I know she doesn't like men going close. She's beautiful. Nose like a tortoise, hair like a squirrel — and a way of looking at you like a hawk in the sky!'

'Her, then,' said the animals and looked at each other, rolling their eyes.

The crow was magic, of course. She built a nest in a tree, then told Frank to cut down the tree and chop it into firewood. This he loaded aboard a horse and cart. Then the crow put Frank inside one of her eggs in the nest, the vixen barked, and the horse trotted off towards the high tower.

When it was still a mile away, Princess High-and-Mighty heard the cart coming, and looked out of one of the twelve windows. She saw the cart, the firewood, the nest and, in the nest, the eggs. 'I see you, fool-in-the-egg!' she shouted.

'Ah! What a voice! Like a bittern booming!' sighed Frank. 'I must try again!'

The toad was magic, of course. She opened her mouth as wide as an umbrella, and swallowed Frank down. Then she hopped into a river, swam down to the bottom, and crept slowly, slowly along it towards the tall tower.

Though it happened a mile away, Princess High-and-Mighty heard a splash and looked out of one of the twelve windows. She saw the river, saw the ripples, saw the toad on the river bed. 'I see you, fool-in-the-toad!' she shouted.

'Ah! The eyesight of a fly!' sighed Frank. 'I must reach her!'

The vixen was magic, too, of course. 'Stand still,' she said, 'and trust your friends.' She flicked Frank with her ginger brush, and turned him, then and there, into a book with a thousand pages. Carrying the book in her soft mouth, she set it down in front of the tall tower before trotting away.

Princess High-and-Mighty looked out of the twelve windows and saw the book. Her sharp eyes counted the thousand pages and read the title: *A Book of Princesses*.

Down her spiral stairs she ran and out to where the book lay. Scooping it up eagerly, she found herself holding . . . a young man in her arms.

'You're even cleverer than I am,' she said.

'Not clever enough to know your name,' said Frank. 'What is it?'

'Rose, though they all call me High-and-Mighty.'

'Why?' asked Frank. 'Rose is a beautiful name — almost as beautiful as you.'

The King came speeding from the palace in an open coach, shaking the reins himself, urging on the horses. In the coach rode a fox, a crow and a toad. 'What's this I hear? Someone passed the test? Someone did it? Will you marry him?'

'Yes, Father, I rather think I will,' said Princess Rose, then added nervously, 'if he wants me to.'

'I rather think I do,' said Frank, and the vixen and the crow and the toad barked and cawed and hopped about with delight, till the King's coach rocked on its wheels.

Their happiness was nothing compared with the joy of Frank and Rose after they were married. Bride and groom lived together in the tall, tall tower. When they sat hand-in-hand on its window sill and looked at the view, they could both see all the way to Ever After. And Rose and Frank liked what they saw.

Mermaid Princess

He thought it was a fish at first — something big and strange washed ashore out of the deep ocean. But when he got closer, he saw it was too silvery to be a dead thing. And there were several of them — a whole shoal of scaly sheaths with huge fluke fins, strewn here and there on the beach. Ivan was a fisherman, but he had never seen fish like these in all his days at sea.

Bending to pick one up, he was suddenly bowled off his feet by a pack of young girls, stark naked but for the shell wreaths in their hair, who leapt from behind rocks and ran for the sea. Mermaids, come ashore to play in the rock pools, had taken off their tails to move more easily on dry land. Now they snatched up their tails and fled, barging him to the ground, plunging into the surf with cries like seal cubs.

But Ivan held tight to the tail in his hands, and clutched it to his chest as the sand and spray flew. When he opened his eyes again, a young girl stood in front of him, hands outstretched, pleading for her tail. 'I shall die if I don't have it,' she said.

'Never. You come home with me. I think I might spare you a plate of sardines. Fancy! A real mermaid! I'll make a fortune!'

The mermaid's seal-brown eyes brimmed with tears. 'I shall die if I don't go back on the falling tide,' she said. 'Will you make such a fortune from a dead mermaid?'

Ivan saw how she was trembling, how her tears spilled, how her hands dropped back to her sides in helpless despair.

'I'm sorry,' he said, laying the tail down at her feet. 'I'm a poor man. Sometimes I lose sight of other people's needs in thinking of my own. Go. Before you miss the tide.'

Delightedly the mermaid slithered into her tail and flung herself headlong into the surf. She was beyond the seventh wave before she raised her head above the water again and called, 'Come with me! My father will want to thank you. You won't be sorry you let me go, I promise!'

Ivan did not know what came over him. He was not a good swimmer and he was still dressed in his fisherman's sweater and seaboots. But he found himself wading out to sea, just to touch the fingertips she stretched out to him. And once he had touched those fingers—

SPLOOSH!

It did not matter that a wave broke over his head and swirled him off his feet. All the while she kept hold of his hand, he was able to breathe — even under the water!

'What's your name?' he shouted, and saw his words, bubble-shaped, rush towards the turquoise surface.

'Marina. Princess Marina.'

It was true. He had not just found a mermaid on the beach; he had found the mermaid among mermaids — only daughter of the King of the Ocean! On the slopes of an undersea mountain range whose peaks broke surface to form a chain of islands, Ivan was introduced to King Neptune.

'He let me go, Father! He could have showed me off like an oddity at the zoo, but he let me go. Wasn't that wonderful of him?'

The King, whose couch was the hull of a sunken galleon and whose belt was made of lobster pots and buoys, pointed his trident at Ivan. 'You are as welcome here as is the sight of our daughter safe and well. Accept our meagre hospitality and stay as long as you wish!' At that, a mermaid blew a conch shell, and the eerie noise of it set the ocean trembling, fetching from every crevice and spinney of weed a host of strange creatures who came to fetch Ivan his every wish.

He ate fruit from the golden weed trees, honey from the floors of the undersea, and shark meat brought home by the great mer-hunters, daring as toreadors. A million brilliantly coloured fish danced in mesmerizing clouds around his head, while cleaner-fish sipped every last grain of dust from his hair and clothes. All the while, Princess Marina kept tight hold of his hand, and told him stories of drowned cities, and great sea storms, of ghost ships, and of meteorites splashing into the sea.

'Stay, won't you?' she said, unsettling him once again with those doleful eyes. 'I don't care a fig for our pale-skinned, hairless, sleek men of Mer. I've always dreamed of a husband from the place of sunshine, with a rough red beard like yours and strong muscles made by good hard work. Stay with me — or do you have a wife waiting for you on the land?'

'I don't,' said Ivan. 'Nor did I ever see a maiden as beautiful as you. But I am from that world and you are from this. You would only have to let go of my hand . . .'

'I never would! Not once! Not even when I fell asleep!'

'. . . And I would drown like a fish on a slab. How could I work with only one hand, no nets and no-one to buy my fish? No. Take me back where I belong. I shall never forget you or your kingdom, but where could we make our home, us two?'

Underwater it is impossible to see a mermaid's tears, but Ivan could taste Marina's — saltier than the surrounding sea. He bowed to the King of Oceans, thanked him for his royal welcome, and led Marina unwillingly away towards shallow water and dry land. The tide was just turning as they kissed goodbye.

'Let me stay with you!' pleaded Marina. 'Perhaps I could live for a year or two on land, if you sprinkled me with water . . .'

'People would stare. People would pry,' said Ivan. 'People would never leave us alone. Go quickly, and let's pretend we dreamed each other.'

For a great many days, back at the slopes of Neptune, Marina did not speak. Her father grew anxious about her. He knew she was thinking of the dry-land fisherman. 'Say the word, daughter, and I will wreck his fishing boat far from shore and fetch him back here to you.'

Marina shook her head. 'No. But if I cannot look after him as a dry-land wife, perhaps I could still take care of him in other ways.'

That is why, when Ivan next wound in his nets he found, in the mouths of the fishes, precious gleaming gems, ancient coins, pearls from the oyster beds.

Far from being poor, Ivan became rich, and the young local girls made themselves look pretty and walked pointedly up and down the wharf when he was unloading, hoping to catch his eye. But Ivan never gave them a second look. It seemed he would never marry at all. In fact he grew thin and dishevelled for a time, as if he had too much on his mind to take proper care of himself.

Sometimes he tangled daisies in the mesh of the nets before he let them down. He was doing this when he accidentally knocked his old torn smock over the side into the sea. It was returned to him, on the next trip, clean and mended, like new. And on Fridays, the catch he brought up had been cooked on the volcanoes on Undersea, herb-sprinkled, crispy and delicious. After that, he lowered down books and mirrors and pretty tin cups — the sort of thing, he thought, that mermaids might find it hard to come by.

The other fishermen did not know what to make of him. 'He talks to himself,' they said. 'He throws things over the side. He talks to himself all the while — or that seal that's always swimming round his boat.'

They could see he was no longer happy on shore. The old fishwives told him, 'You work too hard, Ivan! Why take your boat out every day? In all weathers! It's not as if you have a wife or children to support. Don't work so hard!'

But Ivan would simply look at them with eyes as round and moist as a seal's, and murmur, 'Children, yes, children. That would have been nice . . . I must be going now. I must get out on the water.'

'Sea fever, that's his trouble,' said the fishermen, scowling. 'Sometimes the sea gets into a man's blood . . .'

Ten years later, one stormy day, when all the fishing boats ran for harbour, Ivan's did not arrive home.

The fishermen took off their caps in sorrow. The fishwives crumpled their aprons and said, 'We knew it, we knew it all along.' And several of the young girls shed a secret tear to think of young Ivan, gone.

But then they heard it — everyone heard it, no mistaking — the muffled clamour of bells ringing under fifty fathoms of sea.

'That's a sea wedding,' mused the oldest fishwife. 'Them's wedding bells. That's one of the mermaids marrying, for sure.' Then she suddenly smiled, and her smile passed along from face to face. The fishermen threw their caps in the air, the fishwives waved their aprons, and everyone shouted together out towards the sea: 'Congratulations, Ivan! Good luck to you!'

SUMIO WHO FELL FROM THE MOON

One night when the moon was full, a little old man and a little old lady held hands and wished a wish. They wished for a child, because all life long they had only had each other.

Suddenly there was a crash behind them, among the bushes. At first they thought some wild animal was prowling through the bamboo. But when they heard the crying, and went to look, they found a little baby girl. The old lady picked her up and gave her a kiss — also, a name as sweet as any kiss: Sumio. Then they took her indoors and loved her as if she were their own daughter. Sumio loved them just as much.

She grew into the most beautiful girl in all Japan, with hair as black as the night sky and a face as white as moonlight. The news of her loveliness spread, like water spilled from a jar, and poets came from far and wide to gaze at this house, hoping for a glimpse of Sumio.

Far away, the Emperor heard tell of Sumio's beauty. 'I may have her for my wife,' he yawned, scratching his grey beard. 'Tell her to come, so that I can take a look at her.'

But Sumio did not come, would not come, and the Emperor waited in vain.

'Well, no-one else shall have her,' complained the Emperor, picking his yellow teeth. 'If I must, I shall go and fetch her myself.'

He called at Sumio's house, and was given green mint tea and macaroons. 'I mean to do you the honour of marrying you,' he told Sumio (who was even lovelier then he had imagined).

'No, thank you, sir,' replied Sumio politely. 'That is not possible.'

The Emperor sucked tea out of his moustache and scowled. 'I don't think you quite understand me,' he said. 'I say I shall marry you and so we shall be married.'

Sumio bowed politely. 'I regret we cannot. You see, your Imperial Highness, I am the Princess of the Moon. My nurse rocked the cradle too hard and I fell down here from my country in the sky. But very soon my people will be coming to take me back to the Land of Silver Soil.' And she opened the door to let him out.

The Emperor scuffed his heels all the way down the hill. When he reached the bottom, he turned and pointed his imperial finger at Sumio.

'Have I not captured castles?' he shouted. 'Have I not captured cities? Prepare to marry, Sumio! I shall return with my army tonight! Princess of the Moon, indeed! Pish!'

The little old lady and the little old man might have begged Sumio to agree. Their daughter married to the Emperor? Think of the honour and riches it would bring them!

But the little old woman closed the windows and the little old man barred the door. 'If you don't want to go with him, you shan't,' he said and his wife agreed.

At sunset the Emperor arrived with seven battalions of troops, and circled the hill as if it were the mightiest of castles. He brought a large box to put the Princess in, and barrels of gunpowder to destroy the little house on the hill.

At midnight, he started up the path. The bamboo trembled at the stamp of soldiers' feet. The stars blinked with astonishment at the sight of so many troops. The moon was just

rising, and its light glinted on a thousand sharp swords, a thousand pointed spears, ten thousand iron-tipped arrows.

Sumio opened the door and stepped outside. The little old man held her hand on one side, the little old lady held her hand on the other. She looked even more lovely in the milky moonlight, and fireflies swooped around her head.

'Give yourself up to me, Sumio!' called the Emperor. 'For I never want a thing but I get it!'

All of a sudden, a broad moonbeam fell across the hill. Like a river of milk it shone, the Princess on one side, the Emperor and his guards on the other. The soldiers moved forward to seize her — and stopped short. They tugged and wriggled. But their boots seemed to be stuck to the ground. They could not take another step.

'Grab her, you fools! What are you waiting for?' boomed the Emperor, and strode forward himself. But — 'Oh! Help!' — he sank up to his ankles in moonlight, up to his knees, up to his waist, up to his chest. He struggled and wriggled, but the sticky moonlight only sucked at his silken sleeves and grey hair.

As seven battalions stared in amazement, a second moonbeam unfurled, like a bolt of white silk unrolling. It had no sooner touched the ground than it stiffened into a silver chute, and down from the moon slid a cascade of warriors in silver armour with stars on their breastplates and moondust in their long hair. Down the slope galloped a pearly chariot drawn by the dappled moon-horses who stopped in front of Sumio; the charioteer lifted her aboard.

'We must take my friends here, too,' she sighed, helping the little old couple into the chariot, 'because I love them as dearly as my own mother and father.'

The Emperor puffed and panted. The Emperor fretted and fumed, wriggled and writhed. His soldiers pulled and his Chancellor pushed. But he stayed stuck fast in the river of gluey moonlight as his would-be bride sped away into the night sky.

And he could not get free till morning.

Town Palace, Country Palace

There was once a King who had so many children that his palace was full to bursting. There were Princesses in the kitchen and Princes in the parlour, more in the morning room and lots in the lofts. So the King took out his chest of gold and said, 'Let all but the littlest leave home. Then your mother and I can have some peace!'

Some took trains to distant countries. Some bought boats and lived on them. Some rented palazzos by the canals of Venice. Some looked in the newspapers and found castles for sale.

But Princess Adelaide and Princess Ottaline chose to build their own palaces from top to bottom, and one chose the country and one chose the town.

'Mine will be finer then fine,' said Ottaline. 'Mine will be grander than grand!' And she built in concrete, glass and steel at the top of the highest hill in the city. 'I want soaring pillars, and ceilings as high as the sky. Every room must be bigger than my father's whole palace, every cupboard as big as a room. I want lift-shafts and spires, I want cloisters and choirs. I want it all finished by June!'

She employed every builder, painter and plasterer in the land. By every strike of the hour on her huge gilded clocks, tradesmen and delivery boys arrived with braids and brocades, satins and rattans, panelling and chandeliers. Ottaline stood at the top of the stairs and shouted, 'Put it there! No, there! Now try there!'

She hired everybody in town as palace servants, because there was so much housework to do. But on the day all the work was finished, she had the biggest palace in the land. That same night, she sent everybody away.

'Can't live here,' she said. 'You aren't royal like me. You must live in the town and only come up here to work each day.'

The servants mumbled and grumbled because the hill was very steep and they would have to get up very early. 'How much will you pay us?' they asked.

'Pay you? I've no money left to pay you! Don't you realize how much this castle cost to build? Besides, I'm a Princess, and everybody wants to work for a Princess in a palace like mine.'

Away went the servants, shaking their heads and rubbing their hands (because the weather was getting cold).

Out in the country, Princess Adelaide found a pretty spot for her palace — but then she had no idea where to begin. So she asked the insects and the animals for their help. 'How should I build?' she asked.

'With paper,' said the wasp and showed her how to chew woodchips and make grey paper and mould a city of tiny rooms each big enough for a wasp.

'That's not how,' said the badger, and he showed her how to dig a sett and line it with fresh grass every day and make it cosy for cubs.

'That's not how,' said the rooks, and they showed her how to weave a nest out of twigs and balance it high up in a tree.

'That's not how,' said the water vole, and he showed her how to burrow in the riverbank — though the squirrels were of the opinion she should live in a hollow tree.

Adelaide did her best to please them all, and soon she had built a sett halfway up a hollow tree, overhanging a river and divided into paper chambers. It was very cosy and she was never short of company, for her animal friends came day and night and danced to the fiddling of the grasshoppers.

Then winter arrived.

Up on the hill, it shook at Ottaline's windows. Draughts howled around the enormous rooms, and set the curtains streaming like sails and the doors banging. Thunder boomed like cannonfire over the roofs. She huddled in bed with her crown on her head, and tried to feel regal. But nobody came when she called, for it was no weather to climb the hill, especially for no wages.

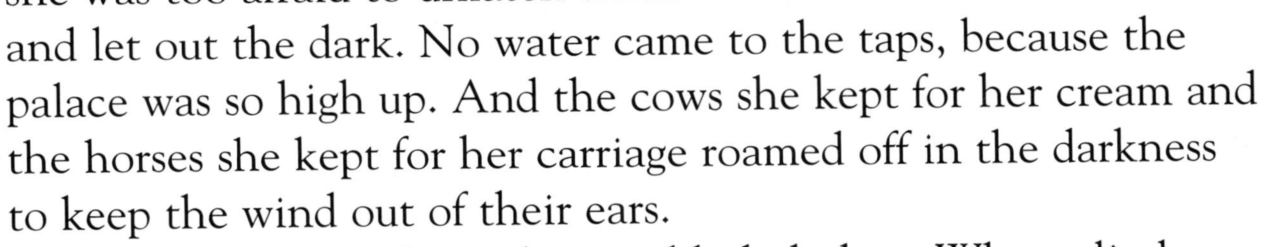

The fires blew out in the grates. The candles blew out in their sconces. And then Ottaline would have gladly crept into a cupboard with her eiderdown, except that the cupboards were all as big as rooms and full of shadows, and she was too afraid to unlatch them and let out the dark. No water came to the taps, because the palace was so high up. And the cows she kept for her cream and the horses she kept for her carriage roamed off in the darkness to keep the wind out of their ears.

Nobody ventured out those cold, dark days. What, climb that hill to be shouted at? So they stayed in their small, warm cottages and said, 'What a waste of gold to give it to one like that.'

Meanwhile, out in the country, down by the stream, Princess Adelaide was snug and warm in her honeycomb palace, curled up among all her friends while the storm raged outside. Only the wasps were missing.

The animals began to argue about what the Princess should eat for supper.

And whom she should marry.

And when she should go to sleep.

'Excuse me,' said Adelaide, 'but I don't want to go to sleep.'

'Oh, but you must, you must,' said the hedgehog. 'All winter. Eat now. Eat. Eat! Then go to sleep for a good four months.'

'The question is, has she stored enough nuts?' said the squirrels.

'Excuse me, but I don't like nuts,' said Adelaide.

'Worms and beetles,' said the badger. 'Worms and beetles, then she'll be fat enough in the spring to marry my nephew.'

'Of course, she may die in winter, like the wasps . . .'

'Excuse me!'

At this point, the palace, which was built halfway up a hollow tree, out of twigs and paper and feathers and turf, fell down, tree and all, into the stream below, washing along like a raft.

They sailed all night, till the tree ran ashore on the city quayside, at the bottom of a hill. Seeing a blaze of light high up, the animals naturally ran away, while Adelaide climbed towards it.

Halfway up the hill, she met Ottaline coming down, and hand-in-hand they walked to the railway station through the driving rain. They caught the train home, where the King and Queen gave them crumpets and kippers for tea. Oddly enough, all the other Princes and Princesses seemed to be visiting that night.

'We have been thinking of building an East Wing,' said the King. 'For the Princesses.'

'And a West Wing,' said the Queen. 'For the Princes.'

'Plenty of room for everyone,' they said, and nothing more was ever mentioned of anyone leaving home.

EAST OF THE SUN, WEST OF THE MOON

There was once a man so poor that he had nothing to feed his children, and barely the firewood to keep them warm. One night, when snow lay level with the windows, and the wind howled in the chimney, someone came beating at the door.

There, towering over the man as he opened the door, was a huge polar bear. 'I am Prince of Bears. Give me your youngest, sweetest girl, and I shall give you home and heat and food to feed your family, and riches besides.'

'No! No!' said the man. 'Take Molly? We'd sooner starve!'

But Molly ran up, her cloak already round her shoulders. 'If it is for the good of you, then how can it be bad for me?' Then, kissing her father goodbye, she took the Bear's paw and went out into the blizzard.

She thought at first that the Bear meant to eat her, but he simply took her on his back and galloped off through the snow.

'Aren't you afraid?' he asked as he loped along.

'For one moment, but never again,' said Molly, and clung on tight to his shaggy white fur.

The Bear took her to a palace as round as a dome. And though it was ice outside, it was warmth and firelight inside, and as cosy as a nest. He gave her robes and ribbons, shoes and books; her plate was always full; and best of all was when the Bear shared their mealtimes and they talked. They talked of earth and sky, of sea and shore. But when the lights burned out and the palace was all dark, Molly reached out to hold his paw, and it was not a paw at all, but a big, gentle hand!

'Bear by day and man by night,' Molly told her sister, 'and as kind as any girl would wish for.' She had only come home to visit her family's new home, where she found them all as rich and round and happy as mudlarks, living in luxury.

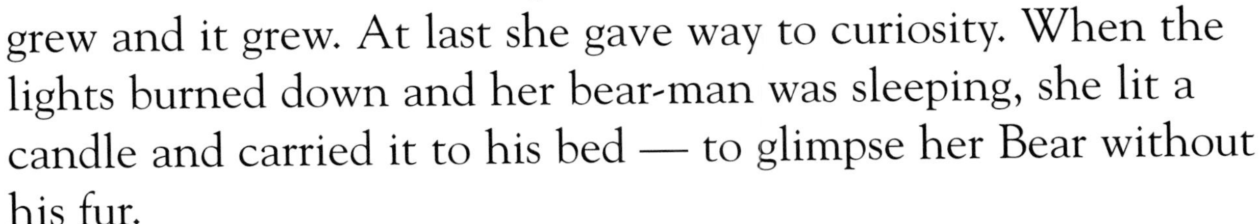

But her sisters, for all their new-found riches, were jealous of Molly's happiness. They dared her, knowing she could never resist a dare: 'Light a light. Look one look. See what it is the darkness hides. You've married a troll, and that's the truth of it!'

She did not want to believe them, but the idea was planted there like a seed in her head, and after she returned from her visit, it grew and it grew and it grew. At last she gave way to curiosity. When the lights burned down and her bear-man was sleeping, she lit a candle and carried it to his bed — to glimpse her Bear without his fur.

'Bless me, if he isn't the handsomest man in all the world!' And her hand shook, so that three drops of candlewax fell on to the young man's shirt.

'What have you done? Oh, Molly, how could you!' he cried in the very moment of opening his eyes. 'If you had cherished me for one whole year, you would have broken her hold over me! But now I must go East of the Sun, West of the Moon. Oh, Molly!' And his eyes reproached her as he melted away — into fur, into snow, into water. The ice palace fell with a crash,

leaving Molly alone in her nightdress on a glacier of ice.

There Molly lifted up her head. 'I'll not rest till I've found you!' she cried, and the frozen sea growled like a bear.

First she wept, but there was no use in weeping.

Then she thought, but there was no good in thinking.

Next she walked, and walking brought her to the house of the East Wind.

'East Wind! O, gentle East Wind! Tell me if you will and if you know: where is the place called East of the Sun, West of the Moon, and how may I get there?'

'I have heard of it,' sighed the mild East Wind, 'but never been there. My brother the West Wind may know; he is stronger.'

So Molly climbed onto the East Wind's back and he carried her far and wide. 'Aren't you afraid, little one?' he asked.

'Only for my Prince,' she said. And when she got down, she found in her hand a golden apple, without knowing how it got there.

At the house of the West Wind she asked again: 'West Wind, O, Wise West Wind! Tell me if you will and if you know: where is the place called East of the Sun, West of the Moon, and how may I get there?'

'I have tasted the scent of it,' said the West Wind, 'but never been there. My brother the South Wind may know; he is stronger and roams farther afield than I.'

So Molly clambered onto the West Wind's back, and he carried her farther and higher. 'Aren't you afraid, little one?' he asked.

'Only for my Prince,' she said. And when she got down, she found in her hand a golden comb without knowing how it got there.

At the house of the South Wind, Molly asked again: 'South Wind, O, Sir South Wind! Tell me if you will and if you know: where is the place called East of the Sun, West of the Moon, and how may I get there?'

'I have blown to the ice reefs,' roared the fierce South Wind, 'and to the edge of the planet, and I have heard the bells of its towers, but I have never been there. My brother the North Wind will know — but do you dare ask?'

'I dare anything for my Prince,' said Molly as she leapt astride the South Wind. And when she slid down again, she found a golden spindle in her hand without knowing where it came from.

She slid down with a bump, because the South Wind was suddenly barged by a blast of icy, icy cold. Clawed with frost and armoured with ice, the North Wind brayed and blared at them: 'WHO DARES COME NEAR?'

Molly curtseyed and said, 'Please, master, tell me if you will and if you know: where is the place called East of the Sun, West of the Moon, and how may I get there?'

'WHO WANTS TO KNOW?'

'Molly, and if you will take me there, I'll ride on your back and weigh no more than a feather.'

Now no-one had ever ridden on the North Wind's back, and he was so startled by the daring of this little scrap of a girl in her nightdress that he let her clamber into his hoary hair and cling on, as he whirled away into the sky. The North Wind, though he was strongest, had never blown such a distance before. 'I'm scared I may fail, little one!' he said.

But Molly stroked and encouraged him. 'You can do it!'

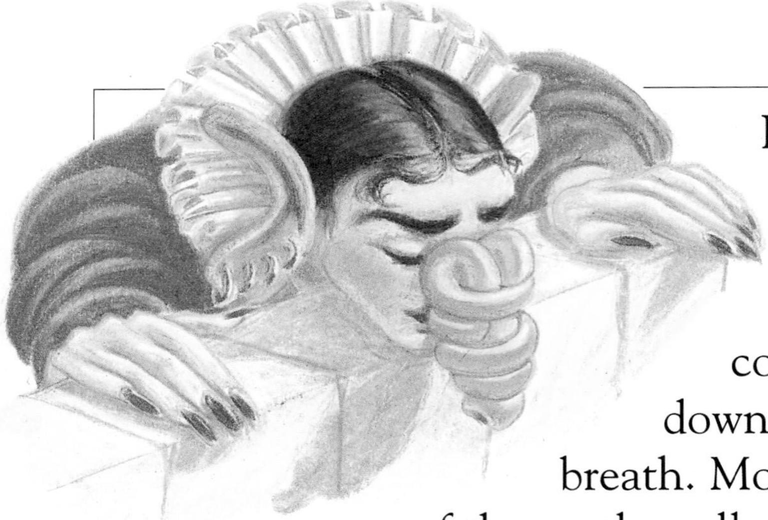

By the time he reached the castle East of the Sun, West of the Moon, the North Wind was winded and hoarse, and could only fling himself face-down and rest till he got back his breath. Molly sat herself down at the foot of the castle wall and played with her golden apple. And when the sun came up, that is what the owner of the castle saw. The owner? A Troll Princess with a nose so long that she tied it in a round-turn-and-two-half-hitches to keep it out of her dinner.

'What's that you have there, beggar maid, and what will you take for it?' called down the Troll Princess, wanting the apple.

'No gold or silver, but a word alone with the Prince who sleeps here,' said Molly, bold as brass.

'I won't deny you that,' said the Troll, but she laughed a nasty laugh, as if she were giving away nothing by it.

Molly was shown to the room where the Prince was staying. Oh, but he was fast asleep! And though she was left alone to shake him and speak in his ear, she could not make him wake.

Next morning, Molly went out and sat by the castle wall, and she combed her hair with the golden comb.

'What's that you have there, beggar maid, and what will you take for it?' called the Troll Princess, wanting the comb.

'Nothing but a word alone with the Prince I saw yesterday,' said Molly.

'I won't deny you that!' said the Troll, but she showed her tombstone teeth in the same nasty grin.

Molly was shown up to the same room, and once again she found her Prince sound asleep. Though she was left alone with him to slap him and shout in his ear —'WAKE UP!' — she could not make him wake. So instead, she pushed a note into his hand, which read, 'Wine drugged: don't drink!'

Next morning Molly was playing again outside the wall, spinning wisps of wool on her golden spindle.

'What's that you have there, beggar maid, and what will you take for it?' called the Troll Princess, wanting the spindle.

'Same as before,' said Molly, and the Troll let her in, knowing she had drugged the Prince's wine and thinking he would not stir.

But this time he was only pretending to be asleep.

'I can't believe you came so far and did so much to find me here!' he whispered, kissing her. 'And all for nothing! Tomorrow I must marry the Troll Princess with her nose in a knot, and nothing can save me!'

'Love can save anyone,' said Molly, 'and here's how . . .'

Next day, Molly sat outside the wall, as ragged as ever. But indoors, the Troll Princess came down to her wedding in silken finery, her nose tied in a bow and her hair fastened back with a silver cartwheel. Ever so many troll maidens tripped behind her in boots as big as boats. But the bridegroom arrived only half-dressed.

'I can't marry you in this shirt!' he complained. 'Someone has dropped three spots of candlewax on it — see here! Wash it for me, won't you, as you'll wash it when we are married.'

Though washing was not to her liking, the Troll Princess flung her nose over her shoulder and dunked the shirt up and down in a tub of soapy water. But the more she washed it the blacker it grew, till a crow could have worn it to a funeral.

'D'you call that washing?' demanded the Prince. 'There's a beggar maid at the door could do better than that!' And he called in Molly.

So Molly washed the shirt, washed it in the sea, and it became so white a dove could have worn it to a wedding.

'Ah now, this is the girl I shall marry!' said the Prince.

When they held hands, the malice of the trolls ran off them like water off a swan, and the trolls grew so mad with rage that one by one they went off – BANG! – so that ordinary people like you and I thought they saw shooting stars East of the Sun, West of the Moon, and made a wish.

Molly and her Prince sailed away in the shoe of the Troll Princess, towing the other behind, full of treasure. And the four winds sped them on their way, calling out to the Prince, 'Aren't you afraid of such a daring wife?'

The Prince replied, 'Only of parting from her, and that I will never do!'

Princess Dora and the Ministers of State

When the King of Ufonia decided to go to the World Congress, he said to his daughter, 'No need to worry, Dora. My ministers of state will look after everything while I'm gone.'

But his ministers threw up their hands in protest.

'I should go to the World Congress — a man of my stature!' said the fat Prime Minister.

'I should be there to advise His Majesty — a man of my worth!' said the Chancellor, gripping the lapels of the expensive fur coat he always wore.

'I should, you mean,' said the Home Secretary, uncrossing her long, elegant legs. The King looked troubled.

'Don't worry, Father,' said Princess Dora. 'I shall be quite all right on my own. You all go. After all, what can happen while you're gone?'

And so they all drove away, the coach swaying under the weight of so many great people.

While the Princess was still waving her handkerchief, she felt a drop of rain fall on her nose, and ran to fetch in the royal washing.

After the rain came hail and sleet and snow. Never in the history of Ufonia had the people seen such weather. Hurricanes blew off their chimneys, and the rivers swelled to bursting.

'What must I do?' said Princess Dora to her dog. 'If only I had some ministers of state to advise me.' The royal bloodhound yawned. 'You're right, Bludnock, I must appoint new ministers to save the city. Let me see. First a Chancellor.'

'And how do we choose a Chancellor?' asked the bloodhound.

'Well, the last one,' said Dora, 'had the biggest fur coat I ever saw. Find the biggest fur coat, and the person inside it is bound to be a good Chancellor.'

'And the Home Secretary?'

'Well, the last one,' said Dora, 'had the longest legs I've ever seen. Find someone with long legs and she is bound to make a good Home Secretary.'

'Prime Minister?' said the bloodhound, taking notes.

'Well, the last one,' said Dora, 'was the fattest man in the kingdom. If we look for someone huge, we can't go wrong!'

So the Princess and the bloodhound put on their waterproofs and waded out into the teeth of the gale. They searched high and low, and near and far, but the biggest fur coat they could find belonged to a polar bear.

Meanwhile, the trees were tumbling, barns collapsing, and ships were driven ashore with sheets of ice where their sails should have been. The people sobbed with cold, and wailed, 'Where's the Princess? How will she save us?'

Princess Dora and the bloodhound were, in fact, searching hither and thither, up hill and down dale, for a Home Secretary. But the longest legs they could find belonged to a giraffe.

Meanwhile, the reservoir in the mountains above Ufonia City was more full of rain and snow and sleet than it had ever been. The dam which held back the water groaned and bellied outwards like a great bow window. If it burst,

the whole country would be flooded as high as the highest church spire. The people jibbered with cold and fright: 'Where is the Princess? How could she desert us at a time like this? We'll all be drowned!'

Dora had not deserted them, nor had the royal bloodhound.

They were busy searching willi-cum-nether and over-li-do for a Prime Minister. Unfortunately, the fattest they could find was a hippopotamus blowing bubbles in the mud.

Dora hurried home to Ufonia City. As they went, she explained the danger her country faced to her new ministers of state.

'Of course, we have no experience of government,' said the polar bear, 'but we will do what we can.'

Just as they approached the city, there was a crack like the end of the world, and a zigzag line appeared from top to bottom of the dam. Everyone who could, climbed onto their roof.

The hippopotamus trotted as fast as he was able, and sat down with his flank against the dam. The pent-up water pushed against him, but could not get past.

Then the giraffe waded through the town, with Dora on her back, her legs so long that the floodwater rushed under her ribs. She rescued small boys from lamp posts, farmers from trees, babies from cradles washed away on the flood.

She carried them all to the palace (which stood on a hill) and went back for more. Soon everyone in Ufonia City lay in a damp heap on the ballroom floor, while the blizzard blew snow in at the windows and the wind howled up and down the spiral stairs.

The polar bear Chancellor spread his paws and clasped them close. He was as warm as an electric blanket, and silky soft. His breath filled the palace with a comforting smell of fish, and his big paws stroked the children till they fell asleep.

The storms blew themselves out that night. When the King and his ministers of state came back from the World Congress, there was hardly a snowdrift or a puddle to show for the great gales. But the whole town rang to the banging of hammers and the clang of scaffolding as people repaired their homes and mended the dam.

'There is a hippopotamus sitting in my office!' complained the Prime Minister furiously.

'Yes,' said Dora. 'I needed a little help while you were gone.'

'There's a giraffe riding in my limousine!' said the Home Secretary, greatly put out.

'Yes,' said Dora. 'She was such a help while you weren't here.'

'There is a polar bear in the counting house!' screamed the Chancellor, running in with his fur coat in tatters.

'Yes,' said Dora. 'He helped me save the city while you were away.'

And when the King heard what had happened during his absence, he said he would not be going to any World Congresses in future, in case his people needed him. 'My ministers of state can go in my place,' he said.

And so they did. In fact, the King entrusted the polar bear, the giraffe and the hippopotamus with all manner of important jobs.

But I have no idea what became of the fat man, the lady with the long legs, or the man who wore his fur coat all year round.

MOUSEY AND SULKY PUSS

'Hear ye! Hear ye! Let it be known in every corner of the land, that a daughter is born to the King and Queen of Bellepays! Let no-one work today, for the King declares this a public holiday!'

At the sound of the herald's announcement, everyone ran out into the streets and began to dance and sing. But when the invitations were sent out for the royal christening of the baby Princess, a terrible mistake was made.

No-one invited Agatha!

Agatha had not always been a crabbed and spiteful witch. But ever since the day she turned her sister by mistake into a large black cat, Agatha had not smiled. Neither had her sister, come to that. In fact her sister was such a sad sack of a cat that she was known as Sulky Puss. Agatha searched the world over for a magic spell which would restore her sister to human form, and it was while she was away on one such trip that Princess Marcia was born. That's why *no-one invited Agatha.*

On the day of the christening, all manner of important and famous people travelled to the celebrations. So did Agatha. She waited until all the other christening presents had been given — spoons and egg cups and china bowls — then she did her worst.

'Because you made little of me, I shall make little of your precious Princess!' cried Agatha, and struck the crib with her wand. When the purple smoke cleared, Agatha had gone, and there in the royal cradle wriggled — a small white mouse.

The Mouse Princess they called her — or Mousey for short. And Mousey was very, very short. Her dresses could be made from a single silk handkerchief, her bed from an open jewel box. She was as pleasant a little thing as you could ever hope to meet — but she was, when all's said, a white mouse who ate cheese with her paws and whiffled her small, pink nose.

The King, terrified for her safety, banished every cat from Bellepays, with one single exception. Sulky Puss, the witch's sister, was allowed to stay because no-one dared tell her to go. Besides, she was a vegetarian.

As the years passed, the other baby girls in Bellepays grew into lovely young women. But Mousey only grew into a lovely young mouse. When she was in a room, it was easy to overlook her, to forget she was there. She squeaked so quietly that she was rarely heard. And not everyone was as kind and as loving as the King and Queen. Some were ashamed to admit they had a mouse for a Princess, and did their best to forget all about her. Just as Agatha had not been invited to the christening, *no-one invited Mousey anywhere*.

Then, as in all such stories and histories, the Prince of the next door kingdom announced his wish to choose a bride.

'Oyez! Oyez! Every maiden of wealth or degree is invited to the palace of the King of Oystria, so that the Prince Michelangelo may have dancing partners at the Grand Ball!'

What queues there were at the dress shops, at the milliners, the hairdressers and the florists! There were carriages at every door and women arrayed in every colour of the rainbow scrambling to be ready in time for the Grand Ball.

'I should like to go, too,' said Mousey, but nobody heard her. She climbed onto the dinner table and shouted as loud as she was able, 'I want to go, too!'

'Nonsense, Mousey dear,' said the Queen. 'You would get trodden on.'

'Besides, there are still cats in Oystria,' said the King. 'Out of the question. Get down off the table, please.'

But the more they said no, the more determined Mousey became to go to the Ball. She put on her finest silk handkerchief dress — it was scarlet with silver embroidery — and a sash made from a velvet hair ribbon. She fetched a pin — to use as a sword if she met any cats — and put on her tiny tiara, then ran to the palace door.

But she was only in time to see the coach, with her mother and father in it, gathering speed as it drove away from the palace down the long, dusty drive.

Mousey sat down and wept.

Then she got up and dried her tears. How could she make the journey to Oystria? By boat?

She found her father's newspaper and folded it ever so many times, until she had made a paper boat. She dragged it to the moat and rowed it out to where the moat joined the winding river which flowed right across both countries. But she had forgotten — the river flowed OUT of Oystria and INTO Bellepays. It was running in the wrong direction!

Mousey paddled ashore and thought again. She would fly to Oystria! But though she was able to fold a paper glider out of the newspaper, she could not get it up the winding stairs to the castle parapet.

She went to the stable, where the royal horses were kept. But the huge mares and stallions towered over her like monsters, and she dared not stay among those swinging hooves for fear she may be trampled and never seen again.

'What I need is a horse more suited to my size,' thought Mousey, and as she crept out of the stable door, she saw the very thing.

A dozen chickens were pecking in the yard, and there beside the dungheap, a splendid red cockerel stretched its claws and surveyed its farmyard kingdom.

Mousey took the sash from her dress, ran full tilt up the dungheap, and launched herself onto the back of the cockerel. The bird was so startled that it set off to run. And after Mousey had got the ribbon into its beak for reins, it was just a matter of guiding the speeding fowl in the direction of the Oystrian border.

The Grand Ball was well underway when Mousey arrived, riding her cockerel. She did not dismount at the gate, nor at the steps, but rode straight on up, for fear the footmen and flunkies thought she was an ordinary house mouse. Indoors, she came to a scarlet-carpeted staircase lit by chandeliers. At the foot of the stairs, she could just make out the Prince.

She missed seeing Sulky Puss.

Oh yes, Sulky Puss was there. The King of Oystria had not made the same mistake as his neighbour. He had remembered to invite Agatha, and Agatha had brought her cat.

Sulky Puss saw the cockerel with its reins of scarlet velvet. She saw the meal-sized white mouse on its back, damp at the hems, stained black with newsprint, tiara awry over her little pink eyes, pin-sized sword raised aloft and tiny mouth open to shout: 'Out of the way! Out of the way! I don't know how to stop this bird!'

It was enough to make a cat laugh.

And that's just what Sulky Puss did. For the first time in her miserable sad-sack cat's nine lives, Sulky Puss rolled on her back in fits of giggles.

The music in the ballroom faltered and fell silent.

Everyone stared. For there, rolling on her back on the staircase, in a most unladylike way, was a large fat witch, laughing and laughing and laughing.

'Sister!' cried Agatha joyously. 'The spell! It's lifted!'

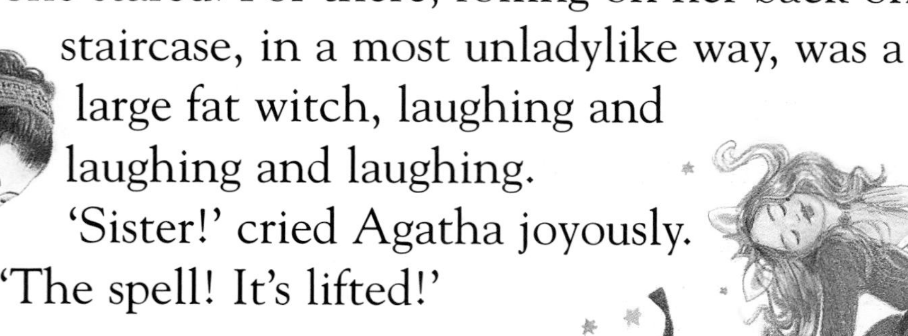

'All I needed was a good laugh,' said Anastasia wiping her eyes and scratching some cat food off her dress. 'And that sight was enough to give me one!'

Agatha looked to see what jester or clown had restored her sister to her. And when she recognized the Mouse Princess, she was filled with tender remorse for the unkindness she had done at the christening.

And she hit Mousey with her wand.

The white mouse flew through the air, somersaulting one, two, three times before landing at the feet of the Prince of Oystria. She landed heavily, perhaps because she was no longer a mouse but a tall, elegant, pale-skinned girl in a ball dress of red silk, with ash-blonde hair tumbling down from a buckled tiara.

'Good gracious,' said the Prince. 'You are the most beautiful young lady I have seen all night. Will you marry me?'

'No, thank you,' said Marcia. 'I just wanted to dance.'

So that's what they did instead.